Building the Free Society

GEORGE WEIGEL is president of the Ethics and Public Policy Center. A graduate of St. Mary's Seminary and University in Baltimore and the University of St. Michael's College in Toronto, he was a 1984–85 Fellow of the Woodrow Wilson International Center for Scholars. Mr. Weigel is the author of eight books, among them *Tranquillitas Ordinis: The Present Failure and Future Promise of American Catholic Thought on War and Peace* (Oxford, 1987), *Catholicism and the Renewal of American Democracy* (Paulist, 1989), *American Interests, American Purpose: Moral Reasoning and U.S. Foreign Policy* (Praeger, 1989), and *The Final Revolution: The Resistance Church and the Collapse of Communism* (Oxford, 1992).

ROBERT ROYAL is vice president for research at the Ethics and Public Policy Center. He holds a B.A. and M.A. from Brown University and spent 1978 in Italy as a Fulbright Scholar. He has taught at Brown, Rhode Island College, and The Catholic University of America. From 1980 to 1982, he was editor-in-chief of *Prospect* magazine in Princeton, New Jersey. His articles have appeared in numerous publications, including the *Washington Post*, the *Washington Times*, *National Review*, *The American Spectator*, and *Crisis*. He is the author of *1492 And All That: Political Manipulations of History*, and has edited (with Virgil Nemoianu) *Play, Literature, Religion: Essays in Cultural Intertextuality*.

Building the Free Society

*Democracy, Capitalism, and
Catholic Social Teaching*

Edited by

George Weigel and Robert Royal

WILLIAM B. EERDMANS PUBLISHING COMPANY
GRAND RAPIDS, MICHIGAN

ETHICS AND PUBLIC POLICY CENTER
WASHINGTON, D.C.

Copyright © 1993 by Wm. B. Eerdmans Publishing Co.,
255 Jefferson Ave. SE, Grand Rapids, Michigan 49503

Some of the material in this volume first appeared, in different form, in *A Century of Catholic Social Thought: Essays on* Rerum Novarum *and Nine Other Key Documents,* published by the Ethics and Public Policy Center.

This edition first published 1993 jointly by
Wm. B. Eerdmans Publishing Co. and the Ethics and Public Policy Center,
1030 Fifteenth St. NW, Washington, D.C., 20005.

Printed in the United States of America

ISBN 0-8028-0120-X

Contents

Preface

FOR good and for ill, as the inspiration of either nonviolent revolution or violent confrontation, religious conviction has re-emerged over the past generation as a powerful influence on the affairs and fates of men and women around the globe. This was not supposed to happen. According to the dominant models of Western social science, "modernization" inevitably leads to secularization, and thus to the decline of religion as a factor in the unfolding drama of human history. Well, the social-science models were wrong—as a minute's glance at the daily paper will confirm.

And if they were, and are, wrong about the general trend, perhaps they have also been wrong about the particulars. Take, for instance, the Roman Catholic Church. It is often thought of as the quintessentially "pre-modern" institution. Yet for several decades now the Church has been a crucial voice in the defense of religious freedom and other basic human rights in venues as various as Manila, Kraków, Prague, Santiago de Chile, Managua, Dakar, Khartoum, and New York. That voice has developed through the evolution of Catholic social teaching on the right ordering of society, a tradition whose modern phase began in 1891 with Pope Leo XIII's encyclical *Rerum Novarum*.

In planning this collection of commentaries on the eleven key documents of the modern Catholic social-ethical tradition, we encouraged the contributors to undertake something other than strict textual exegesis. We have tried instead to put the encyclical and conciliar documents into conversation with what the Second Vatican Council called "the joys and hopes, the griefs and anxieties" of people today.

These commentaries are most certainly not to be taken as a substitute for the originals; we hope rather that they will motivate readers to explore the documents themselves. Like the tradition on which they are based, these reflections are an invitation to an ongoing conversation about the moral dimension of social, political, economic, and cultural life today.

The writers of the commentaries do not agree about every detail of modern Catholic social teaching; one of the surest signs of the tradition's fecundity is that those who agree on its great principles still find in these documents considerable stimulation for further development of thought and application. What these writers do have in common is certain qualities of mind, character, and conviction. They respect the teaching authority of the Roman Catholic Church, expressed through popes and general councils. They value Catholic social thought as an important effort to give meaning to the concept of the "public Church." They accept the tradition's sense of its own limitations in matters of "prudential judgment." And they take seriously the Catholic tradition's invitation to a conversation on public matters with all people of good will. We asked our authors for thoughtful, courteous, critical, ecumenical, and accessible essays. And that, happily, is what they have given us.

Many friends have helped to bring this book to fruition, and we thank all of them: the commentators whose essays are collected here; our colleagues Jacqueline Stark, Carol Griffith, Marianne Geers, and Gretchen Baudhuin at the Ethics and Public Policy Center; Richard John Neuhaus, the author of the foreword; and our friends at the William B. Eerdmans Publishing Company.

We offer this book as a tribute to the genius of Pope Leo XIII, who began the tradition of modern Catholic social teaching; as a small gesture of gratitude and affection to Pope John Paul II, who has both extended the tradition and brought it to bear on world affairs with singular effect; and as a modest contribution to the future development of Catholicism's reflection on the many public tasks still facing the Church in the modern world.

GEORGE WEIGEL
ROBERT ROYAL

Washington, D.C.
Pentecost, 1993

Foreword

RICHARD JOHN NEUHAUS

CHRISTIANS of all times and all communions have had a big problem with the concept of "Christian social thought." Some have contended that there is no such thing as a distinctively *Christian* way of thinking about society. They have usually been in the distinct minority. Most Christians have harbored the troubling intuition that there *should* be something distinctively Christian about everything a Christian thinks and does—including his thinking and doing about society. Then there are those Christians who are quite certain that there is a distinctively Christian way of relating to society. Moreover, they are quite certain that they have a firm hold on that way, and are prepared, indeed eager, to do battle against all the un-Christian and anti-Christian forces that oppose their way. Such Christians are a big part of the big problem mentioned above.

An odd thing about Christians is that they are both here and not here. Put differently, they cannot help but be worldly, since they are inescapably part of the stuff and time that we call the world, but their identity depends most critically on their devotion to another world that is already present in the form of a promise, in the form of the Promised One. A Christian who is not other-worldly is very doubtfully a Christian. That is to say, he or she is very doubtfully devoted to the One who said that his kingdom is not of this world. It would be nice to argue that other-worldliness, in fact, makes one more effective and responsible when it comes to worldly affairs. There is something to that argument. For instance,

Richard John Neuhaus is president of the Institute on Religion and Public Life and editor-in-chief of *First Things: A Monthly Journal of Religion and Public Life*.

self-surrendering love for the neighbor comes easier to someone who knows that, in laying down his life for a brother or sister, he is not losing everything. On the contrary, if the Christian promise is true, he is actually gaining his life by losing it. That cannot help but make a difference when he is faced with the heroic demands of radical love.

But most social thought and practice is not composed of heroic demands of radical love. Social responsibility, as it is called, has to do with the more or less right ordering of the everyday. In attending to that task, we pay special attention to the ordering of power relationships, so that people who have power are, at least in part, restrained from being mean to those who don't. Much of social responsibility comes down to the "who/whom" question—who does what to whom. At a more elevated level, social responsibility means trying to conceive and advance something like a "common good." One says that cautiously, knowing that the passion to advance the common good has all too commonly meant trampling on the goods cherished by particular people who make up the commons. What despot or tyrannical regime has not claimed to be advancing the common good? The principle of "subsidiarity" in Catholic social thought attempts to make sure that sometimes vaulting notions of the common good are always held accountable to the everyday goods necessary to the dignity of everyday people.

Setting our hearts on the eternal trains our minds to respect the quotidian. Christian other-worldliness does not necessarily lead to greater clarity or effectiveness about the ordering of this world. Rather, it results in our being unable to give this world the full attention that some people believe it deserves. We Christians are, and are supposed to be, otherwise preoccupied. To be sure, the reality with which we are otherwise occupied interpenetrates this that the spiritually myopic call—simply and exhaustively—reality. We know that they are wrong about what constitutes reality. The world is shot through and through with what Václav Havel calls "the hidden sphere." I suppose nobody has explained better than Saint Augustine the difference it makes if this "city of man" is the only city we've got. People who have only one city understandably take it with awful seriousness, and with often awful consequences.

Of course we, too, are to take the world seriously. The best known of Bible passages declares, "God so loved the world. . . ." We are told that we should love the world the way God loves the world, and that is true. But people who say that sometimes fail to take note of the "that" of John 3:16. What God does as a consequence of his love for the world is to free us from the world. That is, those who believe in the One he sent are to have everlasting life in another world. The reality that is usually meant by "the world" is bounded by death. Those who have only that world, those who have only one city, must try to convince themselves that death is optional. Today's culture is powerfully pervaded by a cult of youth and health. It is nothing less than a societal immortality project in which people are tutored to worry more about the well-being of their lungs than the well-being of their souls. We should not be surprised. Those who have only one city, and therefore one citizenship, must, as I said, take the world with an awful seriousness.

Little wonder that from early on Christians were viewed as being unreliable by one-city citizens. If we are even half-serious about Christian discipleship, we will always be a security risk in the eyes of the guardians of earthly securities and the proponents of grand projects for social transformation. On the fringes, and sometimes nearer the center, of American life, Jews and Catholics are accused of harboring a "dual loyalty"—Jews to Israel and Catholics to a "foreign potentate" in Rome. The charge of dual loyalty is fully warranted, or at least it would be were we more faithful Jews and Christians. The duality is not between America, on the one hand, and Israel or Rome, on the other. It is between this world and the world promised in the Messianic Age. Put differently, ours is a single loyalty, a loyalty to God and his promised rule. Our understanding of his working out his rule through time involves the command that we be responsible for the world that participates in his rule-in-the-making.

There is no one entirely satisfactory way of describing our awkward situation. We can say that our loyalty to God's rule is ultimate while our loyalty to every order short of that rule is penultimate. There is much to recommend that way of putting it. But then, we do not want to suggest that there are really two loyalties, or that we apportion our loyalty, this much for the city of man and that much for the City of God. Nor is it entirely satisfactory to say that we are ultimately devoted to the promised future and penultimately to the present. The more complex reality is that the present participates in the future, and that the future, in the risen Christ, is already proleptically present in the present. To confuse things a bit more, when we say the present participates in the future, we do not mean that there is a smooth progression from present to future. The way to the kingdom is not evolutionary ascent but eschatological triumph of good over evil. Augustine's cities are at war with each other. The one is on its way to heaven and the other, as Christians used to say without embarrassment, to hell. The stakes are very high, and it matters terribly to which city we give our hearts.

Just to make our situation more interesting, we cannot always discern the city limits of these cities; the battle lines are often obscured; good and evil are maddeningly entangled with each other. "The servants said to him, 'Then do you want us to go and gather them?' But he said, 'No; lest in gathering the weeds you root up the wheat along with them. Let both grow together until the harvest; and at harvest time I will tell the reapers, Gather the weeds first and bind them in bundles to be burned, but gather the wheat into my barn' " (Matt. 13:28–30). Working against such an eschatological horizon puts a sharp crimp in Christian designs to establish a "just society." Yet our loyalty to that just society for which we pray each time we say "your kingdom come" turns us back to concern for the historical "stuff" that participates, in ways beyond our sure discerning, in the realization of what God is up to.

It is better, then, to think of our having not two loyalties but one loyalty, and that one loyalty is reflexive. The loyalty to what is to be ever turns us back to what is. To love God is to share God's love for his world. He loves the world by freeing the world from its bondage to itself, so that it may be itself. We have not even broached the profundity of Christian social thought until we see its connection with the mystery of salvation. Moral theology is not simply ethics or the science of rights and wrongs. Moral theology is, first of all, theology. Christian social thought, and most emphatically Catholic social thought, cannot be understood apart from what Cardinal Ratzinger has called the "structure of faith." God's loving purpose in creation, his covenantal election of Israel, his self-disclosure in Jesus the Christ, the Spirit's guidance of the Church, and all this set against an eschatological horizon—here is the "structure" within which Christians discern their responsibilities in society.

The first and utterly normative thing that Christians say is that Jesus Christ is Lord. Nothing can be permitted to compromise or fudge our allegiance to his lordship. The reflexive nature of that loyalty is grounded in the incarnation of God in Jesus of Nazareth. The distinctive thing about the Hebrew prophets, wrote the late Rabbi Abraham Joshua Heschel, is that they were able to hold God and man in one thought. So the Christian cannot think of God without thinking of man, nor of man without thinking of God. For us, these are held together in one thought because they are held together in the one person, the God-Man Jesus Christ.

We participate in the person of Christ, and therefore in the trinitarian life of God himself, through our initiation into Christ's body, the Church. All who are baptized belong to the Church. According to the Second Vatican Council (*Lumen Gentium*), that one Church "subsists" in the Roman Catholic Church. Therefore Catholic social thought is not just for Catholics. Put differently, it is thoroughly catholic (lower case), intending to address all Christians and, indeed, in many instances, "all people of good will." Certainly all Christians are deeply implicated, so to speak, in Catholic social thought. Through the centuries and numerically at present, Roman Catholicism constitutes the largest part of the Christian presence to the world. Anyone who cares about that presence must care about Catholic social teaching. This does not mean, of course, that non-Catholics will always agree with that teaching, or even agree with it most of the time. Nor does it mean that there will not be continuing conversation and controversy among Catholics with respect to social teaching. On the contrary, conversation and even controversy are part of the development of Catholic thought under the authentic guidance of the magisterium of the Church.

My point here is a simple one, although it is a simple truth oft forgotten. Christian social thought is theologically grounded in the revelation of God in Christ. That revelation invites a relentlessly singular loyalty that is reflexive in nature and issues in the claim that Jesus Christ is Lord. That claim, in turn, is borne though history by the community, called the Church, that witnesses to his lordship. However tragically divided into churches and communions, that community is ultimately one. The Catholic Church claims to embody and anticipate the unity of all Christians. Whatever non-Catholics make of that claim, it should be obvious that it is not possible to speak of the Church without major reference to the church called Roman Catholic. It is not possible, that is, unless one is prepared to excommunicate, so to speak, the great majority of the Christians of both the past and present.

Christian social thought, then, is both Christological and ecclesiological. The reflexivity of Christian loyalty requires that to say yes to the head is to say yes to his body, the Church. To say that Christ is Lord is to commit ourselves to the people who say that Christ is Lord. The Church is a community ahead of time. It proclaims now what will one day be acknowledged by all. "Therefore God has highly exalted him and bestowed on him the name which is above every name, that at the name of Jesus every knee should bow, in heaven and on earth and under the earth, and every tongue confess that Jesus Christ is Lord, to the glory of God the Father" (Phil. 2:9–11). Christian social thought, and Catholic social thought in particular, is premised upon that sure expectation. Social responsibility requires the doing of many things. We must aim to ameliorate suffering, to avert great evils, and to establish whatever modicum of justice is possible in a world grievously wounded by sin. But, above all, the purpose of Christians is to prepare the world for that day when the seventh angel sounds his trumpet and all creation declares, "The kingdom of the world has become the kingdom of our Lord and of his Christ, and he shall reign for ever and ever" (Rev. 11:15).

Social thought that is Christological and therefore ecclesiological can result in Christians taking quite different postures toward our worldly responsibilities. Citizens of the City of God may at times feel themselves to be besieged by a world that has declared war on its true Lord and its own promised fulfillment. Then Christians may think that the most imperative call is to "come out from among them and be separate" (II Cor. 6:17). This may result in what is pejoratively termed a "fortress mentality"—a mentality that critics say marked the Catholic Church in the several centuries prior to Vatican II. We should try to nurture a measure of charity when it comes to judging what Christians of other times and places discerned to be their duty. When under attack and momentarily facing overwhelming odds, a fortress might seem like a pretty good idea. It was not a Tridentine Catholic, after all, who wrote "A Mighty Fortress Is Our God."

A fortress mentality can be associated with either sectarianism or triumphalism. In the former case, the Church is thought of as a very fragile fortress, being little more than a small community of believers, supporting one another in the life of discipleship, having no expectation of influencing the surrounding culture, and drawing comfort from the Lord's promise, "Fear not, little flock, it is the Father's good pleasure to give you the Kingdom" (Luke 12:32). In the triumphalist case, the fortress is very big, formidably organized along martial lines, and those within are only waiting for the propitious moment to storm out of the gates and carry the day against the enemies of Christ and his Church. It is somewhat more difficult to find solid biblical support for this interpretation of the Church as a fortress.

A good many thoughtful Christians today—Protestant, Orthodox, and Catholic—lean toward the sectarian model when thinking about Church and culture. They are to be found on both the right and the left of the political spectrum, for Christian discipleship is no respecter of partisan lines. They agree that ours is a post-Christian or even anti-Christian culture. Some argue that the very notion of a "Christian culture" is wrongheaded, and always has been. They are robustly skeptical of the proposal that the Church can or should engage the culture. The Church cannot engage the culture, they say, because the two represent entirely different and antithetical cultural-linguistic traditions. The Church's witness and way of life has no purchase—no place to take hold, no common ground for debate—with the ways of the world. And, they add, the Church should not attempt to engage the culture because experience demonstrates that attempted engagement leads to accommodation, and accommodation leads to capitulation. "Do not be conformed to this world," the Apostle Paul instructs us, "but be transformed by the renewal of your mind" (Rom. 12:2).

There is much to be said, I believe, for the sectarian model in thinking about the relationship between the Church and society. Anyone who understands the radical distinctiveness—what the New Testament calls the *scandalon*—of the Christian claim has to have considerable sympathy for the sectarian model. "Sectarian" is not necessarily pejorative; it can be a synonym for faithful. In times of cultural vibrancy, Christians may tend to dismiss it lightly. But in times of cultural degeneracy, such as our own, it has a powerful appeal, and rightly so. Any discussion of the Church and society that is not marked by a sympathetic awareness of the sectarian option is not to be fully trusted. In Catholicism, the monastic tradition keeps alive the awareness that there is a radically "other way," and that, in some circumstances of cultural disintegration and hostility to the gospel, it may be the best way, indeed the normative way. No matter how impressive its institutions or how large its numbers or how palpable its cultural influence, the Church must never forget that it is, in the final analysis, the "little flock" completely dependent upon the promise of its Lord.

And yet, while the sectarian model must always be in play, it is not dominant in Catholic social thought, as I understand it. As distinct from both sectarianism and the transformative expectations associated with triumphalism, Catholic social teaching conceives of the people of God as *penetrating* the temporal order with the seed and spirit of Christian truth. The Church eschews worldly means of domination. From the eleventh century on, a new pope was crowned with the papal tiara, symbolizing both spiritual and temporal power. The tiara was expanded by Boniface VII (d. 1303) and reached its final and most ambitious form as a symbolic statement of power under Clement V (d. 1314). It has not been used since the death of Paul VI. The retirement of the papal tiara is of great significance in understanding the development of Catholic thought.

The Second Vatican Council says this about the Church's relation to the world: "It is to be a leaven and, as it were, the soul of human society in its renewal by Christ" (*Gaudium et Spes* [GS], paragraph 40). The Council cites the second- or third-century "Letter to Diognetus": "What the soul is in the body, let Christians be in the world" (*Lumen Gentium* [LG], paragraph 38). The Church is the conscience of society when questions are raised that are fundamental to human dignity. Thus it is "the sign and the safeguard of the transcendence of the human person" (*GS*, 76). But the Church signs and safeguards the sphere within which Christians, especially lay Christians, exercise their prudential judgement according to their own conscience (*LG*, 36; *GS*, 43). The relationship between the Church and culture is hardly one-way. The sciences, literature, philosophy, and the arts can contribute to a fuller understanding of the faith and its implications for the right ordering of society (*GS*, 62).

There is no doubt, then, that the Catholic disposition with respect to social responsibility is one of engagement. It is engagement in full awareness of the temptations to accommodation and capitulation. It is engagement joined to an appreciation of the sectarian model as a cautionary counterpoint within the life of the entire Church, and as a controlling theme of communities especially called to exemplify the radical "otherness" of the Christian vocation. It is engagement that is disciplined by the knowledge of the universal nature and mission of a church that cannot be limited to any temporal order but provides a bond of unity for all sorts and conditions of men (*GS*, 42). Finally, it is an engagement that is necessarily ambivalent. The Church's ambivalence is a saving ambivalence. It is a saving ambivalence in that social responsibility is understood within the context of salvation—of the Church's constituting commission to direct human beings to their ultimate end, which is to say, to God. And it is a saving ambivalence in that it saves us from the imperiousness of all present and proposed social orders short of the right ordering of everything in the rule of God.

Christian social thought, it has always seemed to me, must be strongly marked by the paradoxical. The paradox is inherent in the reflexivity described above. On the one hand, we are to take social responsibility with intense seriousness, indeed with religious seriousness. On the other, the same imperative requires that we not take the social task all *that* seriously—certainly not as seriously as it is often taken by those who have only one city and one citizenship. This is the abiding awkwardness of people ahead of time, of people who have here no abiding city (Heb. 13:12). The "Letter to

Diognetus" cited by the Council goes on to describe Christians this way:

> Though they are residents at home in their own countries, their behavior there is more like that of transients; they take their full part as citizens, but they also submit to anything and everything as if they were aliens. For them, any foreign country is a homeland, and any homeland a foreign country.

Resident aliens. That pretty well sums it up. What that means for specific actions, policies, and political directions, Christians will be discussing and disputing until the End Time. Along the way, the tradition of Catholic social teaching represents the most comprehensive body of reflection available to us. For Roman Catholics, it is a peculiarly authoritative guide. For all the covenantal children of Abraham, it is a guide that must not be ignored.

1

In the Beginning
Rerum Novarum (1891)

WILLIAM MURPHY

CATHOLIC social teaching certainly did not begin with the appearance of *Rerum Novarum* ("Of New Things") on May 15, 1891. Social doctrine has been a constant element of the Church's life from the beginning; it is a logical application of Catholic philosophical and theological thought to the questions of person and society.

Yet *Rerum Novarum* did mark a historical and theological turning point both for papal teaching and for social thought and action. It broke through some barriers that had impeded Catholic social thought and in many ways has become the standard for the Church's social teaching.

Rerum Novarum was also very much the product of its day and of the pontiff who wrote it. Regrettably, there is no modern critical biography of that pope, Leo XIII, born Gioacchino Pecci. René Fulop-Miller's *Leo XIII and His Times* was translated into English in 1937. Its subtitle gives a sense of its prose: "Might of the Church—Power in the World." Portions of Eduardo Soderini's

Monsignor **William Murphy** is director of the Office of Social Justice and secretary for community relations for the Archdiocise of Boston. He teaches social ethics at Saint John's Seminary and at Pope John XXIII Seminary. He was undersecretary of the Pontifical Commission for Justice and Peace from 1980 to 1987.

standard work were published in 1934 as *The Pontificate of Leo XIII*. It remains odd, however, that the pope who first opened the Vatican archives to modern historical research should himself not have attracted a more eager core of researchers.

Let us look briefly at the life of Pope Leo XIII and at the context of *Rerum Novarum*. This will prepare us to confront the encyclical itself and to evaluate its significance, particularly in light of current circumstances and the reflection that Pope John Paul II offered us in his 1991 encyclical *Centesimus Annus*.

Gioacchino Pecci: Leo XIII

Vincenzo Gioacchino Pecci was born in the small town of Carpineto Romano on March 2, 1810. His family came from the minor nobility and was characterized by two elements that would shape the formation of young Pecci: a deep religious nature and a high appreciation of education. The young man studied at the Jesuit college of Viterbo and in Rome. In 1824, just before the death of his mother, he took ecclesiastical dress. After obtaining his doctorate in theology in 1832, he entered the service of the Holy See and quickly gained the attention of Pope Gregory XVI, who was to become his protector.

Administering Benevento and Perugia

Pecci was ordained a priest in December 1837. Just two months later Gregory XVI named him apostolic delegate to the city of Benevento. Benevento, a papal enclave within the kingdom of Naples, was traditionally ruled by a prelate named by the Holy Father. However, the actual administration of the city had for some time been controlled by some powerful families and their allies, and the nominal ruler was very much at the mercy of those who held the reins of the city's economic, social, and political life. Add to this the fact that the court of Naples had for some time wished to acquire this piece of property, which it surrounded, and the delicacy of the position Pecci occupied becomes apparent.

While Gregory XVI was able to withstand the blandishments of the court of Naples, young Pecci was far less successful in governing

Benevento. Groups occupied his palace. He found himself in disputes with the judges of the law courts, and he was unable to
countermand a rising tide of violence. Correspondence between
Pecci and the Vatican secretary of state shows that, while Pecci
wished to confront the leading figures of dissension and to bring
about a major change in the political and social climate, the
secretary kept insisting upon prudence and circumspection.

There were rumors that Msgr. Pecci would be moved out of
Benevento, and in fact less than a year after his arrival, he was
offered a post in Rome. He chose to stay in Benevento. Despite his
energetic efforts, the situation did not improve. Yet Gregory XVI,
faced with contrary opinion, continued to have great confidence in
the young man, and in 1841 he sent him as delegate to Perugia,
then the capital of Umbria. There, Pecci immediately became active
in reorganizing the justice system and the municipal government.

Nuncio to Belgium

Two years later, upon the advice of Cardinal Lambruschini, the
secretary of state, Gregory XVI named Pecci archbishop of Damiata
and made him papal nuncio to Belgium. Belgium was considered a
second-class nunciature, ranking below such places as France and
Spain, but was usually seen as a testing ground for rising young
diplomats. Like Benevento, it did not present Pecci with an easy
situation. The Church was trying to find its way within Belgian
society. In 1830 the Belgian constitution had guaranteed freedom
of religion, and the Belgian bishops felt this guarantee presented a
moment of opportunity for the Church. They had gone forward
with their desire to create at Louvain a new Catholic university that
would become a premier seat of learning. But the political situation
complicated this move. The king was non-Catholic, the parliament
was split between Catholics and liberals, and some in the Catholic
party were attempting to use the Holy See for political ends.

Msgr. Pecci, who arrived in 1843, was instructed by the Vatican
Secretariat of State to be supportive of the Belgian bishops but to
be prudent in the political situation. However, the interrelation
between religion and politics would prove to be his undoing.

In the elections that year the Catholics, though they remained a
numerical majority in parliament, lost most of their influential

leaders. This left the Catholic party without the kind of sophisti-cated leadership that might well have been able to maintain a Catholic presence in an increasingly complex political situation. Later that year the bishops issued a circular letter against "bad books." Simple enough in itself, this had the effect of galvanizing Catholics and drawing lines within Belgian society regarding cen-sorship. Some felt Pecci should have restrained the bishops. The Austrian chancellor Metternich complained to Cardinal Lambrus-chini, and the consensus in diplomatic circles was that Pecci had erred. All the elements were in place for a confrontation.

The catalyst was provided by a new bill on higher education requiring that two-thirds of the state examining board be appointed by the government. The bishops saw this as an attack on the Catholic university, and they protested vigorously that it would be an infringement on academic independence. Coming from those whose letter against "bad books" had made them, in the eyes of many, proponents of censorship, this call for academic freedom was not well received. Thus a comparatively unimportant piece of legislation became the catalyst for significant social and political upheaval.

The Catholic position ultimately won, but not without certain costs. One was the removal of the papal nuncio. The Belgian government, which was being watched by Austria, Prussia, and France, had suffered a defeat and without doubt needed someone on the diplomatic level who could be seen as the culprit. It decided to ask for the recall of Msgr. Pecci. Cardinal Lambuschini agreed but did not want to give in immediately. However, with Vienna as well as Brussels criticizing Pecci's support of the bishops, his removal was only a matter of time.

On October 24, 1845, Cardinal Lambruschini wrote to inform Pecci that the Holy Father was to name him the bishop of Perugia. Pecci was implicitly assured, however, that even though he had to leave Benevento as an unsuccessful apostolic delegate, and even though in Belgium he had become the object of the ire of not only that government but others as well, he would in time be made a cardinal.

Bishop of Perugia

Pecci's new appointment was not an unmixed blessing. Perugia was a backwater town. The promise of the red hat, while a consolation certainly, was for the future and not the present. Indeed, it was not fulfilled until eight years later, at the consistory of December 1853, by Gregory's successor, Pius IX.

Yet the secret of the success of the pontificate of Leo XIII lies in Perugia, where for thirty years Bishop Pecci exercised his pastoral mission. While many might have seen it as banishment to a position without influence, Pecci came into his own in Perugia, intellectually and pastorally. He turned his home into a center for conversation and the exchange of ideas. He read widely and deeply, not only in Italian but also in French and German, and his house became, in the words of his biographer Soderini, "a reading room." Seminarians were invited to his table often and were encouraged to pursue their intellectual interests and their academic careers. Pecci also maintained a prolific correspondence. And no bishop of any importance who came to Rome failed to make a side trip to Perugia. There the visitors contributed to the bishop's grasp of current events—political, social, and economic as well as ecclesiastical.

Pecci's pastoral letters ranged in subject from the prerogatives of the pope, to the sacrament of marriage, to the current condition of the Church, to various aspects of domestic and civil life. He took an active interest in the social and economic conditions of the people of his diocese and helped organize cooperatives that offered people not only the money they needed for agricultural development but also food in times of scarcity. He was acutely aware of the situation in the Papal States and the growing desire for the unification of Italy. To that end he did not hesitate to urge upon Pius IX a greater understanding of the political unrest and the need for appropriate response by the papacy.

In short, Pecci's pastoral ministry in Perugia was marked by a keen sense of his mission as a bishop, intellectual curiosity and wide-ranging interests, and a desire to bring about social and cultural as well as religious development among the people. His contemporaries cited him as a man of wide political understanding and vast knowledge. Small wonder that when he was named papal chamberlain in 1876, a number of the cardinals saw this as an overdue recognition by Pius IX of a man of tremendous talent and very real accomplishment.

Back to Rome

Pecci's appointment as chamberlain came at the end of the pontificate of Pius IX and, significantly, after the death of Cardinal Antonelli, secretary of state through the major part of the Pius IX pontificate, who had long disliked Pecci. With Antonelli gone, Pius's selection of Pecci was widely applauded inside the Sacred College. Pecci was now in a position to be considered as a future pope.

Pius IX died in 1878. In the conclave to elect his successor, there were two tendencies in the College of Cardinals. One group wanted a person who would be intransigent in maintaining the policies of Pius IX. The other group remained loyal to Pius IX but was eager to go beyond those positions that had become associated with his long pontificate. The first group opposed nineteenth-century political developments as "modernist" and pernicious. These cardinals looked for a pope who would be known for piety and holiness rather than for intellectual gifts or political skills. The second group desired new opportunities for progress and dialogue.

Cardinal Pecci fell very clearly into the second group, which prevailed, and on February 20, 1878, he was elected pope. He took the name Leo XIII in admiration for the pontiff of his youth, Leo XII, who had died in 1829.

Early Initiatives as Pope

A few points about the beginning of Leo's pontificate are significant in relation to *Rerum Novarum*. It is the custom for a new pope to send letters of greetings to the heads of state of countries accredited to the Holy See. These letters very often are simply formal notices that the new pope has been elected. Leo XIII, however, wrote into each letter an expression of his concern about the relationship between the Holy See and that particular country.

Thus from the very beginning he showed that he intended to move beyond the political intransigence of Pius IX and to seek a more subtle and supple relationship with the nations. So, too, his choice of Cardinal Franchi as secretary of state showed that he wanted someone broadly experienced in both ecclesiastical and political matters who would be more than simply a martinet of Vatican opinions.

Also, from the very beginning Leo's writings indicated that his pontificate would go in its own direction, not rejecting the past but moving forward to examine the important issues of the day. His first encyclical, *Inscrutabili*, developed his view that there should be positive relations between the Church and society. He did not hesitate to point out the "current misdeeds" that beset the situation in Europe, but he held out the olive branch, explaining how the Church and society could work together for the common good. In that same year, 1878, he published the letter *Quod Apostolici Muneris*, in which he tackled head-on the international socialist movement. While condemning the movement, he also expressed his concern about social questions.

As for more ecclesiastical matters, Leo's interest in reviving Thomism constituted a radical move away from the stagnation of Catholic intellectual life. A kind of positivism had become the order of the day in the theological institutes and universities. The revival of Thomism, which Leo had begun in Perugia, was a means for critical Catholic thought to have an influence on intellectual life. Leo's work on Scripture further enhanced his commitment to a revival of intellectual life in the Church. Allied to that were his interest in historical studies and his encouragement of the archaeologist DeRossi and of Christian archaeological studies.

In fact, what the pontificate of Leo XIII showed prior to the appearance of his great social encyclical in 1891 was his determination, despite his age (eighty in 1890) and despite the hesitations of others, to move the Church forward in a new dialogue with society. That dialogue would find expression most productively in *Rerum Novarum*. The encyclical would also give direction to the forces inside Catholicism that had been grappling with the economic and social challenges of the day.

THE CHRISTIAN SOCIAL MOVEMENT

It is often said that the Church lost the working class in the nineteenth century. Just what is the Church's record during that century noted for so much progress and so many new social problems?[1]

It is true that the Church did not anticipate the rise of a new social class. The Industrial Revolution created the need for a large body of workers, a need made more acute by the decimation of manpower during the Napoleonic Wars. Every available able-bodied man, woman, and child was brought into the work force in industrialized England, Belgium, Holland, northern France, and Germany. The wretched condition of many of the workers gave rise to the socialist option. The socialists recognized that a new class had appeared, a class that needed to struggle to vindicate its rights. The proletariat was established. But Christians for the most part failed to see that. They looked on workers not so much as a new class but as *new poor* whose wretchedness as individuals and families stimulated Christian concern.

The Christian social movement in the nineteenth century was not born as a philosophy or ideology, a movement or a political party. Rather, it was the Church's response to specific problems it faced in various countries as it tried to minister to the new poor. Only after a certain amount of experience had accumulated did the Church grasp the deeper implications of what was happening.

1848: Sweeping Social Change

Major changes, political and social, swept across Europe in 1848. It was a year somewhat like 1989. The French bishops attempted to respond to the ferment by calling attention to owners' insensitivity to the needs of their employees. They called for a sense of partnership in which both the owner and the employee would be given due respect. These bishops explicitly rejected the developing socialist interpretations of "the proletariat" and any attempt to reduce the problem to a mechanistic interpretation of economics. Their appeal was to conscience. It was a moral appeal that sought to change society, not through the overhaul of systems, but through personal spiritual renewal.

A major shift occurred with the ministries of two bishops, Affre of Paris and, more importantly, Ketteler of Mainz. Bishop Affre addressed the situation by looking not only at the suffering of the worker but also at the situation that produced it. He asked whether the integral laws of the economic system demanded the constant diminution of the worker or whether in fact certain virtues could check this.

Affre's response was threefold. First, he spoke about egoism, what he called the cupidity of the owners. In a traditional and classical way he called for an end to egoistic greed. Second, the bishop said it was necessary to modify economic systems in order to safeguard the rights of workers, who he said are "not chattel." Third, he distinguished between the "industrial phenomenon" and the philosophical systems that direct it. People who are indifferent toward God, he said, very often cause economic systems to operate in ways that work against the common good.

Affre did not attempt to analyze economic systems in themselves but focused on the person within the systems. He pointed to human shortcomings, such as cupidity, and saw agnosticism and atheism as root causes of the problem. He spoke about the rights of workers and insisted that they should not be treated as merchandise or chattel.

Ketteler: Laying the Groundwork

The man often called the "founder of social Catholicism" is Bishop Wilhelm Emmanuel von Ketteler (1811–77), whom Leo XIII spoke of as "my great predecessor, the man from whom I learned." Ketteler moved beyond moral concern and moral suasion to a rigorous intellectual analysis that laid the foundations for Leo's *Rerum Novarum*. Outspoken in his opposition to the atheistic and agnostic academic circles of his day, Ketteler did not limit himself to condemnation. He had the ability to expose the intellectual weakness of the professors at Frankfurt, where he lived as a young curate, and to offer an alternative understanding of social and political problems.

The predominant theorists proposed a kind of economic liberalism that placed total faith in the laws of supply and demand, as if they were laws of nature. Ketteler offered a different reading. He proceeded on three levels: first, an exposé and analysis of the social and economic misery of the working class; second, a challenge to the faulty intellectual underpinnings of the system that caused this misery; and, finally, the alternative, a Christian vision of the person and society.

In 1848 the bishop of Mainz invited the young curate to come from Frankfurt to take part in a series of Advent services in the Mainz cathedral. Ketteler's five sermons focused on the questions of property, moral freedom, the final end of man, the family, and the authority of the Church. He pointed out that egoism is a constant problem and that avarice must be fought at all levels in the economic system. Then he went beyond the phenomenon of sin to confront the philosophies and ideologies that controlled the economy: they were unable, he said, to respond to the fundamental needs and rights of the workers. Ketteler offered a set of doctrinal principles by which to judge these prevailing ideas and to present a fuller understanding of man and society. That set of principles became the basis of the Christian social movement.

Ketteler was able to look at two dimensions: the *personal*, the life of virtue or vice and the choices that flow from it, and the *social*, the systems that reflect or fail to reflect ethical values. For perhaps the first time he raised the important subject of how religion and temporal affairs relate to each other. Both traditional liberalism and socialism dismissed religion from the world of affairs. The liberal attitude saw religion as a private affair that had nothing to do with business practices. The socialist was even more negative, not simply relegating religion to the private realm but dismissing it as part of the means by which the proletariat was held in subjection. Ketteler argued that religion must concern itself with temporal affairs and that temporal affairs must be judged by and influenced by the values that come from a religious vision of man and society. His argument would later be developed by Leo XIII in *Rerum Novarum*.

From Theory to Action

Ketteler did not limit himself to theory. He felt that analysis was important only to the extent that it influenced social action; theory must lead to, and be validated by, action. All the elements of the Christian social movement were now in place.

When Ketteler became bishop of Mainz in 1850, he in no way saw himself as a major thinker or the leader of a new movement. As his biographer George Goyau points out, his major concern was pastoral. He wrote on religious subjects and busied himself with pastoral duties. However, within a few years he realized that not enough Catholic leaders were dealing with the problems of society, particularly the plight of the workers.

Therefore Ketteler began to address specific social questions, always from a doctrinal foundation. He spoke about the need for cooperatives to help workers and to improve production. He said that workers' salaries should be commensurate with work done, and that working hours should not be so long that the workers had no time for recreation and for family life. He criticized child and female labor and said that women should be at home to take care of children. He was, however, quite diffident about the right of workers to unionize and seemed to skirt that subject in order to defend the importance of cooperatives. He rejected revolution as unworthy of the human spirit and ultimately destructive of society.

Ketteler did not create a new theological or sociopolitical system. Nor was he an intellectual of the first magnitude. Yet he, more than anyone else, was the main influence behind *Rerum Novarum*.

Ketteler was important for at least three reasons. First, he saw clearly that social organization depends upon underlying philosophical and ideological presuppositions. In his view, social organization must be mediated by doctrinal principles that uphold the value of the person and the equal dignity of all human beings. Second, he realized that the transformation of society is tied to the transformation of souls. Ketteler saw that the encouragement of virtue must also unleash the potential of virtue into the social situation. Third, Ketteler argued that social action springs intrinsically from Christian concern. A person cannot be a Christian, he insisted, if his convictions do not flow into social action, and if his social action is not guided by the Christian principles that shape his personal life.

Other Influences

Many other persons contributed to the Christian social movement. Charles Perin of Belgium, Baron von Vogelsang of Austria, and Guiseppe Toniolo of Torino were among the social scientists who analyzed society from a Christian point of view. And local groups such as the Union de Fribourg and the School of Angers also had an influence on Christian thought and action.

England and the United States faced problems similar to those confronting continental Europe, though each of course had its own particular circumstances. In the United States the principal issue was the Church's response to an early trade union, the Knights of Labor. The Catholic Church in the United States was traditionally suspicious of secret societies, fearing that they could have an adverse effect on the social fabric as a whole, and many Catholics thought the newly organized Knights fell into this category that was normally banned. But James Cardinal Gibbons, the archbishop of Baltimore, took a different tack: he offered "cordial approval" to the Knights when they struck against the Southwest Railway System of Jay Gould. While it would take us too far afield to chronicle the development of the famous Gibbons Memorial (or petition) on the Knights of Labor, prepared in 1887 for the Holy See, the importance of the cardinal's undertaking for the future of church-labor relations in the United States can hardly be exaggerated. The debate over the Knights was watched keenly in Rome and could not have failed to have had some influence on the mind of the pontiff.

Gibbons examined the constitution of the Knights of Labor, supplied to him by a friendly priest in Pennsylvania, and concluded that the organization was compatible with Catholic teaching. The Knights had also made it clear that they were willing to amend their constitution should anything be found at odds with church doctrine. Gibbons's defense of the union served the purpose of separating the idea of labor movements from the suspicion about secret societies in general. For laborers to organize themselves was "only natural and just," said Gibbons, and the ends they sought were correct and deserving of church support. By responding to two important issues—the right of the workers to organize themselves and the responsibilities of workers to insure that their organization did not harm the common good—Gibbons helped develop a new Catholic attitude toward organized labor, at least as it evolved in the United States.

Paradoxically, the Knights of Labor were in decline in 1888, when Rome responded positively to Gibbons's appeal. But that did not dampen the enthusiasm for the approval given to the Knights. While Rome continued to be concerned about socialism and about the need to protect private property, the Holy See's positive response to Gibbons indicated the direction in which its thinking was going. On the other hand, while there is no doubt that Gibbons did much to promote a positive relationship between the Church in the United States and labor, John Tracy Ellis concludes in his biography of the cardinal that there is "no clear proof that the Pope was directly influenced by Gibbons and his memorial on the Knights of Labor" in his writing of *Rerum Novarum*.[2] Perhaps the ultimate influence of Gibbons was to prepare the way for a good reception of the encyclical in the United States when it appeared in 1891.

Across the Atlantic, Cardinal Henry Edward Manning, archbishop of Westminster, had a more direct influence on the development of *Rerum Novarum*. His intervention in the London dockworkers' strike of 1889 was a important moment for the leadership of the Church in resolving social disputes. Manning had indicated earlier his interest in the Knights of Labor by supporting the position of Cardinal Gibbons in letters to persons in Rome. Manning's influence in Rome was considerable, for influential persons in the Curia saw him as the epitome of the church leader involved in the transformation of society.

Manning's most direct influence on Leo XIII probably resulted from the letter he sent to the Social Congress at Liège in 1890. Unable to be present himself, Manning in a letter that was read at the congress advocated Sunday rest, freedom of association and arbitration, and an eight-hour daily limit on the labor of women and children. Manning also pressed for just wages and for free contracts between capital and labor. Leo himself wrote Manning in January 1891, expressing his concern over Ireland and noting the interest he and Manning shared in "the condition of the working men." Thus it seems clear that Manning's social thought and social activism had a significant influence on the pope himself, as well as on the Roman Curia.

In a succinct history of the writing of *Rerum Novarum* published in *L'Osservatore Romano* (March 18, 1992), Gino Concetti cites Monsignor Antonazzi's conclusion that this first modern social encyclical "had several editors and several drafts." There is ample evidence, however, that while Monsignor Volpini and Father Liberatore composed the first draft and Cardinal Zigliara prepared the second and third, Pope Leo XIII supervised these drafts step by step, making sure that each fully expressed his thought and the fruit of his own efforts.

Three Unanswered Questions

With all the various advances made by Ketteler, Manning, and others, certain important questions remained unanswered. First, unions: are they justifiable or not? The Christian social movement either denied the right of unions or skirted the issue by proposing guilds. Most Christian social theorists of the time thought the ideal of the medieval guild seemed more in keeping with Christian social tradition. But this had intrinsic problems. The guild was a gathering of persons who all were members of the same trade, owned their own means of production, and worked singly or in groups to make their own products. It was a cooperative of equals; there was no owner to whom they had to respond.

A second problem had to do with philosophy and ideology: were the choices only liberalism and socialism? Catholic social thought could find a home in neither one. Liberalism generally seemed more favorable to religion, at least in the private sphere. Socialism was clearly anti-religious and explicitly anti-Catholic and anticlerical. Yet the socialists responded to the needs of the workers in ways that the liberals did not.

A third unresolved problem was the attraction to socialism. Many workers, including many Catholics, heard the Socialist International defend them and struggle in their behalf. Why should they not support those who supported them? Many pastors and Christian social thinkers were at a loss to propose an alternative.

The Christian social movement varied from country to country, and the Congress of Catholic Social Works, which met in 1866, 1867, and 1890, became a meeting ground for various tendencies and proposals. At the last congress, in 1890, those tendencies not only met but clashed.

What the Encyclical Says

Leo XIII's great encyclical *Rerum Novarum* did not reconcile the differing tendencies in the Christian social movement or gather them together into one. It did, however, set forth a broad-based middle course that in time would become the standard against which Christian social action would be measured.

Leo XIII opens the encyclical with a clear statement of the social problem (section 1–20).[3] Next he analyzes the proposal made by the Socialist International, including its view of private property, the person, and the family (3–12). Then Leo makes his counterproposal (13–45), which is divided into three areas: the action of the Church, the action of the state, and the relationship of employers and employees. He concludes the encyclical by speaking of the duties of the state, of the rich, of the poor, and finally of the clergy.

In his introduction, Leo XIII raises the subjects of capital, labor, the disparity between rich and poor, the wretchedness and misery of the poor, and the injustice suffered by the majority of the working class. It is interesting to note that from the very beginning he speaks of "relative rights and mutual duties"; he casts his argument in terms of a society that is inclusive rather than exclusive, a society that insists on collaboration ·rather than conflict and polarization.

In Defense of Private Property

Moving immediately to the challenge of the socialist solution, Leo XIII centers his concern on the matter of property. The Socialist International had argued for the necessity of the abolition of private property and transfer of the ownership of the means of production to the proletariat. This not only would harm the interests of the worker himself, says Leo, but would destroy the structure of the home by enabling the state to exercise control of the family.

The pope points out that property operates for the good of people and that the possession of property is, therefore, a natural and legitimate object of the work that men and women undertake: "If one man hires out to another his strength or skill, he does so for the purpose of receiving in return what is necessary for the satisfaction of his needs; he therefore expressly intends to acquire a right full and real, not only to the renumeration, but also to the disposal of such renumeration, just as he pleases." This leads the pope to his conclusion that the remedy the socialists propose is manifestly against justice. For "every man has by nature the right to possess property as his own" (4).

Given the absolutizing of the right of private property that has held sway in certain quarters in the United States and other industrialized countries, it is interesting to note that Leo XIII views it within a broader context. In what sense has God given the earth to mankind? Leo's answer is: "not in the sense that all without distinction can deal with it as they like, but rather that no part of it was assigned to anyone in particular, and that the limits of private possession have been left to be fixed by man's own industry and by the laws of individual races" (7). Subsequent pontiffs will nuance this position. However, it is important to see that at the time when private property was one of the major points of contention between socialism and liberalism, Leo XIII spoke strongly in favor of private property but immediately placed it within the context of another principle of Catholic social teaching, namely, the universal purpose of created things.

Importance of the Family

The second major point in the encyclical (9–12), the importance of the family, is a central theme of Catholic social thought and, like the rights and duties of the person, is a non-contradictable point of reference. Leo uses traditional terms, speaking of the family as a true society. By referring to Genesis (9) and to the rights of the family (10), he sets out the two directions that reflection on the family will subsequently take. One direction, going back to the scriptural foundations, establishes the relationship between male and female as the highest expression of God's intention for creation. The second points forward toward a whole stream of thought about rights and duties that will culminate in the "Charter of the Rights of Family," published by the Holy See in 1983.

Leo's conclusion is simple but profound. First, because the family is the basic cell of society, the state and the institutions of society have an obligation to foster and protect it. Second, the family is so

fundamentally important that the socialist argument for the abolition of property and the community of goods must be rejected
precisely because it stands against the natural desires of human
beings and against the institution of the family as the basic cell of
society. These two points will be fundamental elements of subsequent Catholic social teaching.

A Role for the Church in Society

Leo's rejection of the socialist proposal does not end the matter.
He goes on to move the discussion away from an exclusively social
or economic analysis of society toward a Christian anthropology as
the way toward the solution of social problems. This significant
breakthrough in papal teaching adopts the insight of Ketteler that
doctrinal principles and social analysis must be used to illumine and
shape social action. Revolutionary at the time, it vindicates a specific
role for the Church that would become commonplace in the
subsequent one hundred years of social thought.

The key to Leo's explanation of the Church's role in society (13–
25) is in section 13: "It is the Church that insists, on the authority of
the Gospel, upon those teachings whereby the conflict can be brought
to an end, or rendered, at least, far less bitter; the Church uses her
efforts not only to enlighten the mind, but to direct by her precepts
the life and conduct of each and all." According to this, the Church
must keep in mind several very specific points. First, it must view the
human condition realistically. In contrast both to nineteenth-century
utopianism and to the socialist call for a new society, Leo XIII was a
Christian realist. He recognized that man's work is compulsory and
painful because of sin, as it says in Genesis 3:17. He recognized that
"to suffer and to endure is the lot of humanity," and that "no strength
and no artifice will ever succeed in banishing from human life the ills
and troubles which beset it." This realism renders the Church better
able to address social ills and to give an answer that is neither utopian
nor cynically pessimistic.

No Inherent Class Conflict

Leo rejects the concept of class conflict, the idea "that the wealthy
and the working-men are intended by nature to live in mutual

conflict" (15). He defends the dignity and rights of every person and the obligations that are proper to that person's state in life and role in society. The Church is to try to "bind class to class in friendliness and good feeling" (18).

Lest this seem utopian, it should be noted that Leo XIII refused to be caught in the social Darwinism of liberalism. He rejects the diminution of the worker in liberalism just as clearly as he rejects class conflict and socialism. The worker is not to be used as chattel, nor can he somehow or another be equated with capital. Rather, in the relationship between capital and labor, the dignity of the worker has priority precisely because he is a human being created in the image of God with certain rights, especially the right to found a family. All other things need to be evaluated in light of that principle. Thus Leo can go on to speak of the use of money, of the importance of almsgiving, and of the connection of justice and charity within the vision of human dignity and family life.

That finally leads him to move beyond rights and duties to strike a note that will be picked up in subsequent teaching, particularly by Pius XI in *Quadragesimo Anno*. After speaking of Christ, who "did not disdain to spend a great part of His life as a carpenter," Leo states, "From contemplation of this Divine model, it is more easy to understand that the true worth and nobility of man lie in his moral qualities, that is, in virtue; that virtue is moreover the common inheritance of men, equally within the reach of high and low, rich and poor; and that virtue, and virtue alone, wherever found, will be followed by the rewards of everlasting happiness" (20).

In the 1930s and in the 1970s, Catholic social theorists debated whether restructuring society should be the first aim of Catholic social teaching. Some said it should; others said that Catholic social teaching is more theological and aims at individual virtue as the basis for the good society. Leo brings the two views together in a linkage that goes back to the time of the ancient Greeks, in which the guarantee of the good state lay in the virtue of its citizens. It also is harmonious with the stress in Catholic teaching on the life of charity as the best guarantee of a good society. And it reflects as well the argument of Aquinas in the *Summa Theologiae* that justice is an *effectus caritatis*, a "result of charity."

Leo argues that the Church, because it knows the innermost hearts of men and has a mandate from Jesus Christ, must not only care for the soul (23) but also intervene directly on behalf of the poor (24). It must act on all levels of society to help to bring about a society in which all persons are treated with justice and are open to the call of charity.

The Role of the State

Leo's experience as bishop of Perugia—and in fact his whole life as an Italian—colors his reflection on the role of the state (26–35). Sympathetic to Italian unification and informed by Catholic political theory going back to Augustine, he was eager to carve out a positive role for the state. The foremost duty of rulers of states, he says, is to make sure that "the laws and institutions, the general character and administration of the commonwealth, shall . . . realize public well-being and private prosperity" (26). What must states do to guarantee public well-being? In the first place, the state has an equal obligation toward all members of the society. "The working classes are by nature members of the state equally with the rich: they are real living parts which make up through the family the body of the state" (27). As for the state's specific responsibilities: "A state chiefly prospers and thrives through moral rule, well-regulated family life, respect for religion and justice, the moderation and fair imposing of public taxes, the progress of the arts and of trade, the abundant yield of the land—through everything, in fact, which makes the citizens better and happier" (26). This echoes book nineteen of the *City of God*, in which Augustine sets forth as the two aims of every state the happiness of its citizens and the harmonious achievement of peace.

Having spoken about the state's duties toward all its citizens, Leo now gets to the heart of his message: the specific demand of justice toward the working class. The state must take into account the disparities that exist among classes:

Justice, therefore, demands that the interests of the working classes should be carefully watched over by the administration, so that they who contribute so largely to the advantage of the community may themselves share in the benefits which they create—that being housed, clothed, and bodily fit, they may find their life less hard and more endurable. It follows that whatever shall appear to prove conducive to the well-being of those who work should obtain favorable consideration. There is no fear that solicitude of this kind will be harmful to any interest: on the contrary, it will be to the advantage of all; for it cannot but be good for the commonwealth to shield from misery those on whom it so largely depends for the things that it needs. (27)

Leo goes on to say, "Whenever the general interest of any particular class suffers, or is threatened with harm, which can in no other way be met or prevented, the public authority must step in to deal with it" (28). Finally he adds, "Still, when there is question of defending the rights of individuals, the poor and badly-off have a claim to especial consideration" (29).

Without prejudice to private initiative, Leo presents the classic notion of the state that has come to us from Augustine, from Aquinas, and from the Spanish theologians, in which the state is not a neutral factor but rather must guarantee the well-being of all. There are at least three aspects of the state's responsibility. First, it must protect and guarantee the rights of every person. Second, it must create the conditions under which the citizens can realize legitimate ends; these include founding a family, being productive, and using one's talents to create the basis for a dignified life. Third, the state must foster the common good, the well-being of all. The "common good" means more than simply the sum total of individual goods; it means those things that the community can reasonably expect as goals for the whole society. This includes the work of distributive justice by which the state provides those goods that are for the advantage of the whole society. It also includes the respect and fostering of those principles, symbols, and values by which a nation forms its own identity through its culture, thus guaranteeing its own future.

The task of justice is not simply to give everyone the same amount but to give to each his or her due, according to a sense of proportion. This obliges the state to try to redress those wrongs that have created or that serve to maintain actual injustices in the society. It does not, however, give the state the right to regulate all of life. The state is rather to respond to those needs in ways consistent with its threefold obligation: toward human rights, toward the free exercise of individual initiative, and toward the common good.

In Leo's mind, the state must exercise a positive role in safeguarding private property, defending the spiritual interest of the working person, and setting standards for the regulation of work. Leo does not content himself with setting forth general principles but points out some very practical applications. The state is to "save unfortunate working people from the cruelty of men of greed" (33). "Man's powers, like his general nature, are limited, and beyond those limits he cannot go. . . . Daily labor, therefore, should be so regulated as not to be protracted over longer hours than strength admits." Strength is "developed and increased by use and exercise, but only on condition of due intermission and proper rest." Very specifically Leo adds, "Those who work in mines and quarries, and extract coal, stone, and metals from the bowels of the earth, should have shorter hours in proportion as their labor is more severe and trying to health." Also, "work which is quite suitable for a strong man cannot rightly be required from a woman or a child. And, in regard to children, great care should be taken not to place them in workshops and factories until their bodies and minds are sufficiently developed."

Strikes and Wages

A subject greatly disputed in the nineteenth century—and still controversial today—is the strike. Leo addresses it directly and without any conditions: "When work-people have recourse to a strike, it is frequently because the hours of labor are too long, or the work too hard, or because they consider their wages insufficient." Thus he acknowledges immediately that workers have the right to strike and that their reasons for doing so are usually real and worthy of respect.

The state should both try to prevent and help to resolve grievances: "The laws should forestall and prevent such troubles from arising; they should lend their influence and authority to the removal in good time of the causes which lead to conflicts between employers and employed" (31). The state's contributions in this area, then, are (1) to make laws that help prevent conflicts from arising and (2) to ensure that strikes are resolved in a just way.

Wages are a key point in the matter of justice for the worker, and here too Leo makes an important contribution. First he points to the then-current practice of regulating by "free consent." This practice meant, in fact, that the employer was free to offer too little, leaving the employee with the choice either to accept a substandard wage or not to have any work. Employers and free-market liberals argued that the contract was just because it was freely entered into, through consent. But the practice was in fact discriminatory and unjust, because the contract was made by two persons who were not on the same ground. The employer could offer or withhold work as he chose; the employee was constrained by his need to accept whatever he was offered.

Leo counterargues that work is personal and work is necessary, and that the remuneration offered must take into account the personal dignity of the wage-earner and the necessity that he labor to maintain his life in dignity. As a result, the worker has a right to a living wage, one that enables him to procure the necessities of life. In Leo's words, "wages ought not to be insufficient to support a frugal and well-behaved wage-earner" (34). Thus he moves the question of wages beyond mere consent to the level of justice in the relationship between two persons. Such a relationship is not measured simply by quantity of work performed. Rather, it includes the quality of the person-to-person contract. The contract, therefore, is not about two commodities, capital and labor. It is between two persons, each of whom has the right to a just remuneration that is commensurate with his person and his productivity and that allows him to live with dignity.

Leo's idea of a living and just wage is one that the Catholic Church in years to come would defend in many spheres. Pius XI would call it the family wage; John Paul II would apply it to a much more complex social situation. At the very beginning of reflection on this idea, Leo takes an important step: he moves the question from a matter of consent to one of human dignity and the person's right to live in dignity. This implies the means necessary to exercise all the rights, including the right to form a family, that are basic characteristics of dignified human life.

Leo's realism now brings him back to the question of property, which he sees as the means whereby a person is guaranteed the necessities of life and protected against destitution. Property thus assumes for Leo an extremely crucial role. It is not an absolute in itself but a means to give people a sense of personal security as well as a stake in the good of the society in which they live. Leo goes so far as to say that "the right to possess private property is derived from nature, not from man." And because this is so, the state here, too, has an interest: "The state has the right to control [private property's] use in the interests of the public good alone, but by no means to absorb it altogether. The state would, therefore, be unjust and cruel if under the name of taxation it were to deprive the private owner of more than is fair" (35). The state's role is limited to fostering and protecting the public good. It does not have the right to take over private property except to defend the public good, and it cannot tax private property to such an extent that the workers are deprived of the good use of their property.

The Question of Unions

Moving on to the relation between employer and employees (36–44), Leo tackles head on the question of unions. The Christian social movement had often argued in favor of the medieval guilds as a model for the modern situation. Leo acknowledges this by referring to the notion of brother helping brother that was the inspiration of those guilds (37). However, he moves beyond the limits of the guild to establish a principle that will become a constant in Catholic teaching.

The right to form associations, the right to unionize, comes from the very freedom of people to gather together into private societies and to use those societies for ends agreed upon by the members. Such societies will serve their own interests as well as the interests of the common good. Trade unions and what he calls workingmen's unions can offer, Leo says, what the guilds offered: "the means of affording not only many advantages to the workmen, but in no small degree of promoting the advancement of art." Such unions "should be suited to the requirements of this our age—an age of wider education, of different habits, and of far more numerous requirements in daily life." There are already some such unions, he says, and it is very desirable "that these unions should become more numerous and more efficient" (36). As justification for this, Leo invokes Thomas's teaching about private societies. This places unions within the theological tradition of the Catholic Church.

Leo realizes that unions can be guilty of excesses and says they may require some regulation. But he associates unions with the rights of persons and says, "Every precaution should be taken not to violate the rights of individuals and not to impose unreasonable regulations under pretense of public benefit" (38). Such associations will have certain characteristics. Their administration "should be firm and wise." And, "being free to exist, they have the further right to adopt such rules and organization as may best conduce to the attainment of their respective objects" (42). While not wishing to enter into particulars, Leo insists that in deciding upon their organization, unions should take into account the work to be done, the experience of the members, the scope of the trade, the characteristics of the community, and ultimately the common good.

The great breakthrough Leo makes in this section of *Rerum Novarum* has to do not simply with sanctioning unions but with giving them an intrinsic legitimacy and indicating internal and external characteristics by which they should measure their own activity. This is similar to the breakthrough he made by rejecting the notion of consent as the only criterion for a just wage. It is linked as well to what he said about property. He not only vindicates property but shows why it is important, placing property under the measure of the person and of the good of society.

Leo concludes his analysis with an appeal for every person to "put his hand to the work which falls to his share" and to contribute to the world of work, to the community, and to the good of all. He promises that the Church will continue to cooperate in the effort to solve social problems, its effect all the greater as its action is unfettered. Finally, he appeals to the "ministers of holy religion" to "cherish in themselves, and try to arouse in others, charity, the mistress and the queen of virtues. For the happy results we all long for must be chiefly brought about by the plenteous outpouring of charity; of that true Christian charity which is the fulfilling of the whole Gospel law, which is always ready to sacrifice itself for others' sake, and is man's surest antidote against worldly pride and immoderate love of self" (45).

THE IMPORTANCE OF *RERUM NOVARUM*

In May 1991 Pope John Paul II marked the centenary of *Rerum Novarum* with a new social encyclical, *Centesimus Annus*—thus continuing the tradition established by Pope Pius XI in 1931 (*Quadragesimo Anno*) and followed by John XXIII in 1961 (*Mater et Magistra*), Paul VI in 1971 (*Octogesima Adveniens*), and John Paul himself in 1981 (*Laborem Exercens*). In fact, the first chapter of *Centesimus Annus* is a rereading of and commentary on *Rerum Novarum*, with an eye to showing how remarkably prescient Leo XIII was about the evolution of modern society and its problems and possibilities. John Paul II fully understood that the world of 1991 was not the world of 1891; but he also taught that Leo XIII had "created a lasting paradigm for the Church" by enunciating the fundamental principles and orientation of what we today call Catholic social doctrine, and by establishing the Church's legitimate role in addressing the great questions of international economic, social, and political life. Just as in 1891, so at the end of this century, social conflict (and especially the social conflicts attendant on modern economies) can be resolved only in a peace built on the foundation of justice.

A major reason for the importance of Leo XIII's encyclical is that it established the idea that the Church has a social doctrine, that there is a body of social principles rooted in Christian tradition and developed through reflection upon the person and society. This idea was adopted by subsequent pontiffs, notably Pius XI, Pius XII, John XXIII, Paul VI, John Paul I, and John Paul II. It has also been the guiding force behind the social pronouncements of individual bishops and bishops' conferences, though the concept has been adapted in different ways from country to country. (The U.S. bishops, for example, have opted for a "leader and citizen" approach that emphasizes their participation in the U.S. public debate.)

Leo's statement is important also because it does not remain on the theoretical level. He enunciated principles and then sought to apply them. He established the approach of addressing real questions with more than generalized statements, applying the principles to particular social questions of the day. He showed that the Church's social teaching is indeed a body of principles, founded on values that have emerged through the Church's experience in living the gospel and its reflection on that experience, but that the principles are incomplete in themselves. They need to be applied.

This suggests two characteristics of Catholic social teaching. First, it is historical. It develops in time. The principles become clearer through experience and reflection upon that experience. For example, Leo placed a strong emphasis on the natural right to private property and its importance as a way of guaranteeing human dignity. Subsequent pontiffs in no way deny or contradict that point. However, a certain shift that comes about with Paul VI and is further developed by John Paul II allows us to see not only the legitimacy but also the limitations of private property. For Leo to have used the terms of John Paul II in 1891 would have caused untold misunderstanding. What Paul VI was able to say in 1967 depended directly upon what Leo XIII had said in 1891. The historical development of social principles, therefore, is an important element in our understanding of Leo XIII and subsequent social teaching.

Second, Catholic social teaching is nothing if it is not pastoral. It is not meant to remain in the academic realm. Catholic social principles are to be used to fashion programs and to institute projects that will change the shape of the societies in which people live, making them more harmonious, peaceful, and just. Leo's remarks about unions illustrate this point.

Linking Justice and Charity

One important element often overlooked by some social activists in the Church is the bond—made explicit in different ways by subsequent pontiffs—between the commitment to social justice and the necessity of the virtuous life. Justice and social charity are intimately linked in Leo's writing. Pius XI carried this theme further in his notion of social justice and social charity. Every subsequent pontiff has upheld the life of charity as the ultimate flowering of the search for justice. John Paul II has pointed out the limitations of justice separated from charity.

This argument goes back to Aristotle and to the Greek ideal of the state. But it is rooted more deeply in the Christian dispensation, which sees the life of the Christian as a whole and demands that the life of virtue should be a *bonum diffusivum sui*, a "good that overflows of itself." An important element in Catholic social teaching is to maintain the intimate link, not only between doctrine and social action, but also between the virtuous life that is founded on charity and the activities of the virtuous person in society.

Another characteristic of *Rerum Novarum* that will be taken up in subsequent social teaching is that it analyzes the inadequacies of certain systems and ideologies. In the case of Leo, the direct contrast he makes is between the socialist position and his own. But he acts similarly in regard to liberalism. This is not a simplistic argument rejecting "left" and "right." It is an ethical argument that depends upon a theological vision of the human person. It therefore proceeds from a Christian anthropology and makes judgments about actual situations as well as the theories devised to deal with such situations.

Leo's critique of socialism and liberalism is not meant to propose another ideology in their place; its purpose is to make a moral judgment on what these systems say about the human person and the proper role of society. The final argument against socialism is not that organizing workers is difficult or that the power of capital is so great that the workers cannot succeed. The ultimate argument is that the socialist conception of humanity radically undermines the dignity of the human person.

Addressing Specific Questions

In *Centesimus Annus*, Pope John Paul II argues that the enduring importance of Leo XIII lies in his affirmation of the fundamental rights of workers, the dignity of the worker, and the dignity of work. Leo's defense of private property and his identification of the complementary principle of the universal destination of the earth's goods also have become classic principles of Catholic social thought.

Leo vindicated the formation of "free associations" as a natural human right and applied it to the right of workers to unionize. In Leo's thought, free associations erect a barrier against the encroachments of a state that wishes to control all aspects of social life. They are formed to work both for the good of their members and for the common good. This means that their proper function is not exhausted once they have attended to the interests of their membership, for those interests must also be measured against the common good.

When the International Labor Organization was founded in the second decade of this century, its principal proponents came from the socialist and secularized sectors of European society. However, the first director general recognized that Leo XIII and the Christian social movement represented an important strand of thought about labor and laborers. For that reason he instituted the post of ecclesiastical counselor and entrusted it to the French Jesuits, something that has continued down to our own day. That singular act is an indication of the importance of *Rerum Novarum*. Not only in Europe but also in Latin America and in parts of Africa, the thought of Leo XIII and of those who were inspired by him has guided great portions of the trade-union movement.

Americans, used to the pragmatic approach begun by Samuel Gompers and carried on by the AFL-CIO through this past century, find it somewhat hard to recognize the importance of the doctrinal and ethical underpinnings that Catholic social thought gave to trade unionism. But it is not wrong to see Leo XIII's encyclical as one of the major strands in the formation of that movement. Nor is it wrong to see in the document a singular contribution of the Church, not only to the workers but also to society and the common good.

Pope John Paul II helps us to discern other areas in which the teachings of *Rerum Novarum* continue to be relevant. For example, John Paul speaks of the ongoing challenge of the just living wage, which must be sufficient "to enable [a worker] to support himself, his wife and his children." That idea is a sharp challenge to a society so supportive of the rights of the individual that it often exalts individual autonomy at the expense of personal and social responsibility. The ancient teaching of the Church—and indeed of Western civilization—that the family, rather than the individual, is the basic cell of society has been unambiguously and consistently endorsed by the popes of the twentieth century. This teaching has very real consequences for social policy and societal values. If primitive capitalism worked against the family by denying a just wage to a worker who was often treated as chattel, today's society, with its disregard for familial and social responsibility, similarly undermines the institution that is the basic component of a healthy society.

Leo's insistence on the worker's right to fulfill his religious responsibilities might sound a bit out of date. This right is, however, a basic tenet of Catholic teaching and a crucial element in the defense of the dignity of the person. The practical application of this in the notion of "Sunday rest" moves the principle beyond the realm of individual preference to become a social norm. We regard seven-days-a-week sweatshops as ancient history. But the contemporary importance of Leo's principle cannot be overlooked in a society in which seven-days-a-week shopping has become common—to the detriment of both those caught in the consumerist rat-race and those who have to work on Sunday to fulfill consumers' demands. Leo's teaching is also relevant in a society that marginalizes religion as a "private matter" and bans religious symbols from public expression lest they "offend" those who do not share that belief.

The social teaching of Leo XIII was based on the conviction that the person is the measure of society, not vice versa. The state has a role to play, but the state is not the guarantor of all that is good and right. By serving what is good and right, the state makes it possible for human beings to work together, to associate with one another, and to build those relationships that will respect the dignity of each and advance the good of all.

John Paul II uses this teaching of Leo to call attention to the notion of "solidarity," which corresponds to Leo's idea of "friendship" and is found in germ in ancient Greek thought. The concept had a powerful influence on the organization of workers. "Solidarity" is a warning against social and political isolationism; it encourages a global outlook and a concomitant sense of social, economic, and political responsibility. "Solidarity" assesses the actual conditions of groups, especially the poor, and seeks to find practical ways of incorporating each person and every group into a productive and socially positive set of relationships. "Solidarity" acknowledges the proper role of the state, without falling into the totalitarian trap of giving the state final responsibility for the good to which all are called.

In his encyclical on work, *Laborem Exercens*, John Paul II referred to *Rerum Novarum* as "the decisively important encyclical" and added that "the Church considers it her task always to call attention to the dignity and rights of those who work, to condemn situations in which that dignity and those rights are violated, and to help guide the above mentioned changes so as to ensure authentic progress by man and society." Similarly, in *Centesimus Annus* John Paul II affirmed the importance of *Rerum Novarum* by stating that "the guiding principle of Pope Leo's encyclical, and of all the Church's social doctrine, is a *correct view of the human person* and of the person's unique value, inasmuch as the human being . . . is the only creature on earth which God willed for itself."

Rerum Novarum marks the beginning of a social teaching rooted in Christian anthropology. Its vision of the dignity and worth of every human person is the basis of the Church's assessment of the institutions of society and how they function. A tradition that began by addressing the economic and social effects of the Industrial Revolution has continued, over one hundred years, to examine the societies that make up this global village with one grand purpose in mind: to help insure that human activity and human aspirations foster and defend "the essential dignity of the human person."

2

In Praise of Little Platoons
Quadragesimo Anno (1931)

THOMAS C. KOHLER

T HE world," wrote Saint Augustine, "is groaning for salvation."
Certainly, its cries were especially acute in 1931, the year Pope
Pius XI issued his famous encyclical *Quadragesimo Anno* ("Forty
Years Having Passed"—i.e., since *Rerum Novarum*). The Great
Depression, by then nearly two years old, had left twenty-five
million Americans and Europeans unemployed. The extreme solutions to which many people turned reflected the bleak anxiety of
the times. In France, Italy, and Germany, the Christian democratic
movement stood feeble and discredited. Fascist and related cult-of-
the-state movements were gaining popularity or had assumed the
reins of government in various parts of Western and Central Europe. The appeal of communism was also growing. Meanwhile, in
the Soviet Union, Stalin had consolidated his power. His expedient
for guaranteeing agricultural plenty—the brutal program for the
forced collectivization of Ukrainian farms—was well under way.

Addressed to an increasingly desperate world, *Quadragesimo
Anno* has a clear mission, which is stated succinctly in its English

Thomas C. Kohler is an associate professor at Boston College Law
School, specializing in labor and employment-relations law. He is the
author of numerous publications on labor law, and is currently working
on a study of groups, associations, and notions of personhood in American law, as well as a book on labor law as discourse.

subtitle: "On Reconstructing the Social Order." In part, the encyclical attempts to sketch the framework for a Catholic "third way" between collectivism (in either its right- or left-wing guises) and radical individualism. The encyclical's core concern, however, is with the sorts of social institutions that are most conducive to the full development of human personality. In a world increasingly dominated by large and often state-controlled institutions, the encyclical seeks to carve out the grounds for authentic individual self-determination. Consequently, the encyclical's most fully developed and nuanced teachings concentrate on the properly delimited role of major institutions like the state, and emphasize the importance of intermediate (or subsidiary) groups and associations in the social order. These themes constitute *Quadragesimo Anno*'s most enduring contributions—ones that have proved to be as timely and insightful today as when Pius XI first offered them to a restless and yearning world.

The Origins of Quadragesimo Anno

The fortieth anniversary of the issuance of *Rerum Novarum* supplied the occasion for the promulgation of *Quadragesimo Anno*.[1] Deeply concerned by the direction of political and economic developments, Pius XI viewed the anniversary as an appropriate opportunity to restate, refine, and extend the "incomparable" teachings of *Rerum Novarum* in light of the present exigencies. Instead of relying on any of the Vatican offices, Pius XI charged his confidante, Fr. Wlodimir Ledochowski, the superior general of the Jesuits, with the task of overseeing the preparation of a draft. Ledochowski, in turn, assigned its writing to a German Jesuit, Fr. Oswald von Nell-Breuning. In keeping with the practice of the time, Nell-Breuning was instructed to conduct his work in secret.

When the task of drafting *Quadragesimo Anno* was delegated to him, Nell-Breuning had held an appointment as a professor of moral theology and canon law at the University of Frankfurt for just three years. His doctoral thesis, published in 1928, presented a study of the morality of the stock exchange, a topic on which he later lectured publicly. Since the time he assumed his teaching post, he also had taken an active part in the debates about the direction of the Catholic social movement. These activities, Nell-Breuning later modestly wrote, resulted in his possessing "a certain name, in the Catholic labor movement in western Germany, and even beyond."[2]

Quadragesimo Anno went through eight drafts before the final version was settled upon. During the period he worked on the encyclical, Nell-Breuning met with the pope only once, shortly after the first draft was completed. Subsequent communications between the two men were mediated through Ledochowski. Apart from paragraphs 91–96 of the encyclical, which the pope himself wrote, Pius XI took little active part in the preparation of the document. Nevertheless, as Nell-Breuning later commented, the close relationship between the pope and Ledochowski ensured that "Pius XI knew the range of what was to be published in his name."[3] The gravity and volatility of the world situation guaranteed that *Quadragesimo Anno* would be the most closely and critically studied encyclical since *Rerum Novarum*, and it remains a vibrant part of the Church's social teachings. Nell-Breuning, incidentally, was nearly as hardy as the document he did so much to propound. The "Nestor" of Catholic social thought, he died in August 1991 at the age of 101, leaving a corpus of eighteen hundred books, monographs, and articles.

Indeed, Nell-Breuning's work has had a substantial impact on twentieth-century life. He was officially silenced and his writings banned by the Nazis in 1936; subsequently, he was arrested and sentenced to prison. After the war Nell-Breuning became a longtime adviser to the West German economics ministry (1948–65) and to the Deutsche Gewerkschaftsbund (DGB), the German trade-union movement (which awarded him their highest honor, the Hans Böckler Prize). Much of Nell-Breuning's thought was also adopted by the Social Democratic Party (SPD) and integrated into its 1959 Bad Godesburg Program, in which the party dropped its Marxist orientation and its opposition to a market economy.[4] Educated in the same gymnasium in which his "great adversary," Karl Marx, had studied, Nell-Breuning lived to see the collapse of communism. He also lived to see one of the basic principles of *Quadragesimo Anno*—subsidiarity—adopted as a core precept for the organization and development of the European Economic Community.[5]

Subsidiarity

Quadragesimo Anno is known primarily for its development of two ideas, the aforementioned principle of subsidiarity and the notion of solidarism, or corporatism. These concepts are best understood when examined in light of their shared intellectual heritage.

When Pius entrusted the drafting of *Quadragesimo Anno* to Ledochowski's supervision, he remarked that the work of its preparation would undoubtedly fall to the German Jesuits.[6] This was a natural supposition. Social Catholicism had received its start in Germany under the guidance of Wilhelm Emmanuel von Ketteler, the bishop of Mainz (1811–77), and Germany had remained a leading center for Catholic social thought.[7] Ketteler's thought, as well as the Catholic social movement, was profoundly affected by the collapse of a relational society and the poverty that attended the rise of the Industrial Revolution. It was also affected by the challenges to Catholicism mounted by liberal and critical social philosophers. As early as 1848 (the year Marx and Engels published the *Communist Manifesto*), Ketteler declared that "the task of religion, the task of the Catholic societies in the immediate future, has to do with social conditions." He continued: "The world will see that to the Catholic Church is reserved the definite solution of the social question; for the State, with all its legislative machinery, has not the power to solve it."[8] The authority of Ketteler's thought became immense. *Rerum Novarum* was so influenced by it that Leo XIII referred to Ketteler as "my great predecessor."[9] Similarly, the Swiss sociologist and Catholic activist Kaspar Descurtins declared that to Ketteler belonged "the undying honor of having met the manifesto of the Communists with a program of Christian social reform that stands unsurpassed to this day."[10]

In contrast to some Catholic social theorists who regarded the entire structure of liberal capitalism as evil, Ketteler was a meliorist. He accepted capitalism and believed that its replacement was not a practical possibility. He instead called for self-help through labor unions, producers' cooperatives, and other workers' associations, supported by a limited program of social legislation. Central to Ketteler's thought was a principle that would come to be known as subsidiarity. This principle insists that the state and all other associations exist for the individual. Societies should not assume what individuals can do, nor should larger societies undertake what smaller associations can accomplish.[11] Conversely, the state or other large social institutions have the responsibility to take up those tasks that neither individuals nor smaller societies can perform.[12]

Although the notion of subsidiarity was integral to Ketteler's thought and to the encyclicals of Leo XIII,[13] it was not until *Quadragesimo Anno* that the principle received either its name or a rigorous formulation. There the idea is expressed as follows:

> It is true, as history clearly proves, that because of changed circumstances much that formerly was performed by small associations can now be accomplished only by larger ones. Nevertheless, it is a fixed and unchangeable principle, most basic in social philosophy, immovable and unalterable, that, just as it is wrong to take away from individuals what they can accomplish by their own ability and effort and entrust it to a community, so it is an injury and at the same time both a serious evil and a disturbance of right order to assign to a larger and higher society what can be performed successfully by smaller and lower communities. The reason is that all social activity, of its very power and nature, should supply help [*subsidium*] to the members of the social body, but may never destroy or absorb them.
>
> The state, then, should leave to these smaller groups the settlement of business and problems of minor importance, which would otherwise greatly distract it. Thus it will carry out with greater freedom, power, and success the tasks belonging to it alone, because it alone is qualified to perform them: directing, watching, stimulating, and restraining, as circumstances suggest or necessity demands. Let those in power, therefore, be convinced that the more faithfully this principle of subsidiary function is followed and a graded hierarchical order exists among the various associations, the greater also will be both social authority and social efficiency, and the happier and more prosperous too will be the condition of the commonwealth. (79–80)[14]

Subsidiarity has been described as "neither a theological nor even really a philosophical principle, but a piece of congealed historical wisdom."[15] The noted theologian Josef Pieper has referred to it simply as a *deutsch-rechtlichen Grundsatz* ("German legal principle"),[16] while Arthur-Fridolin Utz has suggested that subsidiarity represents a reaction to the claims made by the modern liberal state.[17] However characterized, the principle has become a well-established aspect of the Church's social teaching. Regarded as a basic norm for the proper ordering of civil society, subsidiarity has been invoked in the social encyclicals of every pope since Pius XI.[18] Joseph Komonchak has described the principle as consisting of nine elements:

1. The priority of the person as the origin and purpose of society: *civitas propter cives, non cives propter civitatem.*

2. At the same time, the human person is naturally social, only able to achieve self-realization in and through social relationships—what is sometimes called the "principle of solidarity."

3. Social relationships and communities exist to provide help (*subsidium*) to individuals in their free but obligatory assumption of responsibility for their own self-realization. This "subsidiary" function of society is not a matter, except in exceptional circumstances, of substituting or supplying for individual self-responsibility, but of providing the sets of conditions necessary for personal self-realization.

4. Larger, "higher," communities exist to perform the same subsidiary roles toward smaller, "lower," communities.

5. The principle of subsidiary requires *positively* that all communities not only permit but enable and encourage individuals to exercise their own self-responsibility, and that larger communities do the same for smaller ones.

6. It requires *negatively* that communities not deprive individuals and smaller communities of their right to exercise their self-responsibility. Intervention, in other words, is only appropriate as "helping people help themselves."

7. Subsidiarity, therefore, serves as the principle by which to regulate competencies between individuals and communities, and between smaller and larger communities.

8. It is a formal principle, needing determination in virtue of the nature of a community and of particular circumstances.

9. Because it is grounded in the metaphysics of the person, it applies to the life of every society.[19]

Solidarism and Other Concepts

Despite the attention *Quadragesimo Anno* pays to subsidiarity, the much larger portion of the encyclical is devoted to enunciating a "sane corporative system" on which a society can be grounded. Like subsidiarity, the notion of solidarism has a German genealogy. Its founder was Heinrich Pesch, S.J. (1854–1926), a well-known German economist. After Pesch's death, Gustav Gundlach, S.J., and the members of the so-called Königswinter circle became the principal proponents of solidarism and Peschian economics. Nell-Breuning met regularly with this group during the time he was (without their knowledge) drafting *Quadragesimo Anno*, and he later acknowledged the pervasive influence Gundlach had exercised over his work. The encyclical, Nell-Breuning stated, "is in fact well-saturated with Gundlach's thought."[20] (Indeed, Nell-Breuning claimed that "both the name 'principle of subsidiarity' and the formulation in which it is expressed in *Quadragesimo Anno* came from Gundlach."[21])

Solidarism, or corporatism, can be seen as an attempt to work out the principle of subsidiarity in the economic order of a society. Meant to represent a "third way," solidarism rejects the premises of both socialism and liberal individualism. It locates in the nature of man and society a principle for the order of the economy as a whole. Repudiating both centrally planned command economies and unrestricted competition, solidarism proposes the establishment of free, voluntary, and self-governing organizations composed of all the members of the various professions and occupations represented in the economy. These organizations, encompassing both employers and employees, are to act as self-regulating bodies, providing the opportunity for an ordered economic freedom. In keeping with the principle of subsidiarity, these occupational groups are to mediate the relationship between individuals and the state; they are to stand apart, and to enjoy a large measure of autonomy, from the state. The state's function is to oversee the activities of the various economic associations only to the degree required by the common welfare. In this view, the economy is a set of social relations composed of various autonomous vocational organizations that are bound together to achieve the welfare of all.

The corporative social order outlined in *Quadragesimo Anno* calls for no specific form of state organization.[22] Indeed, the very idea of a "corporative state" would contradict the subsidiarity principle. Thus, as Chantal Millon-Delsol points out, the social encyclicals never promoted corporatism as a political-economic system.[23] This distinguishes the sort of "Christian solidarism" contemplated by *Quadragesimo Anno* from the corporatist systems championed by twentieth-century fascist regimes. It similarly distinguishes it from the resolutely non-centralized, but ultimately paternalistic if not romantic, forms of corporatism associated with such nineteenth-century Catholic activists as René de La Tour du Pin and Karl von Vogelsang. Both those thinkers assigned the state a large role in establishing the socioeconomic order. Moreover, at least for de La Tour du Pin, the individual's identity and capacity to act come only through the social group of which he is part.[24]

Despite the intentions and goals that informed them, the portions of *Quadragesimo Anno* that deal with solidarism stand as some of the most controversial ever set forth in an encyclical. Nell-Breuning stated that he found it "oppressive" that "this heart of the encyclical . . . has brought about misunderstandings and has been disparaged in the widest circles of Catholic social teachings as 'statist' or 'restorative' or 'reactionary.' "[25] Mussolini's furious reaction to *Quadragesimo Anno* undercuts any suggestion that Il Duce found comfort or sanction for his form of fascism in the encyclical. Moreover, less than six weeks after the publication of *Quadragesimo Anno*, Pius XI issued the encyclical *Non Abbiamo Bisogno* in which he condemned Mussolini's fascist order. This was followed by the condemnation of Hitler's fascist regime and its anti-Semitic racism in the encyclical *Mit Brennender Sörge*. Nevertheless, the claims by various fascist orders that their regimes were constituted along the lines approved in the social teachings left the notion of solidarism with, at best, an ambiguous image and an unsettled legacy.

Unlike the principle of subsidiarity, solidarism did not long continue as a part of the Church's social teachings. During the early 1940s Pius XII continued to champion it as the means for reconstructing society. Since Gundlach was then writing Pius XII's social allocutions, this is not especially surprising.[26] As one observer has remarked, however, since John XXIII, solidarism "has been allowed to undergo a quiet and seemly death."[27]

Quadragesimo Anno spoke to several other issues besides subsidiarity and corporatism, the most important of which can be summarized briefly:

1. Wholly *sub silentio*, the encyclical corrected the non-Thomistic understanding of private property that was set forth in *Rerum Novarum*. Ironically, the notions that informed the 1891 encyclical were based on the theories of John Locke, which had been incorporated into neo-scholastic thought by the nineteenth-century Jesuit theologian Taparelli d'Azeglio.[28]

2. Consistent with the thought of Leo XIII (and Bishop Ketteler), *Quadragesimo Anno* taught that capitalism "is not vicious of its very nature," but becomes wrong only when it ignores the personal dignity of workers and demands of social justice.

3. It continued the flat condemnation of socialism of every description found in the pages of *Rerum Novarum*.

4. It reasserted the right and duty of the Church to deal authoritatively with social and economic problems.

5. *Quadragesimo Anno* was the first encyclical to use the term "social justice," which it did eight times.

A Distinct View of Human Nature

Like the other social encyclicals, *Quadragesimo Anno* deals with the temporal. It represents an evaluation of and statement about "the signs of the times." Indeed, this encyclical's very purpose was to reiterate the teachings of *Rerum Novarum* in light of the changes that had taken place in the political and economic order since 1891. Of course, the conditions that *Quadragesimo Anno* assessed, and the world to which it spoke, have long since passed. Yet the document, and the principle of subsidiarity it enunciates, reflects a view of human character that has a long development in classical and Catholic thought. This enables the encyclical to speak across time and provides a durable principle for guiding the way we choose to structure our lives.

Key to the notion of subsidiarity is the understanding that what makes men distinctly human is their capacity for reflection and choice. This implies a great deal about human potential, stressing as it does the primacy of persons as intelligent, reasonable, free, and responsible beings. It also suggests that the world, and all that exists, is intelligible and that humans have the capacity to understand it. To the extent one truly understands what is real, one participates in an understanding of God, who is the One, the True, the Beautiful, and the Good. Since the most basic and most authentically human of desires is to know—to know the true, the real—humans by their nature are oriented to know God. Thus, as Aristotle insisted, "the good is in the concrete" (or, as the medievals had it, "God is in the details"). In attending to the questions raised by even the most mundane of life's experiences, one accepts the invitation, issued constantly and to all, to know Being. Consequently, pursuit of the undistorted and unrestricted desire to know, through the activities of inquiry and reflection, ultimately results in the satisfaction and perfection of the most authentic of human longings. "Thou hast made us for thyself, O Lord," wrote Augustine, "and our hearts are restless till they rest in Thee."

As Augustine suggests, truth is not a private preserve. To the extent that anything is true, it is radically "public," and a matter in which all have the potential to share. Because truth is independent of any particular individual, participation in it requires self-transcendence, going beyond the world of private imaginings, suppositions, and feelings to something completely different, to what *is*. Thus, as we appropriate the true, we increasingly become different people. Paradoxically, however, because God "is all in all" (1 Cor. 15:28), the more we "die to the self," the more we become our authentic selves. Since, as Augustine teaches, "God is closer to me than I am to myself," God becomes the ultimate point of reference for achieving one's full humanity.

God invites us to become truly one with him by knowing him. Through perfecting our liberty, we can transcend ourselves—indeed, the whole natural world—and enjoy identity with God. This is the purpose for which we were created. But our intellect also gives us the freedom to refuse to know God, to reject the gifts of grace freely offered to all. We thus bear the awesome responsibility of working out our own salvation "in fear and trembling" (Phil. 2:12), for implicit in every decision we make is a choice for or against God.

Humans being are not just thinkers but doers: *verbum caro factum est*—"the spirit is in the body." Since we cannot long stand the contradiction between our knowledge of what is good and actions that fail to conform, we either constrict our understandings and rationalize our shortcomings, or we change our behavior. Each of us is constantly choosing to be the kind of person who tends either toward, or away from, his or her God-given end. Thus, we can realize our human potential only through our actions, in cooperation with God's grace.

Man as Social Being

We do not reflect and act in isolation. As humans, we exist only in communities. This fact fundamentally conditions the scope of our effective freedom and the likelihood that we can realize the completeness of our humanity. The questions we can raise, our recognition of the ramifications that attend our choices, the scope of our actions, are all affected to a large extent by the communities in which we live. This understanding of humans as situated beings also illuminates *Quadragesimo Anno*. As James V. Schall has observed, this encyclical is "more significant than we are wont to realize precisely because it did suggest that economic and political structures [are] basic to enabling men to lead fully human lives."[29]

The metaphysics that grounds *Quadragesimo Anno* carries significant implications. It undermines the notion that the Church's place in society can properly be confined to some "spiritual" realm, walled off from the affairs of actors in the "real" world. This notion rests upon a fundamentally flawed understanding of the character of human beings. Since spirit and body are co-principles in the constitution of the person, no such distinction can be made. The temporal and spiritual have a mutually conditioning effect on the person, who exists as an inseparable whole. Consequently, everything that touches upon the well-being of the person is of interest to the Church. This does not mean that all theological matters may be reduced to questions of economics or politics, but it does mean that all economic and political issues have "theological" dimensions, which invite the reflection, instruction, and insight of the Church. By man's very constitution, the Church has a public role of central importance. Its function is not to govern but to advise and offer commentary on the arrangements by which we order our lives.

In highlighting the fact that human beings are not deterministically controlled, *Quadragesimo Anno* also suggests that economic and political regimes are not the result of the ineluctable forces of nature or history. Instead, these orders are the products of human choice, and are subject to our liberty. The economy, the law, and related social institutions are not "value-free," nor are the disciplines devoted to their study. Despite frequent disclaimers to the contrary, these institutions, like the disciplines that examine and comment upon them, assume an anthropology of the person, by which the meaning and purpose of life is interpreted. This anthropology also serves as the reference point for determining the desirability of social arrangements. Since the social sciences and the institutions they study concern themselves directly with the habits of being, they should be open to the insights on human character and human ends that the Church's teachings have to offer.

Practical Implications

Quadragesimo Anno establishes the pertinence of the Church's voice in the conduct of our public lives. It also supplies the foundation for the practical program that the encyclical outlines. As mentioned, the principle of subsidiarity forms the heart of this project.

Subsidiarity is a truly conservative principle. In its insistence on ordering arrangements that reserve to individual persons the maximum opportunity to reflect, choose, and act for themselves, it seeks to protect and promote the full development of human potential. Recognizing that man is a political animal, subsidiarity urges the creation of a social order consistent with our authentic liberty. Man's sociability—his political nature—arises from his character as the "speaking animal." As Aristotle points out in the *Politics*, human beings differ from other animals, whose utterances are restricted to expressing pleasure or pain, by their ability to speak of good and evil, the just and the wrongful. Indeed, human community is constituted by solidarity around these issues. Characteristic of any discussion of needs or desires is the effort to justify them by reference to a hierarchy of goods or "values." Principles of fairness—however vague—are invoked whenever people attempt to achieve consensus about a public question. Because speech is the vehicle for the expression of reason, conversation is inherently a normative activity. Our involvement in what Thomas Aquinas termed the *civilis conversatio* actuates our potential for authentic self-rule. Likewise, the shared capacity for reason (and hence, the mutual potential to participate in Truth) serves as the basis for community. As Aristotle states in the *Nicomachean Ethics*, "In the case of human beings, what seems to count as living together is this sharing of conversation and thought, not sharing the same pasture, as in the case of grazing animals."[30] In its fullest development, community transcends particular times and places and achieves its completion in a state of union with God.

Through its emphasis on mediating groups and its insistence on vesting authority in the smallest possible social unit, subsidiarity evinces a nuanced understanding of the character and purpose of human sociability. Small groups facilitate discussion and deliberation, encourage friendship among the participants, and establish the conditions for serious conversation and consensus about the way we conduct our lives. As Edmund Burke observed:

> To be attached to the subdivision, to love the little platoon we belong to in society, is the first principle (the germ as it were) of public affections. It is the first link in the series by which we proceed toward a love to our country and to mankind.[31]

Subsidiarity is a universal principle that provides insights into all varieties of human institutions. To the extent that institutions contradict subsidiarity—by replacing personal and local decision-making authority with distant bureaucracies and experts intent on doing other people's thinking for them—they presume that the average person is incapable of self-rule. Such arrangements are truly dehumanizing. Moreover, as *Quadragesimo Anno* points out, institutions that deviate from the principle of subsidiarity tend to hinder material prosperity. Hierarchical, top-down schemes ultimately suggest that administrative specialists and organizational planners can anticipate not only what people's ideas, needs, and desires will be but when they will have them. When we are denied opportunities for self-determination, we are stripped of the conditions through which we actuate our human potential. We become objects of administration, instead of persons free and encouraged to engage in successively more significant acts of self-realization.

Libertarianism and Communitarianism

Subsidiarity takes its bearings from the character of our abilities and the end for which we were created. Since the principle asserts that communities exist only for the individual, it requires that social arrangements be ordered to enable individuals to assume personal responsibility. Accordingly, subsidiarity condemns as perverse the various strains of libertarian individualism that deny man's social character and that pretend we bear no responsibility toward one another unless we voluntarily assume it. Similarly, the principle denounces orders and ideologies, however denominated, that submerge the person into the mass, and which thereby deny the distinct and unique individuality that we each embody. Subsidiarity also rejects the axiom—from which contemporary political and social discourse typically proceeds—that politics and all other forms of human relationships ultimately are intelligible only as struggles for power.[32]

It is appropriate here briefly to consider what, if any, similarities and points of agreement exist between subsidiarity and the relatively new "communitarian" movement. Communitarianism explicitly posits itself as an approach that cuts across the traditional and ideological differences separating conservatives from liberals.[33] Intended as an "umbrella" movement, communitarianism represents no single set of views or consistent body of thought; even those who consider themselves part of the movement hold a wide range of opinions as to what constitutes the essence of communitarianism. Consequently, those who are identified as or who call themselves communitarians make up a rather diverse lot: they include persons whose views might be characterized as simple majoritarianism; persons whose positions suspiciously resemble those of old-style, top-down statists and cultural homogenizers; and lastly, those who understand the movement as an effort to provide a constructively critical perspective on policies and ideologies that ignore the social nature of human personhood.[34]

As much as anything, communitarianism seems to represent an attempt to instigate a new social, political, and moral discourse from the bottom up. As its motto, "rights with responsibilities," suggests, the movement seeks in part to restore the idea of personal obligations to our well-developed language of individual rights. To accomplish this, and in recognition of the natural sociality of humans, many communitarians call for the revivification of the small groups and mediating bodies where citizens learn the habits of self-rule and respect for others. The 1991 communitarian "plat-form" also recognizes the "rich resources of moral voices" within such bodies that can help restore the ethical foundations necessary to sustain American democracy.[35] Moreover, communities and polities have a duty to be responsive to their members and to foster participation and deliberation by individuals in social and political life.

The subsidiarity principle obviously has much to say to many who would identify themselves as communitarians, and much of the communitarian platform itself appears to draw from the social magisterium and the insights that the subsidiarity principle offers. The understanding of the human person that grounds, orients, and illuminates this principle, however, is its most significant insight. It is this distinct metaphysics that both explains the lasting signifi-cance of *Quadragesimo Anno* and accounts for the moral force that the subsidiarity principle possesses. If the communitarian project is to prosper, it will have to confront unflinchingly and adequately the question of our personhood. Failure to do so will make the movement's prescriptions irrelevant—or worse. In short, while the character of our associations and situations may differ, our character as humans is constant; institutional orders and social philosophies incompatible with our human character will not survive. Hence, the most pressing question of our time is whether and to what extent our notions of the human person are accurate. Everything turns on our answer to this question.

Lessons for the Workplace

Quadragesimo Anno is not, however, a theoretical essay. Rather, it is devoted to developing in broad outline a series of practical principles that real people can apply in their daily lives. This is a strength the encyclical shares with the other social encyclicals, all of which recognize that people constitute themselves through every-day habits of thought and action. Consequently, the social encycli-cals direct much of their attention to the conditions that shape the seemingly mundane aspects of day-to-day life.

Quadragesimo Anno's concern for life in the workplace indicates the importance it attaches to the consequences of routine. The encyclical shows a clear realization that, in contemporary times, a job is typically both a primary source of wealth and a determinant of social status. The encyclical also demonstrates an admirably early understanding of the growing tendency of people to become overly preoccupied with their jobs and relations in the workplace. Because of its abiding interest in the institutional arrangements that affect the development of human personality and the potential for self-realization, *Quadragesimo Anno* is compelled to focus on the relations between employer and employee. Consistent with the meta-physics that informs it, the document repeatedly points out that work is both individual and social in character. The encyclical broadly supports collective bargaining as well, and strongly urges employees to form labor unions.

Advocacy of unions has been a central feature of the social teachings since *Rerum Novarum*, and the Church's enthusiasm for such employee associations continues undiminished to the present day.[36] As *Quadragesimo Anno* makes clear (and as the more recent *Laborem Exercens* and *Centesimus Annus* reiterate), unions and the practice of collective bargaining can serve as a practical and highly effective means of implementing the principle of subsidiarity in contemporary society. To understand how this is so, one must first understand something about the nature of collective bargaining and the functions unions can perform as subsidiary institutions.

Collective Bargaining

Most people tend to think of collective bargaining as simply a method for setting rates of compensation and the hours required to receive it. While this part of collective bargaining is important, it is but a small part. Collective bargaining can best be thought of as a private law-making system. Thus, the U.S. Supreme Court has stated that a collective-bargaining agreement "is more than a con-tract; it is a generalized code" representing "an effort to erect a system of industrial self-government" by which the employment relationship may be "governed by an agreed upon rule of law."[37] The affected parties alone are responsible for promulgating and administering this law, and its reach extends to virtually every condition of employment.

Typically, collective-bargaining agreements even erect a private adjudication system—the grievance arbitration process—that the union and employer jointly administer. These systems generally have jurisdiction over nearly every sort of dispute that might arise between the parties. The existence of an arbitration system usually precludes courts or other arms of the state from deciding matters that fall within the coverage of the parties' private dispute-resolution scheme. In short, collective bargaining requires the parties to work out and maintain the order of their relationship for themselves.

Inglorious as it may seem, collective bargaining is an important social institution. For it is through their involvement in the process that average people can become engaged in deciding the law that most directly determines key aspects of their daily lives. Participating in decisions about eligibility for promotions or advanced training, health and education benefits, the discipline of a fellow employee, or the best way to handle a difficult employment-relations question may seem trivial; certainly, such matters lack the sense of moment and glamour that attend Supreme Court deliberations or major Congressional debates. But it is a real mistake to consider these issues as unworthy of serious attention. As the principle of subsidiarity so well understands, individuals and societies become self-governing only by repeatedly and regularly participating in acts of self-government. It is the habit that sustains the condition. Likewise, we actuate our human potential through reflection and choice about the concrete details of life. As we become what we do, so are we stunted by our failure or lack of opportunity to assume personal responsibility.

Unions as Mediating Structures

Subsidiarity emphasizes that humans can achieve self-realization only in and through relations with others. Unions reflect this aspect of human character. Autonomous associations, unions derive their existence from the concerted efforts of individual employees. The activities of unions, whether at the workplace or in the form of the many (and often unnoticed) social-welfare programs they sponsor, depend on self-direction and self-organization. Unions can therefore play a useful role in reducing the indifference and the unthinking dependence that are such a threat to self-realization.

To be successful, the course of action a union pursues on any matter must reflect the consensus of the rank-and-file members. Consensus arises from discussions about what ought to be valued and why. Such discussions are truly normative, challenging the participants to examine and explain to others the basis for their positions. What is so crucial about such conversations is that they require people to decide and take direct responsibility for the type of people they will be. In a social setting increasingly dominated by large institutions and where opinions are so often subject to the influence of the media, such opportunities are indeed rare. This sort of discourse also furnishes an opening for something almost wholly absent from American public life: the discussion of the participants' religious beliefs as a possible guidepost for decision-making. In all these ways, unions can serve as vehicles for an authentic *civilis conversatio*.

A principal concern of *Quadragesimo Anno* is the restoration and support of the various groups and associations that mediate between individuals and large institutions. As the encyclical poignantly observes, "We once had a prosperous social system which owed its development to the wide variety of associations, organically linked together. That structure has been overturned and all but demolished. Individuals are left alone with the state" (78). And, one might add, with the other large institutions that characterize contemporary life.

The encyclical's support for unions is the direct result of this concern. Unions, which stand independent both of the state and of the institutions on which their members are economically reliant, can check and diffuse the power these institutions exercise over individuals. In doing so, they enhance the status of the individual. Like other mediating structures, unions rely upon local (usually workplace) organization and direct participation for their success. A well-ordered union represents a form of what Richard Weaver termed "social bond individualism,"[38] and can provide individuals with "defense in depth" against the overweening power of larger institutions.[39]

Unions' potential as subsidiary institutions explains the unwavering support they have received in the Church's social encyclicals. But the Church's view of unions is hardly dewy-eyed. The Church is well aware that, like other human institutions, unions have the capacity to fall short of their promise. *Quadragesimo Anno* thus reminds us that the principle of subsidiarity applies to unions no less than to any other social institution. The encyclical also emphasizes that unions have an obligation to serve the common good; it warns them against acting as a self-aggrandizing interest block, and admonishes them to recall that they ultimately exist for individuals.

In the final analysis, the fate of well-ordered unions is tied to that of other mediating groups. No single subsidiary structure—be it the family, parish, religious congregation, neighborhood, service club, fraternal organization, or union—is likely to survive in the absence of other such bodies. All require and can inculate the same habits of reflection, choice, personal responsibility, and self-rule. When people lose these habits, no single institution alone can restore them. The existence and decline of subsidiary structures is mutually conditioning; the loss or deformation of any threatens the rest. It is for this reason that *Quadragesimo Anno* calls for a "social reconstruction," and pays such close attention to the seemingly mundane institutions that should be a remarkably unremarkable part of a flourishing life.

Timely Truths

Of course, the lessons of subsidiarity are hardly confined to the workplace. As noted, the principle is an organizational norm applicable to institutional arrangements of every description, from town government and the other organizations of day-to-day life to transnational schemes like the European Economic Community.[40] Subsidiarity applies as well to educational institutions and programs, social-welfare schemes, health care, and policies that bear on the well-being of the foundational institution of civic and political life, the family.[41] In every context, the lesson is the same: since all rightly ordered societies exist for the individual, the emphasis in establishing any sort of social order must be on setting the conditions that will enhance opportunities for individuals to deliberate, choose, and act for themselves. Only by so doing do we treat people as human beings. Orders that fail to do so, because they are inconsistent with human character, eventually will collapse. To be authentically responsible, social and political orders must be structured in a way that permits individuals the maximum opportunity to act responsibly. Persons, not institutions, are the end of any society worthy of the name. If we are to avoid the iron cage that results from seeing bureaucracies or the market as our sole alternatives, subsidiarity stands as our only guide.

Sixty years have passed since *Quadragesimo Anno* was issued. While much has changed during that time, human nature has not. What we truly are, what our potential is, the purpose and end for which we have been created, remain the same. Subsidiarity takes its bearings by looking to this unchanging character. The metaphysics of the individual that informs the principle of subsidiarity gives it lasting relevance. Subsidiarity is therefore a Catholic principle in every sense of the term. It proceeds from an understanding of human character and end that is distinctly Catholic in development but hardly parochial in nature. Consequently, *Quadragesimo Anno*, and the principle of subsidiarity it so famously enunciates, speaks to all people of good will.

The concept is valuable in accounting for both human individuality and the fact that our authentic individuality can be realized only in community with others. In other words, subsidiarity understands that well-ordered human solidarity sets the conditions for the realization of authentic human freedom. Genuine and complete self-realization, the full perfection of our liberty, is indeed "the pearl of greatest price." Application of the principle of subsidiarity can help maintain a healthy liberal democracy. But the promise and significance of subsidiarity goes well beyond temporal arrangements. At a time when thoroughgoing social reconstruction is being undertaken around the globe, the lessons of *Quadragesimo Anno* are all the more valuable.

3

A Teacher Who Learns
Mater et Magistra (1961)

ROBERT A. SIRICO

M ERELY to mention the name of Pope John XXIII in most circles is to evoke warm feelings. This was, after all, the optimistic and accessible pontiff, the pope of the *aggiornamento*, a kindly pastor who was determined that his ancient church would take account of the positive developments of the modern world and offer that world the medicine of mercy.

John XXIII issued *Mater et Magistra* in May 1961.[1] *Mater et Magistra*, like *Rerum Novarum* before it and *Centesimus Annus* after it, was written in a time of great social upheaval: the world was confronting atomic weapons; a Catholic president occupied the White House for the first time in American history; the devastating impact of the Second World War was still fresh in many minds; a communications revolution was turning the world into a global village; Khrushchev was leader of the Kremlin; and Castro was actively setting up his island prison camp in Cuba. In each of these encyclicals, we see an effort to apply the Church's ageless teaching to a contemporary context. Thirty years after John XXIII wrote his

Robert A. Sirico, C.S.P., is a Paulist priest and president and founder of the Acton Institute for the Study of Religion and Liberty, in Grand Rapids, Michigan. He currently serves on the staff at the Catholic Information Center in Grand Rapids.

letter, his successor John Paul II would describe his similar endeavor as "an invitation to 'look around' at the 'new things' which surround us and in which we find ourselves caught up . . . it is an invitation to 'look to the future' " (*Centesimus Annus*, paragraph 3). Because Catholic social teaching can be understood only as a whole, we do well to view the developments in Catholic social thought that *Mater et Magistra* initiates through the lens of subsequent documents of the magisterium.

John XXIII faced unprecedented changes in the human condition, but the pastoral style of this encyclical reflected the vigorous spirit of the times: optimistic, forward-looking, practical, and enthusiastic about the future. The last encyclical written before the Second Vatican Council, *Mater et Magistra* was also the last of the papal encyclicals to be addressed solely to the Catholic faithful. John XXIII's next social encyclical, the 1963 *Pacem in Terris*, written a short time before his death, broadened the Church's horizon by addressing itself to "all men of good will."

The pope drew on a number of influential individuals for help in drafting the document. Five Jesuits, including the German social philosopher and active proponent of solidarism Gustav Gundlach, were selected to work on the first draft. Msgr. Pietro Pavan and Agostino Ferrari-Toniolo eventually joined the project, which was completed by Pavan, a professor at the Gregorian University and founder of an institute for Catholic social teachings at the Lateran University. J. Hirschman, S.J., translated the final draft into the official Latin version.[2]

Mater et Magistra was written to commemorate the seventieth anniversary of *Rerum Novarum*, with which Leo XIII initiated the modern social teaching of the Church. Leo XIII and Pius XI, in *Quadragesimo Anno*, had focused their attention on the "social problem" of the industrial working class in an age of rapid modernization. By broadening the discussion to include the circumstances of non-industrialized nations, and by stressing the role of the laity in carrying out the practical implications of the gospel, John XXIII introduced new dimensions to Catholic social teaching. Later, in *Sollicitudo Rei Socialis* and especially in *Centesimus Annus*, John Paul II further expands these new dimensions by considering the role of lay men and women in their capacity as entrepreneurs; he explores the ways in which their practical functions reflect God's own creativity and exhibit Christian virtues.

Overview of the Document

In the opening section of *Mater et Magistra*, the pope seeks to establish a link with his predecessors and to demonstrate how he developed his major points from their teachings. He refers to *Rerum Novarum* as the "Magna Carta for the reconstruction of the economic and social order" (*Mater Magistra*, paragraph 26). From Pius XI's 1931 *Quadragesimo Anno*, written in the midst of the Great Depression, John XXIII borrows the principle of subsidiarity and two other key notions: that economic undertakings should be governed by justice and charity, and that a "juridical order" is essential to insure that economic activities are carried out "in conformity with the common good" (30, 40). By the phrase "juridical order" John no doubt recalled Leo's embrace of the tripartite division of power into legislative, executive, and juridical branches (*Rerum Novarum*, section 121), somewhat of an innovation in Catholic thought at the time. Writing in the wake of totalitarianism's collapse in Central Europe, John Paul II would develop the concept even further:

> It is preferable that each power be balanced by other powers and by other spheres of responsibility which keep it within proper bounds. This is the principle of the "rule of law," in which the law is sovereign, and not the arbitrary will of individuals. (*Centesimus Annus*, 44)

Pope John also draws upon Pius XII's 1941 Pentecost radio broadcast—largely a celebration of *Rerum Novarum*—for its discussion of material goods, labor, and the family. John XXIII then briefly identifies the great economic, scientific, social, and political developments that have taken place in the intervening years and concludes by stating that his purpose in writing *Mater et Magistra* is to go beyond a mere commemoration of previous social teachings by seeking to "confirm and explain more fully" current applications (50).

The second section begins and ends with a discussion of private initiative and private property, themes that John Paul II would vastly expand in *Sollicitudo Rei Socialis* and *Centesimus Annus*. Here, John XXIII asserts that private initiative should enjoy "first place" in economic affairs, and, by invoking the principle of subsidiarity (that decision-making should be left to the lowest possible level in the social hierarchy commensurate with the pursuit of the common good), suggests that the role of the state in economic matters should be limited. The section then addresses the controversial notion of "socialization" (which will be discussed in more detail below). The pope also calls for standards of justice and equity in remuneration for work, advocates experiments in cooperative or profit-sharing ventures to promote economic harmony, and encourages businesses to form cooperative associations (68–103). The section closes with a reaffirmation of the rights and responsibilities inherent in private property and restates the principle of subsidiarity.

The third section of the encyclical focuses on "New Aspects of the Social Question." It advocates a host of state-administered policies—including tax laws, social security, public services, and price protections—to make rural and underdeveloped areas more attractive and stable. The Church, owing to its universal nature, can infuse its "energy into the life of a people" to bring about a "unity which is profound and in conformity with that heavenly love whereby all are moved in their innermost being" (181–82). Pointing to the "inexhaustible productive capacity" of the human race, the pope underscores the sacredness of human life, "since from its inception, it requires the action of God the Creator" (189–94). Finally, John XXIII stresses the need for international cooperation in confronting worldwide problems.

The fourth and final section of *Mater et Magistra* deals with the need to strengthen the fabric of social relationships and analyzes the hindrances to such a reconstruction—among them, philosophies that rest on distorted perceptions of what it means to be human. Here the pope underscores "the cardinal point" of the Church's social teaching, that "individual men are necessarily the foundation, cause, and end of all social institutions" (219).

Toward the end of the encyclical, the pope raises the sometimes subtle distinction between the core teachings of the Christian faith and the practical applications of these teachings in the life of the world. For example, in his discussion of the Young Christian Workers, a popular international movement founded to confront social problems without resorting to socialist solutions, the pope notes that "when it comes to reducing these teachings to action, it sometimes happens that even sincere Catholic men have differing views. When this occurs they should take care to have to show mutual esteem and regard, and to explore the extent to which they can work in cooperation among themselves" (238).

A Controversial Openness

As he would later express it in his opening speech for the Second Vatican Council, John XXIII believed that the Church should not cast itself in a reactionary stance but should "look to the present, to the new conditions and forms of life introduced to the modern world," because these developments "have opened new avenues to the Catholic apostolate." This change would, he argues, require a refinement of the Church's ancient message. For "the substance of the ancient deposit of faith is one thing, the way in which it is presented is another."

In turning the face of the Church toward the world it was established to serve, John XXIII displayed an openness his predecessors would not have countenanced. In 1937, for example, Pius XI stated that "communism is intrinsically perverse and no one who would save Christian civilization may collaborate with it." Yet in *Mater et Magistra* John XXIII expresses a somewhat different view. While certainly not endorsing communism, and acknowledging the risk of working with those who do not share the Catholic worldview, he suggests that Catholics "should be prepared to join sincerely in doing whatever is naturally good or conducive to good" (239) with others of different convictions.

Many commentators have construed this as an "opening to the Left" on the part of Catholic social teaching, and *Mater et Magistra* is frequently cited today as legitimizing the central role of government in achieving social goals. Indeed, the controversy surrounding this point was immediate. Upon its publication in the United States, the conservative journal *National Review* greeted the papal letter with chagrin. "The large sprawling document released by the Vatican last week," read its editorial, failing even to identify the document as an encyclical, "may become the source of embarrassed explanations."[3]

Mater et Magistra, it must be admitted, combines a good deal of Christian wisdom with a somewhat conflicted and perhaps even inconsistent message about the role of the state in economic affairs. It may be useful, then, to examine the extent to which Catholic social thought is, at heart, tied to statist assumptions and policies, to ask whether these policies promote the ultimate moral goals of the Church's social and economic teaching, and to see the ways in which later authoritative social teaching casts additional light on some of these conflicts and inconsistencies.

Indeed, while it may be correct to say Pope John did moderate the Church's posture toward the political Left, it would be equally correct to say that his successor, John Paul II, in the aftermath of the Left's worldwide collapse, opens the possibility of a new dialogue with market liberalism.

Private Property and the Common Good

Catholicism's understanding of private property is based on its view of human nature: that human beings are persons who come to the fullness of their individuality in community and society. Hence, in *Mater et Magistra* the individual is described as existing prior to society, and the proper end toward which society is organized is man himself. The right to personal property is "permanently valid," John XXIII believed, and in a key section of the encyclical he outlines his reasoning: because social arrangements exist with "individual men as their end," the freedom and the right to property of these individuals must be protected. Liberty and property thus enjoy a reciprocal relationship because, "in the right to property, the exercise of liberty finds both a safeguard and a stimulus" (109).

Moreover, there is a social obligation attendant on private property, an obligation derived from human nature itself (119). The question for economics and politics is how this obligation is best met. The notion of private property as the key to a wise, efficient, and productive social arrangement dates back to Thomas Aquinas.[4] But the pope's call for a wider ownership of property (115)—based on national policies to facilitate access to private property—has been regarded by some as an innovation in Catholic thought.[5]

Individual liberty has been persistently linked in Catholic thought to the notion of the "common good," and John XXIII's concern was to promote the common good in a "suitable manner" by "the production of a sufficient supply of material goods" (20). Such a goal is consistent with the Christian worldview, but Christian social ethicists have never agreed on the morally appropriate and economically effective means to achieve that desirable worldly end. Some would argue, and not without reason, that *Mater et Magistra* tends to overlook the ways in which state intervention in the economy obscures the price mechanism, thus distorting information exchange and patterns of production and consumption and inviting excessive bureaucratization.[6] Such an oversight may well be due to the Church's tendency to give weight to the social order of the Middle Ages as a normative model of Christian society.

This criticism of the Church may have had some validity in the past. In recent times, however, John Paul has taken a more cautious approach to the role of the state, both as the regulator of the economy and as the remedy for social problems.

In what is perhaps one of the most notable innovations in the encyclical tradition, John Paul speaks cautiously about the danger of the welfare state. Looking at welfare in light of the principle of subsidiarity, he warns:

> By intervening directly and depriving society of its responsibility, the Social Assistance State leads to a loss of human energies and an inordinate increase of public agencies, which are dominated more by bureaucratic ways of thinking than by concern for serving their clients, and which are accompanied by an enormous increase in spending. (*Centesimus Annus*, 48)

Michael Novak's observation on *Quadragesimo Anno* and Pius XI's understanding of the common good applies as well to *Mater et Magistra*. Novak demonstrated how Catholic economic thought, while sharing many of the same goals as classical liberal thought, differs on the practical manner by which the common good is to be attained, and in its understanding of the social dynamics of the pursuit of justice in society:

As part of their medieval inheritance, Catholics tend to believe that a common vision is best enunciated by a public authority and suffused throughout the society from above. By contrast, the liberal method is to multiply the number of active intelligences at the base of society, to maintain free and open discussion, and to arrive at consensus through democratic methods. Similarly, in economic matters, the liberal view is that constraints inherent in economic activity oblige individual intelligent agents to be guided by the needs and desires of others. Thus, economic activities impose by their very nature a coordinating, cooperative tendency. No one intelligent agent needs to have a single vision of the whole in order to discern the specific steps he or she must take in order to adjust to the common flow, in all its variety and sub-departments. Yet, a certain other-directedness is absolutely essential to success.[7]

Contrary to the Marxist view that there is something basically immoral and unjust in the nature of private property per se,[8] the Church's teachings reveal a different concern: ownership of property, absent the protection of a juridical framework, may contain the seeds of its own destruction, by creating conditions in which the right of access to property will become endangered and the pursuit of the common good will be rendered impossible. While there can be legitimate disagreement over the weight the encyclical and its predecessors give to the role of the state in the achievement of the common good, there should be no disagreement on the principles involved: that people have a basic right to own private property; that the exercise of that right contributes to a well-ordered society; and that all men, regardless of their economic condition, have an obligation to contribute to the common good.

Christianity and the Material World

Christianity's somewhat ambivalent attitude towards the material world in general has also shaped its views about private property, at times causing it to lean in a direction distinctly uncomfortable for classical liberals. But whatever its ambivalence about certain aspects of economic life, orthodox Catholicism has always rejected dualism and the ancient Manichaean temptation to regard the material world as essentially evil. The God-given goodness of

Creation, which we read about in the first pages of the Bible, and the classic Catholic understanding of the Incarnation shape the entire social doctrine of the Church.

In stark opposition to Marxism, which contends that religion seeks to anesthetize people to their present-day miseries in order to suppress the revolutionary impulse, Catholic social teaching has sought to infuse the worlds of politics and economics with the leaven of the gospel—the assumption being that the world is capable of being thus leavened. "Total depravity" is not a concept with a well-developed Catholic pedigree. Indeed, one could say that the Catholic moral imagination has a certain "holy worldliness" about it—a worldliness not surprising in a church whose basic sacramental materials are bread, wine, water, salt, and oil.

Reflection on these two grand theological themes, Creation and Incarnation, allows us to discover the spiritual reality "breaking out," as it were, of the material world.[9] And so while tensions exist within the Catholic tradition with regard to the uses of the material world, the Church has never rejected the material world or its components as intrinsically evil. Private property—in fact, the whole material order—should always be regarded as a means rather than an end. In this way, Creation can even be viewed as the locus and material for the self-disclosure of the world's creator.[10]

The Notion of Commodities

Mater et Magistra broadened the Catholic concept of private property as a wealth-producing entity to include much more than land (115). But the encyclical stops short of extending the notion to human labor. The document stresses that

> work, inasmuch as it is an expression of the human person, can by no means be regarded as a mere commodity. For the great majority of mankind, work is the only source from which the means of livelihood are drawn. Hence, its remuneration is not to be thought of in terms of merchandise, but rather according to the laws of justice and equity. (18)

The moral principles at play here are sound, but one may wonder about the application of principles to practice. It may be philosophically consistent to affirm in all instances the priority of moral over pragmatic calculations, but too rigid a distinction between morality and utility can lead to some troublesome contradictions. Moral ends, under certain circumstances, emerge from a morally neutral process. In a free-market system, for example, establishing the price at which labor is renumerated in the same way that one establishes the price of a commodity does not dehumanize the worker; rather, it empowers him by freeing him from forces outside his control. The worker becomes a player who can offer his talent, labor, and product to the highest bidder, just like any other entrepreneur. The ability to work makes each laborer a sort of capitalist in his own right, protected by the availability of economic alternatives.

In its graceful celebration of human labor, *Mater et Magistra* makes an important contribution to social analysis. History shows, however, that justice and equity are best served by allowing individuals to ply their trades and talents freely—that is, as a kind of commodity. While John Paul also warns against treating labor as a "mere commodity" (*Centesimus Annus*, 19, 34), he firmly links the right to property to individual creativity and intelligence. Both of these basic human attributes underpin technology and economic skills, which require freedom to emerge. John Paul distinguishes between free labor and slave labor in a way not envisioned by John in *Mater et Magistra*.[11] John Paul says that "initiative and entrepreneurial ability" should be viewed favorably because, "besides the earth, man's principal resource is man himself" (*Centesimus Annus*, 32).

Papal teaching is reluctant to examine labor in market terms because of a commendable fear that labor will be divorced from the human person, who is the locus of labor, thus degrading his status to that of a machine. It may help, however, to speak of labor not as a noun but as a verb—that is, as a service one individual renders to another. As a service, labor is scarce, which in turn means that those who hire labor place value upon it. This economic assessment of the service function of labor is surely not sufficient (labor must always be seen with all the complexity of the human person who performs it), but it is necessary. Neglecting such an analysis shows a lack of appreciation for labor's total reality, which includes scarcity and abundance. The economic consequences of this neglect are dire.

If wages are paid without regard to the factors of supply and demand, overcompensation will result. At first glance this may appear to work out well, but it does so only for those who are employed. Those left unemployed pay the price of overcompensation, as do consumers who will be offered fewer products at higher prices than they would have been had the unemployed workers been hired.

It is doubtful that the popes, in expressing their concern for the treatment of labor as a "mere commodity," intended to foster such imbalances. Rather, they were underscoring the importance of seeing labor as uniquely *human* action. Viewing labor as only "an economic service of a personal character engaged in production with other factors" would rob this free human activity of its dignity by reducing it to the level of a machine.[12]

In his *Summa Theologiae*, Saint Thomas Aquinas addressed the charge that property rights result in an inequitable situation in which the success of some means the deprivation of others. It is not the case, Saint Thomas argued, that the possessor of private property is analogous to a person who, by attending a play, thereby prevents others from coming. On the contrary:

A man would not act unlawfully if by going beforehand to the play he prepared the way for others: but he acts unlawfully if by so doing he hinders others from going. . . . A rich man does not act unlawfully if he anticipates someone in taking possession of something which at first was common property [i.e., existing in a state of nature], and gives others a share: but he sins if he excludes others indiscriminately from using it.[13]

Appropriate Social Planning

Saint Thomas's distinction is a valuable one and can serve as a useful guide in charting a course between the injustices and inefficiencies of a centrally planned economy and the excesses of some participants in the free market. There are those—including a fair number of Catholic theologians and social theorists—who maintain that market competition inherently harms people. But a more positive case may be made for competition, a case that derives from the principles of private property and justice spelled out in the Church's own encyclicals.

Whatever may be the temporary inequities of a free market, they are vastly preferable to the systematic and permanent inequities of a monopoly. Competition results in a dispersal of economic planning throughout the whole of society. As F. A. Hayek explains:

> Planning in the specific sense in which the term is used in contemporary controversy necessarily means central planning—planning of the whole of the economic system according to one unified plan. Competition, on the other hand, means decentralized planning by many separate persons. The half-way house between the two, about which many people talk, but few like when they see it, is the delegation of planning to privileged industries, or in other words, monopolies.[14]

If, as *Mater et Magistra* teaches, "individual men are prior to civil society," then a practical application of that principle would be the constitutional establishment of a limited state. Liberal capitalist democracy, while deliberately designed for men, not angels, has proven far more resistent to abuse and tyranny than has centralized government in its various forms. The limited state has also shown more respect for, and given more protection to, the individual human person, who is quite properly the beginning and end of Catholic social teaching. As John XXIII makes very clear: "The cardinal point of this teaching is that individual men are necessarily the foundation, cause and end of all social institutions" (219). A rigorous interpretation of this statement places the Catholic tradition far more in alignment with the liberal tradition, and its consistent rejection of the subordination of the individual to the group, than with collectivism in any of its pre-modern or modern forms.

The issue of the-liberal-state-versus-collectivism raises the question of the Church's teaching on the role of the state in economic life. Jean-Yves Calvez, a Jesuit theologian and expert on Catholic social teaching, has traced the ebb and flow in the manner and extent to which the Church has endorsed government involvement in economic affairs. *Mater et Magistra*, according to Calvez, approaches the issue in "calmer and less belligerent tones" than previous papal pronouncements. John XXIII defines the principle of subsidiarity such that "in the very action of intervention is contained its limitation." And given the nature of the human person, only highly specific and restricted forms of assistance can be permissible. Calvez explains:

> Help is not bestowed on human beings in the same way that care and relief are applied to overtaxed machinery. Since human beings are free persons, help should be given them according to their freedom. They are truly helped only when they are allowed to develop their various potentials and achieve a greater freedom. Moreover, freedom is best assisted when there is reliance, as much as possible, on freedom itself, by stirring it up, by awakening it and by restraining it only in its less basic forms and in a measure that is absolutely necessary.[15]

Productivity and Abundance

In cautioning his readers against repeating the mistakes that have bedeviled economic development in the past, John XXIII argues:

> It seems only prudent for nations which thus far have made little or no progress, to weigh well the principal factor in the advance of nations that enjoy abundance. Prudent foresight and common need demand that not only more goods be produced, but that this be done more efficiently. Likewise, necessity and justice require that wealth produced be distributed equitably among all citizens of the commonwealth. Accordingly, efforts should be made to ensure that improved social conditions accompany economic advancement. (167–68)

The latter half of this passage has been seized on by some theologians and activists to justify wide-ranging state-based central economic planning and redistributive economic policies, and no doubt there is a redistributive tug in certain portions of *Mater et Magistra*. But a balanced reading of the encyclical cannot ignore John XXIII's admonition that we must consult history in order to discern why some societies have achieved a higher material standard of living than others. The encyclical unfortunately fails to elaborate on what it would mean for goods to be produced "more efficiently." But it seems reasonable to conclude, weighing the historical evidence, that those nations that have emphasized free trade, defended the right to private property, and stressed the inviolability of human rights against the claims of the state, the party, or "history," have been the nations that have enjoyed abundance and economic progress. Certainly, John Paul II makes precisely this point in *Centesimus Annus* when he calls for "an economic system which recognizes the fundamental and positive role of business, the market, private property and the resulting responsibility for the means of production, as well as free human creativity in the economic sector" (42).

Empirical evidence, which according to John XXIII has to inform any moral analysis, has only recently begun to dispose Catholicism to a favorable assessment of liberal economics. *Mater et Magistra*'s failure to make that assessment forthrightly illustrates how the Church's quite legitimate fear of the atomism, materialism, and radical individualism of modernity can become an obstacle to the empirically informed social ethics that modern church encyclicals have tried to foster.

Socialization and the Market

Perhaps the most widely discussed theme of *Mater et Magistra* is what has been variously translated as the new reality of "socialization" or "the multiplication of social relationships" (59, 62, 63). The Latin phrase *socialium rationum incrementa* may have encouraged a number of commentators to regard this theme as amounting to an endorsement of political or economic socialism. That this was clearly not the encyclical's intent ought to be clear upon careful consideration.

The context in which John XXIII raises the issue of socialization is crucial to understanding the term's meaning. In the same paragraph that he uses this term, the pope notes the changes that have taken place in contemporary society, particularly "technical and scientific progress, greater productive efficiency, and a higher standard of living among citizens" (59). Several paragraphs later he describes the Christian concept of a true community—the standard by which to judge the process of socialization and the common good. Contemporary life, the pope argues, requires strong mediating institutions capable of protecting the primacy of the human person while affording him a means of pursuing the common good, a theme always at the heart of Catholic social concern. Socialization, or the "multiplication of social relationships," is thus a necessary accompaniment to the advancement of civilization and an important component of the integral development of the person.

In short, "social relationships" are at the service of man, not the other way around. Or, as *Mater et Magistra* puts it:

Accordingly, as relationships multiply between men, binding them more closely together, commonwealths will more readily and appropriately order their affairs to the extent these two factors are kept in balance: 1) the freedom of individual citizens and groups of citizens to act autonomously, while cooperating one with the other; 2) the activity of the State whereby the undertakings of private individuals and groups are suitably regulated and fostered. (66)

To interpret this modest, balanced set of standards for relating individual liberty to the common good as a rallying cry for the radical politicization of life or for a socialist approach to economics is to do a severe injustice to the pope's intention. The fact that these passages in *Mater et Magistra* have so frequently lent themselves to socialist interpretation tells us something about the deficiencies of Latin, the inadequacies of some translations, the partisanship of some commentators, and the inability of even the Holy See to effectively control the interpretation of papal documents. But there is nothing in these passages of *Mater et Magistra* to sustain the radical claim that massive state interventions are essential to the achievement of the moral goals the Church has set for society and for the individual.

Indeed, if it can be shown that a given intervention or series of interventions will have harmful consequences for people, either immediately or over time, then such interventions, according to the heart of Catholic moral teaching, should be resisted, no matter how well intended. And if the very things that are so often denigrated in a command economy—private ownership of goods and means of production, the liberty to exchange products and resources without undue interference, and a sound currency—can be shown to promote social harmony and progress, they should be pursued and given full intellectual and moral legitimization.

John Paul II offers just this intellectual and moral legitimization by developing the theme of socialization within a global perspective. In his discussions of human labor in *Laborum Exercens* and especially in *Centesimus Annus*, he outlines the interconnecting social relations, or "community of work," that emerge in the context of economic liberty. Such relations should be fostered among the peoples of the Third World by including them within "a society of free work, of enterprise and of participation" (*Centesimus Annus*, 32, 35).

Persistent Suspicion

That being said, it has to be conceded that, in the encyclical tradition from *Rerum Novarum* through *Mater et Magistra* and even in some of the writings of John Paul II, there remains suspicion about liberal capitalism. One reason for this hesitancy is the popes' claim that liberal economists attribute everything in their field of inquiry to "inescapable, natural forces" that are somehow beyond the order of morality. As John XXIII put it in *Mater et Magistra*, "Hence it was held that no connection existed between economic and moral laws. Wherefore, those engaged in economic activity need look no further than their own gain" (11).

Reasonable analysts, respectful of the Church's contributions to social thought, may still find Pope John's history here to be a caricature of reality. Were Roman Catholic social teaching to reflect more deeply on Adam Smith as a moral philosopher and not "merely" as an economist, a richer, more compelling, and less stereotyped discussion might evolve. Smith, after all, wrote not only *An Inquiry into the Nature and Causes of the Wealth of Nations* but also *A Theory of Moral Sentiments*—and he understood the two works to have an intrinsic connection. Similarly, modern Austrian economists like Wilhelm Röpke, Ludwig von Mises, Henry Hazlitt, F. A. Hayek, and Israel Kirzner certainly show a concern about moral matters, even if on particular points they would parts ways with the Church's teaching.[16]

One can even argue that the Church has lost an important opportunity in its failure to develop a case for the free market from its own preferred natural-law method of moral reasoning. Why should an economic order that results from the interaction of free individuals, peacefully pursuing what they deem is best for themselves and their families and influenced by the norms of natural law as explicated by the Church, be seen as somehow unnatural or even vaguely immoral? In fact, a Catholic capitalist ethic is not so much in need of creation as of retrieval and extension, as a study of the Spanish scholastics Francisco de Vitoria, Domingo de Soto, Domingo de Banez, Pedro Fernandez Navarrete, and Luis de la Calle suggests.[17] One could also approach the question phenomenologically, as is the custom of John Paul II. Far from there being no connection between economic and moral laws, economic actions within a free economy embody the actors' own moral premises. Freedom is not immoral; only its abuse.

Nor can "profit," a term frequently given a derogatory connotation in religious discussions, be dismissed as axiomatically immoral. Profit is less a moral category than a point of accounting; moreover, it has proven essential in ameliorating poverty. In *Mater et Magistra*, unfortunately, John XXIII, like many of his predecessors, seems drawn to the faulty yet popular image of the pie—i.e., that the economic gain of some represents the creation of poverty for others. Here, again, more attention to economic creativity and the creation of wealth as expressions of man's stewardship over the material world, and a more rigorous study of the empirical realities, might well lead the Church to a deeper moral understanding of the profit motive and "profit" itself.

Unfinished Business

Mater et Magistra's spirited willingness to bring the modern world into dialogue with Catholic understandings of society, polity, and economy was a watershed in the encyclical tradition of modern Catholic social teaching. Yet *Mater et Magistra* was not and did not claim to be the final development of that tradition. Almost thirty years later, Catholics and others awaited a papal statement that would take full account of the dramatic historical events of the past few years (including the trend away from centrally planned to free-market economies) and that would enter into serious conversation with free-market theorists.

The waiting ended on the one-hundredth anniversary of Pope Leo's inaugural social encyclical with the promulgation of *Centesimus Annus* by the first pope to have lived under a command economy. With its appearance, an entirely new dialogue has begun.

No doubt it will take some time for the old mode of centralized governmental approaches to social problems to pass from the scene, but the process has begun.[18]

A broad-minded and empirical approach to social questions is fully in keeping with the developmental nature of Catholic doctrine, and with the "holy worldliness" that has distinguished the tradition in its mainstream for well over a millennium. It has been nothing short of astounding to watch the market experiments now being undertaken by Catholic political leaders in the new democracies of Central and Eastern Europe and Latin America, and to witness how these efforts have already had an important impact on the evolution of encyclical tradition in *Centesimus Annus*. *Mater et Magistra* anticipated some of these developments. John XXIII reminded the people of God that the Church is, indeed, a teacher. It is indeed the finest kind of teacher: one that not only teaches but also listens and learns itself.

4

The Human-Rights Revolution
Pacem in Terris (1963)

GEORGE WEIGEL

Issued on Holy Thursday in 1963, Pope John XXIII's encyclical *Pacem in Terris* quickly established itself as the most beloved text in modern Catholic social thought. The reasons why involve the timing, tenor, and authorship of the letter as well as its specific contents.

The spring of 1963 followed hard on the heels of the most frightening episode of the Cold War, the Cuban Missile Crisis, which was itself the culmination of a period of great international tension marked by the sundry East/West confrontations over Berlin, the Congo, and Southeast Asia. As *Commonweal* editor John Cogley put it in his commentary on the encyclical, the world seemed to be looking, at times even desperately, for an answer to the question, "Who speaks for Man?"[1] *Pacem in Terris* offered one possible response.

The tenor of *Pacem in Terris* also contributed to its warm reception. Subsequent mythologizings notwithstanding, John XXIII was fundamentally a conservative in matters of doctrine and spirituality. But he exuded a warm confidence in humanity that was reflected in his encyclical. A world that had come to regard Roman Catholicism as an implacable critic of modernity now found itself presented

---

George Weigel is president of the Ethics and Public Policy Center.

with a magisterial document that celebrated (if too effusively for some tastes) mankind's capacity to order public life according to the dictates of reason and morality. Pope Pius XII had, of course, addressed questions of international politics on a host of occasions over nineteen years. But the tone was, well, different. *Pacem in Terris* marked the point at which the highest leadership of the Roman Catholic Church fully inserted itself into the modern quest for peace with freedom and justice and did so in the confidence that its appeal would be heard by "all men of good will."

Finally, the enthusiasm that greeted *Pacem in Terris* had to do in considerable part with the personal stature of its author. By the spring of 1963 John XXIII, the "interim" pope elected in 1958 to provide a short breathing space after the lengthy pontificates of Pius XI and Pius XII, had become a kind of *pater familias* to the world. And that the pope died just two months after the publication of the encyclical gave the document a kind of testamentary authority: here was the last, valedictory message of the pontiff who had struggled bravely against cancer in order to leave as his final legacy a plea for peace on earth.

SIX KEY THEMES

According to stories circulated shortly after John XXIII's death, the pope had Msgr. Pietro Pavan, the drafter of the encyclical, rewrite it several times until, as the pope was alleged to have put it, even he could understand it. Be that as it may, *Pacem in Terris* is a lengthy document not without its subtleties and complexities. Six principal themes, however, establish the encyclical's originality and have had a great impact on the subsequent Catholic (and ecumenical) debate over the morality and politics of peace and freedom.

1. Pope John believed that the world had entered a *new moment in history*, characterized by "the conviction that all men are equal by reason of their natural dignity" (*Pacem in Terris*, paragraph 44). Beneath the surface of the world's agitations over racism, decolonization, and the status and role of women, the pope discerned a deeper current: the world had become "conscious of spiritual values, understanding the meaning of truth, justice, charity, and freedom" (45). Because of this, men and women could grasp anew

that "the ties that bind them to God [are] the solid foundation and supreme criterion of their lives," both as individuals and as members of society (45). In short, the human community had entered a new phase in its development, a spiritual evolution that would lead to new forms of political organization.

2. This meant, the pope continued, that the classic Catholic social-ethical principle of the "common good" now had to be understood in global terms. There was a *universal common good* that individuals and nations were obliged to advance. Moreover, the pope argued, the universal common good could not be secured by the efforts of states operating according to the principles and practices of state sovereignty that had shaped world politics since the Peace of Westphalia in 1648. What the world lacked, in other words, was a political instrumentality with effective authority to advance the universal common good, or, put differently, to solve the myriad problems that no state or alliance of states could satisfactorily address on its own.

3. John XXIII did not hesitate to draw the obvious structural implication of this analysis: the world needed a *universal public authority* that was capable of acting in the name of humanity in the pursuit of the universal common good (137). To fulfill its duties, this universal public authority had to be established by consent, not by force; it had to respect the legitimate prerogatives of sovereign states, according to the principle of subsidiarity (i.e., no decisions should be taken at any higher level than necessary to achieve the common good); and it had to acknowledge and foster the protection of basic human rights.

4. This last theme, that the *protection and promotion of basic human rights were the fundamental purposes of governments and of the universal public authority*, was the fourth distinctive element in *Pacem in Terris*. Human rights, the pope insisted, were the rights of persons precisely as persons: as men and women endowed with reason and free will, and thus the capacity to think, judge, and choose. "Human rights," properly understood, were not benefices granted by government. On the contrary, the legitimacy of government was determined in part by a government's recognition that it was accountable to norms that transcended (and stood in judgment on) its own sovereign will. The pope then adduced a lengthy list of

the human rights that it was the function of governments and the universal public authority to protect and promote, running the gamut from the basic right to life, through the rights of religious liberty and association, and on to economic, social, and cultural goods (9–27).

5. The fifth distinctive element in *Pacem in Terris* was the approach Pope John took to the *problem of communism*. Pope Pius XI had taught that "no one can be at the same time a good Catholic and a true socialist" (*Quadragesimo Anno*, paragraph 120), and forbade Catholics from engaging in common public activity with communists. Pius XII had been rigorous in his denunciation of communist tyranny as the Iron Curtain fell across Central and Eastern Europe and a great persecution of the Church followed there (and in the China of Mao Zedong).

A career diplomat, John XXIII was not unaware of the dangers of communism. But he seemed to believe that important changes had occurred in the communist world since the death of Stalin in 1953. Ever optimistic about the human person, the pope urged a distinction between errors in political and economic theory and practice, and the erring person who was the bearer of those theories and the embodiment of those practices. Moreover, the pope seemed to intuit that the communist project was doomed over the long haul, for the human thirst for truth could never be completely extinguished; in the interim, one had to treat the erring person as a human being with an inherent dignity and capacity for grasping the truth. In a more controversial vein, the pope claimed that one ought to distinguish "between false philosophical teachings regarding the nature, origin, and destiny of the universe and of man, and movements [i.e., Marxism-Leninism] that have a direct bearing either on economic and social questions, or cultural matters or on the organization of the state, even if these movements owe their origin and tenets to these false doctrines." Those movements, the pope believed, "are readily susceptible to change" and sometimes "contain elements that are positive and deserving of approval" (159). Thus did Pope John effect, if not a full-scale "opening to the Left," at least the initiation of a dialogue between the leadership of Roman Catholicism and communist leaders: one which, to be sure, should be undertaken "with the virtue of prudence" (160).

6. Finally, Pope John addressed the issue of *deterrence and disarmament*. The pope understood the political reasons for, and the dynamics of, the arms race, and did not reduce them to the alleged psycho-pathology of the "enemy mind-set," as a later generation of activists would charge. On the other hand, the pope deplored "the enormous stocks of armaments that have been and are still being made in more economically developed countries, with a vast outlay of intellectual and economic resources" (109). And then John XXIII made his plea for general and complete disarmament, inspected and enforced:

> Justice, then, right reason, and consideration for human dignity and life urgently demand that the arms race should cease; that the stockpiles which exist in various countries should be reduced equally and simultaneously by the parties concerned; that nuclear weapons should be banned; and finally that all come to an agreement on a fitting program of disarmament, employing mutual and effective controls. (112)

Disarmament could not be effective and complete, the pope concluded, unless it "proceeds from inner conviction," which meant that the "true and solid peace of nations" would consist, not in deterrence, but "in mutual trust alone." This, the pope believed, "can be brought to pass" (113).

THE REALISTS DEMUR

Christian realists of various denominational persuasions did not readily share the general enthusiasm for *Pacem in Terris*.

The Jesuit social ethicist John Courtney Murray welcomed the encyclical's opening to a conversation with modernity, and agreed with the pope's emphasis on the importance of the problem of *order* in international public life: "This does seem to be the contemporary issue. . . . The issue is not whether we shall have order in the world; the contemporary condition of chaos has become intolerable on a worldwide scale. The question is, then, on what principles is the world going to be ordered."[2] Murray was also grateful for the pope's tacit endorsement of democracy and limited government, and argued that the pope had added a fourth, key element—freedom—to the Church's traditional concern for truth, justice, and charity in the social order.

But Murray also thought that the pope's call for an international public authority, while a plausible conclusion from moral reasoning, was simply impossible in the current empirical and historical situation: for the world lacked the moral and political consensus on which such an authority would, by the pope's own logic, have to rest. Murray also worried that the pope had not adequately measured the "fundamental schism" in the modern world, between democracy and totalitarianism.

The Perils of Perfectionism

Murray's concern about the pope's sense of the possible was shared by Reinhold Niebuhr, who argued that the encyclical "speaks as if it were a simple matter to construct and reconstruct communities, not by the organic processes of history but by an application of 'the sense of justice and mutual love.'" The pope's portrait of a "community of mankind" was at once true and false, a reality and an ideal, "since mankind is divided by a multitude of languages, customs, traditions, and parochial loyalties." Niebuhr worried that the encyclical evoked a Pelagian spirit of human perfectibility, rather than an Augustinian spirit of man's limited capacities for concretely achieving the good society, and compared the pope's decency and charity to the idealism of a Francis of Assisi, whom medieval pontiffs could admire while conducting the affairs of state according to a rougher calculus of the human condition.[3]

Perhaps the most acute analysis of the encyclical came from the Methodist theologian Paul Ramsey, who conceded that John XXIII had taught many "sound and exceedingly important political truths that were in search of a voice humanly great enough to utter them." But Ramsey noted that only two sentences in *Pacem in Terris* referred to the realities of sin. And the public meaning of man's sinfulness was that politics would always be an arena of indeterminacy, recalcitrance, and damage control. Ramsey worried that the pope's idealism, in the world of politics, would decay into a romanticism that ignored the cardinal political virtue of prudence.

Pacem in Terris was enthusiastically welcomed by pacifists and others concerned that the Church's traditional just-war doctrine was evangelically irresponsible and prudentially inapplicable in a world of weapons of mass destruction. Ramsey turned this position on its head and argued that the only morally acceptable way to achieve the pope's vision of an orderly international public life was *through*, not around, the classic just-war canons: "for these criteria are also the principles intrinsic to purposeful political action; they specify the moral economy governing the use of force, which must always be employed in politics—domestically within nations; internationally in the post-feudal, pre-atomic era; and under the public authority of any possible world community that may be established during the nuclear age."[4]

In sum, one could accept, as a moral and religious vision, Pope John's call for an international public authority; but getting to it, and then operating it successfully for the common good, required harder thought about the problem of power and political community than the encyclical offered. The just-war tradition, Ramsey believed, included far more than the rules of war: it contained a sophisticated political wisdom about the right ordering of states and their relations that had to be tapped if *Pacem in Terris* were not to suffer the fate of those liberal Protestant pronouncements on international affairs that, "while rightly stressing what positively needs to be done for the attainment of the universal common good, fail to grapple with the problem of power" and the realities of power as inextricably enmeshed in the pursuit of peace, security, freedom, justice, and prosperity.

Necessary Correctives

In the retrospect of thirty years, many of these fraternal criticisms of *Pacem in Terris* seem warranted, and others might have been added. At the level of the encyclical's politics, the concerns of Murray, Niebuhr, and Ramsey revolved around the question of whether *Pacem in Terris* had adequately addressed the relationship of ends and means in the pursuit of the common good of humanity. The pope, these friendly critics seemed to imply, jumped rather precipitously from the order of politics to the order of spirituality when the crunch question of "how" reared its head: the political organization of the world would be accomplished through the exercise of "mutual trust."

But was "trust" the basis on which *political* communities formed? Surely some minimum of confidence in the rectitude of the basic structures of governance was a precondition to "peace on earth," within or, ultimately, among nations. But that confidence was itself a function of the capacity of structures of governance to protect basic human rights and advance the common good. And those structures ought to assume, at least according to the Anglo-American understanding of democracy, that men are not angels; that conflict is in the nature of things political; and that governments ought to be designed precisely so that men's inevitable disagreements over individual prerogatives and public policy can be directed into creative, rather than destructive, channels. Put in terms of theological worldviews, the creative tension between the Augustinian or realist pole of the classic Catholic tradition of social ethics and the Thomistic or idealist pole tended to collapse in *Pacem in Terris*, to the point where idealism was in danger of decaying into naiveté or romanticism about the human prospect.

The encyclical's failure to order "basic human rights" schematically was also troubling. *Pacem in Terris* did not address (and indeed it may have exacerbated) the problems that arise when two notions of "basic human rights" are wedded together: immunity from the coercive power of government (including the freedoms essential to the right ordering of the political community), and economic, social, and/or cultural goods or entitlements. The empirical evidence strongly suggests that the effective protection and exercise of civil rights and political freedoms is an essential precondition to a society's sustained success in the attainment of economic, social, and cultural goods. Some rights, in other words, make the achievement of other goods (even when these goods are construed as "rights") possible.

By muddling the distinctions between, and relationships among, various categories of rights, *Pacem in Terris* also helped create an intellectual climate in Roman Catholicism in which what was oxymoronically referred to as the "Marxist human-rights tradition" could achieve, in the 1970s, a kind of cachet. This was most conspicuous in the various theologies of liberation, many of which actually scorned the tradition of civil rights and political freedoms as so much "bourgeois formalism."

The encyclical would have been strengthened as well by more clarity on the question of the relationship between peace and justice. Even nations that are traditionally pacific have different understandings of the requirements of justice in a rightly ordered society (much more in an international political community). What could the world agree to disagree on and still enjoy peace—a peace that permitted the argument over the demands of justice (in the economic and social spheres, for example) to be carried on without resort to the use or threat of mass violence? *Pacem in Terris* did not do much to illuminate this issue, which would become hotly controverted throughout world Catholicism in the decades to follow. The trauma of the Church in Central America in the 1980s would illustrate, tragically, just how such controversies could lead to the very violence *Pacem in Terris* deplored.

AN ENCYCLICAL AHEAD OF ITS TIME?

Viewed through the prism of subsequent history, the Murray/Niebuhr/Ramsey critique of *Pacem in Terris* graphically illustrates both the necessity and the limits of Christian realism.

A realist sensibility is an essential component of the intellectual furniture of any Christian analyst or practitioner of international politics who would observe, in that dangerous arena, the first principle of sound medicine: first, do no harm. Idealism untethered to an Augustinian sense of the limits of human perfectibility can erode into romanticism, and the bill, ultimately, will be paid in human lives and suffering. Neither the defeat of Nazi totalitarianism nor the collapse of Marxism-Leninism has invalidated the enduring importance of the realist sensibility.

But realism absolutized carries its own dangers. It can lead to a prematurely foreshortened view of the possible. It can obscure the potential for good that arises from the ideas and activities of individuals and movements who work "off the headlines" of diplomacy and commerce, and whose impact cannot be readily calculated according to the standard realist weights and measures of military power and economic capability. An absolutist form of realism can bifurcate the worlds of politics and morality by creating the false (and, in classic Catholic moral terms, unacceptable) image of international public life as an "amoral" arena. Finally, by minimizing the fact that, while it is certainly true that man sins, it is equally true that it is man who makes the judgment that he sins, absolute realism can blind itself to the opportunities for incremental improvement in the human condition that do exist because of the tug of conscience.

The Human-Rights Revolution

As the history of world politics in the intervening years has demonstrated, both realist critics and idealist celebrants of *Pacem in Terris* tended to miss or minimize the crucial importance for subsequent history of what was perhaps the key intellectual and political move in the encyclical: Pope John XXIII's linkage of the cause of peace to the defense of basic human rights. The pope's summary affirmation—that "peace will be but an empty-sounding word unless it is founded on the order which this present document has outlined in confident hope: an order founded on truth, built according to justice, vivified and integrated by charity, and *put into practice in freedom*" (167; emphasis added)—may have appeared, at the time, to be mere ruffles and flourishes at the end of a long papal statement. But as the course of European, Latin American, and East Asian history has effusively illustrated in recent years, the pope had intuited here a central dynamic of international politics in the 1980s and 1990s. For the democratic revolution that has swept through Eastern and Central Europe, parts of East Asia, and Latin America over the past decade has been built upon the ideas and political labors of men and women whose first concern was, not to seize power, but to defend fundamental human rights and freedoms against the depredations of totalitarian and authoritarian governments.

The European case is perhaps the most dramatic example of this process. The Helsinki Final Act, signed by thirty-five nations on August 1, 1975, was intended by the Soviet Union as a ratification of its postwar hegemony in Central and Eastern Europe—an intention to which Western governments, including the United States under the Kissinger foreign policy, tacitly acquiesced. But in an extraordinary historical reversal, the Final Act turned out to have contained within itself the forces that eventually brought down the

Berlin Wall and destroyed the Warsaw Pact: the so-called Basket Three agreements on basic human rights, which were given diplomatic and political weight through the concurrent creation of an ongoing "Helsinki review process" by which governments' adherence to those human-rights standards could be publicly judged— and precisely as an issue with profound relevance for the future of European security.

Shortly after the Final Act was signed, Helsinki monitoring groups began to spring up throughout the Soviet Union and Eastern Europe, supported by an impressive network of human-rights organizations in the United States, Canada, and Western Europe. These non-governmental organizations, oppressed (often viciously) in the East, had a dramatic impact on international diplomacy. For three years (1980–83), for example, at the Madrid review conference on the implementation of the Helsinki Final Act, the Western democracies held the human-rights record of the Soviet Union and its client states up to the harsh light of international scrutiny and publicity, and demonstrated how the security problems of Europe could not be understood (much less ameliorated) apart from a clear understanding of the differences of regime in East and West. Totalitarian regimes, in other words, were the primary causes of Europe's postwar instability.[5]

Then Leonid Brezhnev, for whom the Helsinki Final Act was thought to have been a great triumph, passed from the scene. *Glasnost* and *perestroika* followed within two years. And the human-rights activists of the Warsaw Pact countries became central figures in the drive for democratization that swept away the communist governments of Poland, Hungary, Czechoslovakia, and East Germany; that toppled aging Leninist dictators in Romania and Bulgaria; that resulted in a hitherto-unthinkable wave of republican secessions from, or declarations of sovereignty within, the Soviet Union; and that, finally, culminated in the collapse of the USSR itself.

If the war that threatened to destroy Europe for almost forty-five years after World War II now seems unlikely, it is not because there has been comprehensive disarmament across the continent but because there has been a dramatic change of regimes: democrats have replaced Marxist-Leninists in the control centers of most governments in Central and Eastern Europe. And that happy circumstance—which has been so crucial to securing the peace—is, indisputably, related to the human-rights activism that followed hard on the heels of the Helsinki accords. Peace became possible, as a working reality rather than a fondly held vision, when Marxism-Leninism, an implacable foe of basic human rights and freedoms, was consigned to the dustbin of history. John XXIII, it seems, had a better insight into the dynamics of European history than Leonid Brezhnev or, for that matter, Henry Kissinger.

Endorsement of Democracy

The Catholic Church's vigorous support for the democratic revolution in Europe, Asia, and Latin America is also an extension of the legacy of *Pacem in Terris*. John XXIII's recognition of the fundamental right of religious liberty (14) was subsequently amplified in 1965 by the Second Vatican Council in its pathbreaking "Declaration on Religious Freedom." And that declaration in turn became the charter for the Catholic human-rights revolution in world politics.[6]

For under Pope John Paul II, the Church has taken up the question of the political structures necessary for the effective protection and defense of the basic right of religious liberty. The mere assertion of a right, according to the contemporary Catholic understanding of these matters, is not enough: the Church has the responsibility to articulate norms for the creation of political structures that are most likely to protect asserted rights in practice. This discussion has been carried out, at the theological level, in the two Instructions on liberation theology (1984) and on Christian freedom and liberation (1986) from the Congregation for the Doctrine of the Faith, and in the encyclicals *Sollicitudo Rei Socialis* (1987) and *Centesimus Annus* (1991). In the world of action, the Catholic human-rights revolution launched by *Pacem in Terris* and given a firm theological foundation in the "Declaration on Religious Freedom" has grounded the Church's support for democratic revolutions in Chile, South Korea, Paraguay, the Philippines, and most especially Poland and Czechoslovakia.

Moreover, Pope John Paul II, in his endorsement of "democratic and participatory" forms of government[7] and his support for the forces advancing that cause around the world, has adopted and developed another theme of *Pacem in Terris*: the encyclical's preference for nonviolent means of social change. In Czechoslovakia, Poland, Hungary, Chile, the Philippines, and Central America, that teaching was a key factor in setting conditions under which dictatorial regimes could be replaced by democratic ones without mass violence: another example of historic change through a process often considered unlikely (if not impossible) by certain realists, Christian and otherwise. The next test of this new Catholic interest in nonviolence as a method for securing basic human rights and forcing democratic transitions has already emerged in the former Yugoslavia; and perhaps an even more difficult, long-term problem is becoming evident in societies dominated by certain forms of Islam. But those tests do not invalidate what happened in Central and Eastern Europe, East Asia, and Central America; they only raise questions about whether those experiences are wholly exportable.[8]

Pope John XXIII's faith in the potential decency of individual communist leaders may have been somewhat misplaced; the period of John's pontificate was in fact a time of intensified persecution of Christians in the USSR. But *Pacem in Terris* should also be remembered as a document that correctly anticipated the crack-up of the Marxist-Leninist project, and precisely along the fault lines through which the revolutionary earthquake of 1989 traveled: the intellectual and moral wrongheadedness, and the political evil, of the Marxist-Leninist understanding of the human person, human society, human history, and human destiny. The falsifications about man and about mankind that communism perpetrated resulted in the gulag system, to be sure; but it also created what Václav Havel of Czechoslovakia would come to call the "culture of the lie." And it was against that thick and clotted morass of official mendacity, against its corrosive effects on social and cultural life, that the human-rights activists in the 1970s and 1980s and the democratic revolutaries of 1989 rebelled and said, "No." That those brave men and women had, in many cases, the Catholic Church on their side was due in no small part to *Pacem in Terris* and its important effects on Catholic self-understanding throughout the world.

INTEGRATION AND DISINTEGRATION

If *Pacem in Terris* looks to have been remarkably prescient in its linkage of human-rights issues to peace-and-security issues, can the same be said of the encyclical's other distinctive geopolitical claim: that the world required a "universal public authority" as an expression of its increasing integration and as a means of resolving problems that no single nation-state could manage on its own?

It is certainly true that integrating forces (some benign, others disruptive) have been shaping important aspects of world politics and economics since the Second World War. Institutions such as the European Community (EC) and the Organization for Economic Cooperation and Development (OECD) give concrete expression to the fact that the economies of the industrialized democracies are thoroughly intermeshed (although expectations that the EC would, in time, evolve into a United States of Europe now seem to have been premature). Moreover, ecological issues—from acid rain, to the pollution of the Mediterranean, to the possibility of global warming—seem likely, over the next decades, to be far more international than national matters. The impact of the technological revolution on communications and transportation has dramatically altered, not only patterns of commerce and tourism, but the very self-understanding of peoples. Human-rights issues, as noted above, are thoroughly "internationalized" in character. Thus there is, without doubt, an integrative dynamic at work in the affairs of men and nations.

At the same time, it has to be admitted that many of the international legal and political institutions created in the wake of World War II, institutions in which Pope John placed great hope, have failed more often than they have succeeded. The United Nations has recently had some success in the international-security field; but the U.N. remains today what it has been since its founding—a stage on which a script written elsewhere is played out. U.N.-related "functional" international organizations (such as UNESCO) have become thoroughly bureaucratized and, worse, politicized: UNESCO has bent "education, science, and culture" toward partisan ends rather than marshalling the resources of the human intellect as a force for integration across traditional national, racial, ethnic, and religious boundaries. Then there are the stupendous and tragic failures of many international development agencies and programs.

Stubborn International Challenges

In this respect, at least, Reinhold Niebuhr's critique of *Pacem in Terris* remains sound: the encyclical did not accurately measure the difficulty of creating even that minimal measure of world political *community* necessary to sustain an international public *authority*. Indeed, paralleling the evolution of the forces of integration noted above have been powerful forces for disintegration and fragmentation in international public life, forces that were simply unanticipated by Pope John's encyclical. In this sense, the encyclical's vision may reflect the influence of an intellectual misapprehension—namely, that technological change would dissolve traditional forms of association and thus their capacity to create conflict—that was widespread in humane Western liberal quarters in the early 1960s. The truth of subsequent history has, of course, proved to be rather different.

Ethnicity, far from being displaced by the economic and technological solvents of modernity, remains a primary source of personal and communal identification, and a *casus belli* when the clash of identities leads to intercommunal conflict. This seems particularly to be the case in countries emerging from under the rubble of Marxist-Leninist totalitarianism. In areas where the writ of the Church runs large (one thinks of Poland, Czechoslovakia, and Lithuania), the reclaiming of a vibrant sense of ethnic identity has been complemented by a moral commitment to nonviolence. But that does not, unhappily, seem to be the case in other areas, as events in Romania, Bulgaria, Armenia, Georgia, and the former Yugoslavia attest.

There is another unsettling dimension of international public life that was wholly unanticipated by *Pacem in Terris*, namely, the rise of a militant and dynamic form of Islam with the wealth, and the military capacity, to attempt to impose its will across a considerable swath of the world. Reading *Pacem in Terris*, and, to be fair, many other seminal documents of the same period, one cannot imagine an Ayatollah Khomeini emerging in the future, much less asserting considerable geopolitical influence; the world wasn't supposed to evolve that way. *Pacem in Terris*, in other words, did not take adequate account of the fact that profound anti-modernity currents would soon ripple across the globe, and that one of their primary carriers would be a religion that asserted the divine mandate to bring all peoples under its sway.

Then there is nationalism. Whatever else can be said about the twentieth century, it has surely not seen the death of nationalism. Perhaps more accurately, the twentieth century has seen an intensification of nationalism that, like the recovery of ethnicity, has run parallel to the increasing integration of world scientific, economic, and cultural life. Among civilized, tolerant, economically prosperous, and democratic peoples, national identity remains a primary personal and communal reference point.[9] In much of the formerly colonized world, nationalism is seen by political elites as an essential (perhaps *the* essential) ideological component of nation-building. And if nationalism can be considered as a distinctively modern expression of tribalism, then we may indeed see just how far from Pope John's vision of international political community the world is in the last decade of the century.

Searching for Solutions

Perhaps these two phenomena—integration and disintegration —feed on each other. The homogenization of the world through technology, commerce, and, increasingly, pop culture has, ironically, given new urgency to older forms of personal and communal identity as men and women seek to retain some measure of distinctiveness and personal/communal integrity. If that be the case, then the short-term global prospect is for a complex and interactive process of simultaneous integration and disintegration.

The world of the immediate future will likely see further rapid economic integration (as the countries of the old "second world" reindustrialize and modernize, and as the new development success stories of East Asia become full-fledged members of the "developed" world); it may also see a modest degree of further political integration in Europe, perhaps between Europe and North America, and just possibly among Europe, North America, and Australia. But it will also likely witness the failures of explicit attempts at political integration (in Latin America) and actual political disintegration in the old Soviet empire, in Africa, and perhaps in South Asia. Compounding the complexity will be a continuing clash between resurgent Islam and the worlds of what used to be called "Christendom."

If anything is likely to ameliorate these disintegrative forces, it might well be Christianity, in several forms. The twenty-first century could, just could, witness the re-Christianization of Europe and a closing of the eleventh-century breach between Rome and Constantinople: events that would have a profound (and almost certainly salutary) impact on Western Europe and North America, and on the post-communist churnings in Eastern Europe and the western parts of the former Soviet empire. On the index of historical possibilities, it is also no less likely, and arguably more likely, that the next century will see the increasing Protestantization of Latin America, and of significant parts of Africa and perhaps even East Asia.[10] This phenomenon will itself cause considerable inter-religious chafing (as it already has in the 1990 Peruvian presidential election, in Mexico, and in Guatemala). But over the longer run, the form of Protestantism involved here—evangelical, fundamentalist, and charismatic—tends toward the "embourgoisement" of its adherents, toward democratic forms of politics, and toward efforts to achieve reconciliation and peace within society and across national borders. Whatever its other implications for world Catholicism, the explosion of Protestantism in the Third World may hasten, ironically or providentially (or both), the realization of John XXIII's vision of international political community.

POST-MODERN CHRISTIAN HUMANISM

The legacy of *Pacem in Terris* is, in sum and at the risk of cliché, a complex one. Remarkably prescient on some issues, deficient in analysis on others, the encyclical nevertheless remains a powerful call to the pursuit of peace with freedom and justice, thirty years after its publication.

In the American 1990s, *Pacem in Terris* may take on a new significance as the debate over U.S. foreign policy returns to its most basic level: namely, should the United States actively seek to shape world politics and economics? The aftermath of the Cold

War has seen new isolationisms (now usually styled "new national-isms") emerge from both the political Right (isolationism's tradi-tional pre–World War II home) and Left (isolationism's post-Vietnam roost). In both cases, the message is strikingly similar: the United States has no duties beyond its borders; its responsibility is to tend its own republican garden and to perfect its experiment in democratic governance.[11]

Against this seductive call to a retreat into the pre-modern past, *Pacem in Terris* may appear—and with good reason—as a potent countervision of human possibility that is not so much modern as post-modern. It is true that, in one sense, *Pacem in Terris* is a thoroughly modern, "liberal" document that breathes a more Pela-gian than Augustinian spirit. But it is also true that the encyclical teaches a host of post-modern themes that are far beyond the classical liberal concern with the autonomous self (or nation) and its prerogatives. It stresses the inherent linkage between human rights and human duties. It calls men and women from raw individualism into communities of responsibility and mutual aid. It insists on transcendent reference points for the moral life, and it rejects any notion of the "irrationality" of morals as a matter of essentially emotive, personal preferences; rather, John XXIII gently but firmly reminds us of the capacity of human reason to discern the good, and of the capacity of the human will to act properly on that discernment. *Pacem in Terris* also unabashedly defends biblical religion as a source of human fulfillment and teaches the crucial importance of civic culture or "civil society" for a decent and humane politics.

These themes of a post-liberal, post-modern politics may not be so easily linked to a full-bore internationalism as *Pacem in Terris* seemed to suggest. On the other hand, these themes, taken to-gether, dramatize at the religious and moral level the poverty of isolationism. What is true of men as individuals is also true for nations: to live as an island, cut off from the whole, is humanly diminishing. To do so willfully is even worse.

Pacem in Terris is a forthright statement of Christian humanism and, as such, it remains an important challenge to the two false humanisms that continue to bedevil modernity in the aftermath of the communist crack-up: secularist positivism, with its reduction of the dilemmas of the human condition to problems of technology and management; and debonair nihilism, which insists that there are no truths to be known or moral norms to be followed, only "needs" to be "satisfied." Positivism and nihilism are both, curiously, anti-political, at least as "politics" has been understood in the West since the Greeks. *Pacem in Terris*, on the other hand, is a call to recover the Western tradition of politics as an extension of ethics, and as the art of persuasion through rational debate among men and women distinguished by reason and free will, by the defining human capacities to think and to choose. And for that reason alone, the teaching of *Pacem in Terris* will, and indeed deserves to, retain its salience as the twentieth century gives way to the twenty-first.

5

Modernity and Its Discontents
Gaudium et Spes (1965)

MARY EBERSTADT

Twenty-five years ago, during the Second Vatican Council, the Catholic Church looked to the world and found "a new age of history" marked by "critical and swift upheavals spreading gradually to all corners of the earth" (*Gaudium et Spes*, paragraph 4). It was an age in which men, "in wonder at their own discoveries and their own might," had become "troubled and perplexed" by a plethora of questions, including "their place and their role in the universe," "the meaning of individual and collective endeavor," and "the destiny of nature and of men" (3). To "clarify" those questions and to express "its solidarity and respectful attention for the whole human family," the council announced its intention of "enter[ing] into dialogue" with the world about the modern age and the problems unique to it (4). The result of that undertaking was the council's "Pastoral Constitution on the Church and the Modern World"—*Gaudium et Spes*. This two-part examination of man, Church, and world is justly considered to be among the most important Catholic documents of our time.

Several features distinguished *Gaudium et Spes*, even among the other innovations of Vatican II. There was, first, the dual nature of its religious ambition. Two thousand years of church history had

---

Mary Eberstadt is a contributing editor of *The National Interest*.

never before seen a "pastoral constitution"; to explicate the very meaning of the phrase became the text's first order of business. As a long footnote to the title explained, *Gaudium et Spes* was both doctrinal, in the sense that it was built on fundamental dogmatic principles; and pastoral, because it attempted to apply those principles to the circumstances of the contemporary world. The document, in other words, involved a kind of internal dialogue as well as a dialogue between "the Church" and "the world": for doctrine has a built-in pastoral dimension, and the Church's analysis of the modern world was inexplicable without reference to the Church's most basic religious convictions.

A second feature that gave *Gaudium et Spes* its distinctive aura was its identification with the agenda of church progressives—an identification that has continued to characterize the document in the years since. This progressive reputation has rested both on particular passages in the document itself and on the major figures associated with its creation. Even before the Second Vatican Council opened in October 1962, senior bishops were pushing for a document that would address the pressing cultural, social, economic, and political questions of the day. On December 4, 1962, late in the council's first session, the debate that eventually gave birth to *Gaudium et Spes* was launched by Cardinal Leo Jozef Suenens of Malines-Brussels, who perhaps more than any other prelate was responsible for the council's finally adopting a statement on "the Church in the modern world" some three years later. Suenens's 1962 initiative was supported by other leaders of the council's reformist wing: Cardinal Giovanni Battista Montini of Milan (soon to be elected as Pope Paul VI), Cardinal Giacomo Lercaro of Bologna, Cardinal Paul Leger of Montreal, Cardinal Achille Lienart of Lille, and Dom Helder Camara, then auxiliary bishop of Rio de Janiero. The archbishop of Kraków, Karol Wojtyla, made important contributions to the document's discussion of labor and modern atheism.

Third, the very scope of *Gaudium et Spes* made the document a singularly complicated exercise, not least in bureaucratic terms. Previous councils had addressed themselves to the internal doctrinal and disciplinary affairs of the Church, as, indeed, did every other constitution, decree, and declaration of Vatican II. Now the council fathers turned their attention to the world beyond the Church in all its plurality and complexity. The longest of the council documents (the final text runs to some 23,000 words), *Gaudium et Spes* was debated, drafted, re-drafted, and re-debated at each of the council's four sessions. As late as October 1965, in the council's fourth and final period, some 20,000 proposed amendments had to be dealt with by the drafting committees. In the end, the document was adopted at the council's last general congregation, on December 6, 1965, and was promulgated on December 7, the day before the official closing of Vatican II.

To these three features that distinguished *Gaudium et Spes* from its inception, the passage of time has added one other that is perhaps most significant of all. That is the unmistakable chasm between what this document has come to signify and the living reality of the text itself. To those familiar with its reputation, *Gaudium et Spes* remains a kind of Magna Carta of the Catholic Left—a text in which the "obsolete" emphases of the "old" Church have presumably been discarded in favor of more current issues and reforms. In fact, this document does nothing of the kind. *Gaudium et Spes* not only fails to repudiate the classic moral teachings of the Church but reiterates them; and not only reiterates but affirms them passionately, positively, and with a lack of defensiveness that is utterly at odds with the way many of those teachings are represented in the more self-consciously "progressive" precincts of the Church in North America and Western Europe today. At the same time, it is precisely those portions of the text bearing the imprint of the reformist hand that only a few decades later sound most out of date, at times even outright antiquated.

The irony of such an outcome is hardly novel; it is, after all, the fate of many efforts explicitly committed to "relevance." Nor is the importance of *Gaudium et Spes* as a whole diminished by the fact that selected portions of the text have grown stale and flavorless with the years. Such occasional disappointments aside, this remains a rich, at times even intoxicating, piece of work. To set forth the most distinctive features of the modern era and to distill the Church's bearing toward each would be a daunting enterprise at any length. To achieve as much in fewer than one hundred pages, as *Gaudium et Spes* does, is nothing less than extraordinary.

Yet to leave the matter there would be a disservice, not only to the text itself, but to its very direct implications for American society today. Like Vatican II from which it sprang, *Gaudium et Spes* presents a challenge to the contemporary reader that its authors could not even have imagined. For what resounds loudest in this document today is not its vaunted novelties but its fiery insistence on what is *not* new. To see why, and to recover at least in part the pastoral intent of its authors, it is necessary to look once more at this remarkable document as a whole.

Sweeping Social Changes

What is it about modernity that sets it apart from other ages? Beneath "the spiritual uneasiness of today" and the "changing structure of life," *Gaudium et Spes* finds a "broader upheaval" affecting all aspects of human society (5). There are "sweeping changes" in the social order—as a result of industrialization, which "radically transfigures ideas and social practices"; of "urbanization" and "emigration"; of the mass media, which have disseminated these and other changes and made people elsewhere in the world "eager to share" in their benefits (6). There is also a "completely new atmosphere" regarding religion. On the one hand, modern man, under the influence of scientific thinking, is "taking a hard look at all magical world views"; on the other, he is encouraged in the name of "humanism" to confuse those worldviews with God and religion itself—a trend evident not only in philosophy but also "in literature, art, the humanities, the interpretation of history and even civil law" (7).

For all its talk of impersonal forces, however, *Gaudium et Spes* continually reminds us that "in the midst of it all stands man" (2). Unlike other treatments of modernity—Hegelianism, Freudianism, Marxism and its many collectivist spawn—this one does not portray man as a mere pawn of larger oppositions. He is made, instead, "at once author and victim" of those forces. "The modern dilemma," as defined by *Gaudium et Spes*, is that "it is up to [man] to control them or be enslaved by them" (9). It is man, therefore—"considered whole and entire, with body and soul, heart and conscience, mind and will"—"who is the key to this discussion" (3).

The emphasis on free will thus established, Part One of *Gaudium et Spes* moves on to discuss the Church's view of man: the dignity of the human person, his nature as a social being, and the role of the Church in educating him to his destiny. It reviews the salvific message and mission of the Church, and "courteously invites" secular humanists to weigh those ideas against the various species of atheism (21). Part Two then brings those teachings to bear on some of the "urgent problems" of the present day: marriage and family life; culture and economy; and society—most famously, political society and the relations among nations.

Gaudium et Spes is perhaps best remembered today for chapter 5, on which its reputation for progressivism largely rests. Here, citing the destructiveness of modern weaponry, the council undertakes "a completely fresh reappraisal of war" (80). The Church's condemnation of total warfare is reiterated, followed by a critical look at modern deterrence theory. Declaring that the "arms race is one of the greatest curses on the human race" (81), *Gaudium et Spes* calls upon nations and their leaders to outlaw war "by international agreement," to "enlarge their thoughts and their spirit beyond the confines of their own country," and to "put aside nationalistic ambitions to dominate other nations" (82). It further calls upon those nations, particularly the richer ones, to engage in collective efforts "to coordinate and stimulate development," noting in conclusion that "we are all called to be brothers" and "ought to work together without violence and without deceit to build up the world in a spirit of genuine peace."

The Relevance of Gaudium et Spes

As even this brief overview of the text makes clear, the council fathers saw the Iron Curtain as the most defining feature of global affairs in the early 1960s. Mindful of its many millions of faithful on both sides of that curtain, the council in *Gaudium et Spes* treated the Cold War with determinedly neutral rhetoric. Communism, capitalism, and Marxism are alluded to but never named; nor is any particular nation or region. Thirty years later, of course, the peoples of the East bloc themselves have decisively repudiated communism, and the West stands virtually unchallenged as the moral and political victor of the Cold War. Both facts, it seems safe to assume, would make for a decidedly less neutral discussion of the Cold War today than the one the council felt compelled to undertake.

For all that, it is worth noting that *Gaudium et Spes* does make a tacit, though never explicit, case for the morality of the Western side. As commentators such as George Weigel and Michael Novak have observed, the forms of government and society that *Gaudium et Spes* judges to be most consonant with human nature bear more than a little resemblance to those in the Western tradition. Private property is upheld as "an extension of human freedom" (71); so too are the "rights" of "free assembly and association, the right to express one's opinions and to profess one's religion privately and publicly" (73). We are even reminded that "citizens . . . should take care not to vest too much power in the hands of public authority nor to make untimely and exaggerated demands for favors and subsidies, lessening in this way the responsible role of individuals, families and social groups" (75).

Meanwhile, of course, the end of the Cold War itself has changed, not only the world as we know it, but also the political preoccupations that once seemed immutable facts of life. Even so, those portions of *Gaudium et Spes* concerned with global events are not altogether without relevance today. But the fears that the text deems paramount—the "arms race," "immense and indiscriminate havoc," and especially nuclear annihilation (80–82)—are not the fears that most people mention first, or even second, when they consider the international picture today.

Some other political concerns of the text have become similarly obsolete over time. One wonders, for example, whether the authors would still insist that "serious and alarming problems" have arisen "as a result of population expansion" (47). Over the past three decades (and beginning, in fact, before *Gaudium et Spes* appeared), fertility rates have actually declined throughout most of the developed world; in most advanced countries, they have hovered at or below replacement levels during those same years. Moreover, the doomsday predictions of such publicists as Paul Ehrlich, whose warnings of the "population bomb" enjoyed wide acceptance in the 1960s, have been refuted in the years since by events themselves.

Meanwhile, and what is even more remarkable, some states and societies have committed infamous crimes in their pursuit of reduced population growth. Forced birth control and abortions are common features of China's "one-child norm" policy; female infanticide persists in population-control-minded India, among other countries. Related evils of "control" in other forms have coincided with advances in medicine. In South Korea, for example, several years of abortions performed for sex selection have actually altered the ratio of boys to girls in elementary schools. In the most developed countries, including the United States, experiments on fetal tissue abound; researchers clearly prefer, and are often able, to extract that tissue from still-living fetuses. As even this cursory review suggests, no discussion of "population" and related issues today, most especially by Catholic authorities, would be complete without recourse to such facts.

Similarly, one wonders whether the authors of *Gaudium et Spes* would be as exercised today about "fostering and acknowledging" the role of women in society and culture. Under just such rhetoric, the feminist movements in much of the Western world have become increasingly radical remnants. Above all, these movements are now explicitly battling a church whose teachings on family and sexuality they fiercely reject, and whose supposed "patriarchy" and "oppression" they find intolerable. Whatever accommodations the authors of *Gaudium et Spes* may have hoped to make with the feminism of the 1960s have been ruled out of bounds by the feminists of today—unless, of course, the Church were to compromise some of its most fundamental teachings, as those same feminists insist that it should.

Enduring Social Concerns

As the example of feminism suggests, the power of *Gaudium et Spes* today—and by extension, that of the modern Church itself—resides far less in its *ad hoc* attempts at relevance than in its systematic defense and development of traditional moral teachings. It is those teachings, rather than the transitory political passions of the 1960s, that bear directly on American society today.

If, in the 1990s, one were to ask most Americans to describe the country's most pressing problems, one would be struck, first, by what they would not say. They would not say "the budget," the "trade imbalance," the "tax rate," or any other description of economic interest *simpliciter*. These are all important issues, to be sure, and they play a perennial part in the country's electoral concerns. But they are not the issues that continue, year after year, to evoke the hottest political debate.

Instead, those debates and the passions they reflect center on what some have come to call "the social issues." In 1985, in an attempt to define that field, writer Nathan Glazer gave a representative list: abortion (first on his list, as it would be on most others); the decline of the family; crime and pornography; and more general questions of authority, hedonism, and responsibility.[1] The most surprising political development in the United States since 1965, Glazer found, was the resurgence of this "social agenda." It was the fact that "issues that many of us considered parochial, backward-looking, symbolic, unrelated to major economically defined classes and interest, have developed unexpected power."

The ensuing years have vindicated analyses like Glazer's with a vengeance. By the 1990s, as most observers would agree, the United States has become divided by a full-blown *Kulturkampf*. Nor is that struggle limited any longer to a handful of readily identifiable issues. It includes all those that Glazer listed, and many more; it has reached into facets of ordinary life that only yesterday seemed very nearly immune to outside forces; and it shows no sign whatever of diminishing.

Consider as a single front in this war the battle now raging over public education. For years the controversy over American schools seemed confined to a single issue: forced busing. Today the issues that divide the schools and those concerned with them defy enumeration. In addition to yesterday's schemes for integration with all their well-known problems, today's parents and students must also contend with the following. There are, in many schools, fundamental questions of order and security; the armed student has become so prevalent that many city schools are now outfitted with weapon detectors and security guards. Drug use, truancy, and drop-out rates persist; in the District of Columbia, to cite the most extreme example, only 60 per cent of high school students graduate on time. Ideological battles over school curricula have roiled districts from city to countryside. At times, as in recent conflicts concerning the teachings of American history, those struggles have been over subjects that are at least recognizably academic. More often, the contested terrain includes issues of moral education so fundamental that a majority of parents finds them off-limits outside the home.

In New York City, for example, the curriculum for grade-school students preferred by most administrators has recently set in motion a series of convulsions. That curriculum included, among other items, instruction in the presumed "equality" of two-parent, one-parent, no-parent, and homosexual-parent homes; explicit instruction in sexual acts, including some that came as news to many adults; instruction in "gender-neutral" play, with exhortations for teacher interventions against too many boys with trucks or girls with dolls; and so on. Nor is New York alone in discovering brave new frontiers of "education." In Minnesota, educators have successfully subjected grade-schoolers to sanctions against "sexual harassment." In Baltimore, controversy now rages over providing Norplant, a contraceptive implant of some five years' duration, to teenage students (this in addition to the contraceptive devices already available in the schools). Almost every district in the country has been afflicted with similarly divisive innovations, from the provision of condoms in the schools to minute instruction in the sexual acts associated with AIDS and other sexually transmitted diseases. The perennial controversies over creationism and evolution may yet live on in places, but they seem positively quaint, even civil, beside the larger traumas that have enveloped them.

The same is true of other items on today's burgeoning "social agenda." Not very long ago, issues of profanity, blasphemy, and pornography seemed distant, even archaic, concerns. Who would have guessed that, by the 1990s, Americans in all parts of the country would come to hold opinions—vehement opinions—about obscure works of post-modern art? Or about the lyrics of lesser-known rock bands, or about who should—or shouldn't—march in New York City's St. Patrick's Day parade? In part, of course, these and other symbolic debates are creatures of the information revolution, which has transmitted so many parochial scenes into the universal American living room. But such controversies can only persist and proliferate in the context of the larger cultural struggle they represent.

No turf in that struggle is more fiercely disputed than that occupied by the subject of abortion. This much is certain: even if *Roe* v. *Wade* were reversed—an unlikely event in this century, to judge by recent decisions of the Supreme Court—the near civil war over abortion would not go away. Too much has happened since 1973. Too many powerful lobbying groups have made abortion on demand the *sine qua non* of their political support; too many politicians, including the current president and his wife, have acquiesced in that bargain. Too many public figures—including leading members of national organizations, such as the American Bar Association and the American Medical Association—have thrown their support behind the pro-abortion movement. But, despite the many setbacks to their cause, millions of Americans remain too firmly opposed to abortion to content themselves with the status quo. In the aftermath of the *Webster* and *Casey* decisions, the clash over abortion continues in the fifty state legislatures, in the national PACs and on the national airwaves, in the streets and on the sidewalks near hospitals and clinics, even in and among most of our churches. It continues to be *the* issue to which those on both sides bring their most passionate and absolutist convictions. It continues, in the words of Nathan Glazer, "to tear the country apart."

Disintegrating Families

Just as politics alone cannot resolve the moral dispute known as the "abortion question," neither can it halt the related trend toward what is sometimes called "family dysfunction." Even the stronger terms, such as "decline" or "breakdown," fall short of describing the radical changes under way in American homes. As the English writer Auberon Waugh has acidly observed:

What has really collapsed throughout vast parts of American life is the institution of the family itself. Even when parents are not swapping partners and cities with reckless abandon, the double-income requirement means that members of a family seldom see each other, practically never have a meal together and, as often as not, spend whatever time they choose to pass under the same roof watching different television programmes in separate rooms.[2]

As almost any American will admit, there is more truth than caricature in that description. Yet Waugh, remember, is describing *intact* families—an increasingly smaller proportion compared to the number of families broken by separation or divorce, or, indeed, the number of households that never formed families in the first place.

Some 67 per cent of all black American babies, and about one-fifth of all white babies, are now born to unmarried mothers. These problems are not limited to the poor. Illegitimacy and divorce rates have risen steadily among all races and classes. Of course those rates have material consequences; when families break up or fail to form, women and children are almost always hardest hit. Hence the sociological phrase, "the feminization of poverty," which has become a rallying cry for politicians seeking expanded services and forms of relief.

Compelling as they may be, the material consequences of family breakdown can at least be alleviated. By contrast, its emotional consequences—particularly for children—seem very nearly intractable. Absent fathers may yet be forced to pay every dollar owed of child support; but those payments will not put those fathers back in the home. Tax breaks and expanded day care may temporarily relieve working mothers; but they will not reduce the number of children who return from school to an empty home, or the number of even younger children who spend more time outside the family than in it. Indeed, most of the political innovations now in vogue will likely *increase* the hours that many children already spend separated from the home.

The behaviors associated with family breakdown—particularly divorce and illegitimacy—have, in fact, expanded in tandem with the welfare state that professes to address them. During the same years in which divorce and illegitimacy rose dramatically, the federal government approved program after program designed to improve the lives of the poorest and most vulnerable Americans. We had a "war on poverty"; later, a "safety net." We have housing programs—services that are not only accessible but advertised ubiquitously on billboards, radio, and television. Yet all the "insurance and security" of the welfare state, all the "legislation and provision" that *Gaudium et Spes* recommends (69, 52), have not led to a diminution of the social pathologies that prevail. On the contrary, those pathologies have grown apace.

This is not to suggest that the actions of civil authorities must always founder in inefficacy. *Gaudium et Spes* speaks for most Americans in its conviction that those authorities can exercise their powers "toward the common good" (73). Nor is it to suggest that the welfare state itself *causes* those same pathologies. If that were so, they would not afflict rich as well as poor, the working as well as the beneficiaries of welfare. Rather, what we do know—or ought to know by now—is that government alone can only ameliorate the many problems that make up today's "social issues." It cannot solve them, because it cannot eradicate the problem that allows such issues to persist: the fact that a great many Americans have come to share a view of human nature that not only takes such behaviors for granted but regards them as immutable facts of life.

A Demeaning View of Man

The view of human nature that prevails in American culture today—"culture" broadly understood, from the universities and government to the popular media and other secular authorities—is radically divorced from the view proclaimed by Christianity since its inception. Today's version is, in fact, a kind of gross amputee of the Christian tradition. In the elegant formulation of Ludwig Feuerbach, Christianity saw man as "half angel, half beast." By current standards he was only half right. As presented by America's cultural arbiters—including many of our churches—man now appears to be all beast.

He is, first, a slave to his every appetite. Once, his weaknesses were called "sins" or "vices"; today, he has only "addictions." Over these he is routinely said to be "powerless." He is no longer a drunk, but "addicted to alcohol"; no longer a gambler, but a "compulsive gambler"; no longer an adulterer or pervert, but a "sex addict"; no longer a glutton, but a "compulsive eater"; no longer a junkie, but a "chemical dependent." The older terms, for all their opprobrium, at least implied the possibility of change. If a woman with a weakness for liquor did not drink, she could not accurately be called a "drunk"; if a man, whatever his temptations, did not engage in sodomy, then he could not accurately be called a sodomite; and so on. The new terms, with their implications of permanence and neutrality, decree only man's abject, immutable prostration.

The difference is more than semantic; it permeates our politics, our social institutions, our everyday lives. Consider the views that prevail in American culture about the human sexual appetite in particular. In this realm, it seems, we are most powerless of all. Teenagers, our educators and health professionals insist, "must" receive "sex education" and access to contraceptives, for the "reality" is that abstinence is obsolete. Homosexual acts "must" be condoned, because they follow what is now viewed as organic "orientation" (no longer even "preference") as night follows day. Abortion "must" remain legal, for babies conceived unintentionally are judged, *ipso facto*, to be permanently "unwanted" or "unloved." Celibacy itself is immensely suspect; it is even said that priests "must" be allowed to marry, because the suppression of their sexual appetite is "abnormal" at best, and at worst a spur to predatory behavior.

The matter of abortion takes such views to their logical depths. Anyone with simple common sense will agree that an unborn cat is more "cat" than anything else, or that an unborn shark is more "shark" than it is, say, "seaweed." Yet the proposition that the unborn of our own species are in fact "human" is somehow controversial. Again, the comparison to the animal world is useful. Imagine what would happen if, in the name of "research" or "convenience," human beings began performing millions of abortions on dogs, cats, seals, whales, and the like. We would doubtless be accused of "cruelty" and of "violating nature"; the practice itself would most certainly be outlawed, or at least widely deplored and severely restricted. Yet our solicitude for the rest of animal life does not extend to our own. We have become, by that measure, even lower than Feuerbach's beast.

Just as the advocates of abortion deny the humanity of the fetus, so too they debase human mothers and fathers. To consent to the legitimacy of abortion, one must first consent to the idea that parental love is supremely *conditional*, that it is weaker than the external stresses—poverty, inconvenience, an absent father—that make a pregnancy unwanted. Whatever else may be said of this view, it is not one that exalts men and women. To the contrary, it denies them one of their highest attributes—the ability to love and care for their offspring even when those acts require sacrifice.

What view of man is discernible in a society where divorce, broken homes, and abandonment of children are endemic? In each case, people are tacitly declaring that they have lost all confidence in their ability to prevail over their troubles. The message of the broken home—as children who grow up in them know very well—is that the family, that quintessentially *human* creation, is a weak reed against the tempests of the outside world. The message of other social pathologies—drug abuse, suicide, criminality—is that millions among us have so lost the sense of their intrinsic worth as to despair of ever recovering it. They have lost all faith in themselves and in humanity itself.

Against this crabbed and despondent estimate of who we are and what we are about, *Gaudium et Spes* offers an exhilarating alternative. In place of a culture that abuses the human body and loathes its imperfection and decay, we are told instead that "man must not despise his bodily life," for "he is obliged to regard his body as good and to hold it in honor" (14). In place of the idea that human coupling is an uncontrollable animal act, we are told instead that sexuality is "wondrous," that its expression in marriage is "noble and honorable" and "enriches the spouses in joy and gratitude"; that it "must be honored with the greatest reverence" (49). (All this, it might be added, from a church ubiquitously mocked and derided for its supposedly "negative" view of sexual activity.)

Do we think more highly of ourselves when we believe, as many Americans today believe, that marriage is just one of various "lifestyles"? Or when we regard it as "a lofty calling," with "dignity and supremely sacred value" (47)? Should we believe, as the culture around us implies, that children are inconvenient, burdensome, and expensive encumbrances? Or that they are our "crowning glory," our "supreme gift," human beings who "sanctify" and "greatly contribute to the good of the parents themselves" (48)? Do we elevate ourselves when we declare the traditional family to be an ambivalent, oppressive, anxiety-ridden prison—or when we consider it, as *Gaudium et Spes* does, "the basis of human society itself"?

What Is Dignity?

The United States today, as anyone within reach of a newspaper or television knows, is rife with therapies and schools of thought aimed at helping people "feel good" about themselves by fostering "self-esteem." Nowhere in those therapies or theories does man appear as the ennobled, majestic, *intrinsically* worthy creature acclaimed in *Gaudium et Spes*. All the most controversial moral teachings of the Church, all those famous "do nots" that make our contemporaries and even some of our clergy uncomfortable, are no *ad hoc* inventions of Rome; they are direct consequences of church teachings on man's "sublime dignity."

At a time when those teachings are so frequently misrepresented and reviled, it is worth reiterating their logic as it appears in *Gaudium et Spes*. *Because* marriage is a sacred state and *because* it demands all that is best in people, it "excludes both adultery and divorce." *Because* people can be "entrusted" with "the noble mission of safeguarding life," abortion—like murder, infanticide, and genocide—"is an abominable crime." *Because* "human life and its transmission are realities that are not limited by the horizons of this life only," the denial of life implicit in sterilization and other artificial contraceptives is unworthy of human beings. *Because* man is a "unity of body and soul," it defiles him to deny that unity by treating his own or other people's bodies—through forms of abuse or selfish sexuality—as ends in themselves.

In the same positive, celebratory spirit, *Gaudium et Spes* affirms the role of the Church itself in educating men and women to fulfill their proper destinies. Here we have a Church proclaiming that "the key, the center, and the purpose of the whole of man's history is to be found in its Lord and Master." It is a church "interested in one thing only—to carry on the work of Christ under the guidance of the Holy Spirit." Only Christ, this church insists, can "show man the way and strengthen him"; "nor is there any other name under heaven given among men by which they can be saved." To an American Catholic, and especially to one whose only living memory is of the post–Vatican II Church, such heat and light in a modern Catholic document are, in the end, the most lingering of all impressions left by *Gaudium et Spes*.

And that is why, nearly thirty years later, such a Catholic can reflect on this document only with a sense of loss. For however the Church has fared elsewhere during these years—and in many parts of the world, it has fared very well indeed—in the United States it is very much on the defensive. Where *Gaudium et Spes* speaks of evangelizing the world, we find an American church struggling—and too often failing—to hold even its own. Where that document, despite the chorus of voices that went into it, speaks as one on teaching after teaching of the Church, we find increasingly prominent and acrimonious divisions among our own clergy and laity. Where *Gaudium et Spes* speaks confidently and humanely about matters of morality, we find many priests who reiterate those same teachings in a spirit of apology, if at all. In the United States, as in much of the West, the daily struggles with a secular and frequently anti-Christian culture seem to have left many lay and clerical leaders exhausted. The contrast between their spirit and that of *Gaudium et Spes*, with its bold and self-possessed challenges to the secular world, could hardly be more profound.

That contrast is particularly unnerving today, when the United States is riven with exactly the modern problems that *Gaudium et Spes* not only foresaw but for which it prescribed enduring and radical alternatives. This is a propitious moment in American political thought to consider those alternatives. On one side, as the recent national election showed, millions continue to cling to the secular panaceas of yesterday—more taxes, more social programs, more political intrusions into daily life. On the other side are those who see mounting evidence that the problems of American life require more than mere politics can offer. In a particularly prescient essay in 1985, Irving Kristol reflected on the government's record to date in ameliorating the problems and pathologies of the black ghettos. He concluded:

> It is becoming more and more obvious that what is needed is the kind of black leadership that goes into the ghettos and works to "uplift" these people. What is wanted is a black John Wesley to do for the "underclass" in the ghettos what Wesley did for the gin-ridden, loose-living working class in eighteenth-century Britain. Reformation has to be on the agenda, not just relief.[3]

"Reformation": the word is exactly right, and it applies not only to the ghettos but to a society in which ghetto mores have now become a general way of life. But the reformation of society at large is a stern demand to make on the many American Catholics who have become more accustomed to apologizing for what they believe than to celebrating it. To those who have forgotten the difference, *Gaudium et Spes* remains an uncomfortable, even accusing, reminder.

6

A Special Kind of Liberty
Dignitatis Humanae (1965)

KENNETH L. GRASSO

THE Second Vatican Council's *Dignitatis Humanae*, known as the "Declaration on Religious Freedom," has received relatively little attention compared with some of the longer and better-known conciliar statements. Nevertheless, as Paul VI pointed out, the document must be numbered among the council's major texts. To appreciate its significance, one need merely contrast two papal statements. In the 1864 encyclical *Quanta Cura*, Pius IX denounced the "erroneous opinion . . . which our predecessors of happy memory Gregory XVI called a madness, to wit, that freedom of conscience and worship is every man's proper right." In 1980, however, John Paul II told the nations signing the Helsinki Final Act that "freedom of conscience and of religion . . . is a primary and inalienable right of the human person." In the century separating these statements, Catholic thought on church-state relations underwent a profound development that crystallized in 1965 with *Dignitatis Humanae*.

The implications of *Dignitatis Humanae*, however, extend far

Kenneth L. Grasso is assistant professor of political science at Southwest Texas State University, San Marcos, Texas. He is co-editor of *John Courtney Murray and the American Civil Conversation*, and his articles have appeared in *Thought*, *Crisis*, *Faith and Reason*, *Interpretation*, and other journals.

beyond church-state relations. The declaration's defense of religious freedom laid the groundwork for what George Weigel has termed "the Catholic human-rights revolution," namely, "the transformation of the Roman Catholic Church from a bastion of the *ancien régime* into perhaps the world's foremost institutional defender of human rights."[1] To appreciate the significance of the declaration and the revolution it touched off, it is necessary to examine the historical context of the document and its understanding of religious freedom.

THE HISTORICAL SETTING

Nineteenth-century Catholic thought on church-state relations developed in reaction to a series of revolutionary movements unleashed by the French Revolution.[2] Toward these movements, and the new social and political order for which they labored, the Church's attitude was one of unremitting hostility. The reasons for this hostility are not readily apparent to us today. The revolutionaries, after all, spoke in an idiom with which we are quite comfortable, appealing to the rights of man, popular sovereignty, freedom of religion, and separation of church and state. But a deeper look at the ideas in which these revolutionary movements were rooted will help us understand the Church's opposition to them.

Continental liberalism was the ideology that informed these movements, and at the heart of this ideology were the concepts of naturalism, which denies the existence of a supernatural order of revelation and grace, and radical individualism, the assertion that each individual is a law unto himself, subject to no objective order of obligations. According to the political philosophy of liberalism, political society is created by naturally autonomous individuals, and the body politic is sovereign in the same manner as the individual citizen. Like the individual, the people as a whole cannot be subject to a standard not of their own making. The democratic state, the state embodying the will of the people, is therefore unlimited in its scope. So understood, the democratic state was coextensive with society and officially agnostic in character. The results were an utterly monistic conception of society and—in the name of religious freedom, and separation of church and state—

the systematic exclusion of the Church from the public life of the community.[3]

Thus challenged, the Church responded immediately and unequivocally. On the one hand, it condemned liberalism: not only were the ideas on which it rested incompatible with Catholic teaching, but the monistic social order it sought to construct was incompatible with the freedom the Church required to carry out its divinely appointed mission. On the other hand, the Church entered into an alliance with the *ancien régime*. This fateful alliance was more than a little ironic, in that the *ancien régime* was the linear descendant of the absolutist state that had emerged from the ruins of the medieval world and had, by virtue of its absolutism and territorialism, long been the Church's adversary. Nevertheless, whatever its shortcomings, the *ancien régime* was at least an ostensibly Christian order. And so the Church rejected religious freedom and the separation of church and state—in the sense in which these terms were used by Continental liberalism—and insisted that the ideal relationship between church and state was the union of throne and altar in the manner of the *ancien régime*.

Shifting Attitudes on Church and State

This outlook persisted through the nineteenth century. But several twentieth-century developments stimulated a rethinking of Catholic teaching on church-state relations. The first is what is perhaps the defining political experience of the twentieth century: the emergence of the totalitarian state. The shattering impact of totalitarianism, whether in Nazi, Fascist, or Marxist-Leninist form, engendered a newfound consciousness of the value and dignity of the human person, and prompted a new exploration by Catholic thinkers of this ancient theme in the Church's tradition.

The second experience was the American experiment in democracy. In its early stages, this experiment was little noticed in Catholic circles. America, after all, was an overwhelmingly Protestant society, and one far away from the European continent, where the Church's attention was riveted by the turmoil of the day. But as the number of Catholics in America grew and the United States emerged as a world power, the Church's attention was unavoidably drawn to American democracy. What resulted was a gradual recognition that neither democracy nor religious freedom was a univ-ocal concept. In the United States, it was apparent, democracy and religious freedom were not rooted in the naturalism and individu-alism of Continental liberalism, and did not entail the formation of a political order informed by a secularist ethos.

These experiences, the rise of the totalitarian state and the American democratic experiment, prompted a profound twofold development in Catholic social and political thought. They spurred the recovery of a medieval tradition in Catholic thought that was committed to the Church's freedom to pursue its evangelical mis-sion free from governmental interference, to the supremacy of law, to constitutionally limited government, and to the ruler's responsi-bility to the community.[4] They also gave rise to a new emphasis on the dignity of the human person as the fundamental principle by which a rightly ordered society must be informed. In Pius XII's classic formulation, man, "far from being the object and, as it were, a merely passive element in the social order, is in fact, and must be its subject, its foundation, and its end." In short, he is "the origin and end of human society."[5]

These intellectual developments found expression in twentieth-century papal thought, which began to embrace the idea of the juridical state, the state whose "principal function" is "to safeguard the inviolable rights of the human person, and to facilitate the performance of his duties."[6] This acceptance of the juridical state was paralleled by a reappraisal of the merits of democratic govern-ment. "The democratic form of government," noted Pius XII approvingly, "appears to many as a postulate of nature imposed by reason itself."[7]

The time was obviously ripe for a renewal of Catholic thought on church-state questions as well. The leading figure in this renewal was the great American Jesuit theologian John Courtney Murray. In a series of articles in the 1940s and 1950s that laid the intellec-tual groundwork for Vatican II's *Dignitatis Humanae*, Murray sought to separate the trans-temporal principles governing Catholic thought on church-state relations from historically conditioned efforts to incarnate these principles in institutions, and to illuminate the differences between the American democratic experiment with its unique understanding of religious liberty and the "totalitarian democracy" of Continental liberalism. Moving beyond the nine-teenth-century Catholic ideal of the union of throne and altar, Murray attempted to formulate a theory of religious freedom rooted in the authentic and enduring principles of Catholic thought. His work, though initially controversial, was vindicated by Vatican II, where he served as a *peritus* and participated in the drafting of the "Declaration on Religious Freedom."[8]

CONCERNING RELIGIOUS FREEDOM

Dignitatis Humanae is a brief document, consisting of fifteen consecutively numbered sections divided into a preamble and two chapters. The first chapter begins by affirming religious freedom as a fundamental human right that must be guaranteed by positive law:

> This Vatican synod declares that the human person has a right to religious freedom. This freedom means that all men are to be immune from coercion on the part of individuals or of social groups and of any human power, in such wise that in matters religious no one is to be forced to act in a manner contrary to his own beliefs. Nor is anyone to be restrained from acting in accordance with his own beliefs, whether privately or publicly, whether alone or in association with others, within due limits.

This right to religious freedom must "be recognized in the consti-tutional law whereby society is governed"; that is, it must be enshrined as a civil right (2; 166–67).[9]

This right, moreover, extends not merely to individuals but also to religious bodies, which must be free to order their internal affairs as they see fit, to bear public witness to their faith and its relevance to the organization of the society's temporal affairs, and "to estab-lish educational cultural, charitable, and social organizations, under the impulse of their own religious sense" (3; 171–72). According to the declaration, the right to religious freedom also includes the right of the family to worship as it sees fit, and to provide children with religious education (5; 172).

Religious Freedom and Human Dignity

The declaration is at pains to dissociate its understanding of the foundation of religious freedom from certain other understandings.

For example, it emphatically rejects the idea that religious freedom is founded on religious subjectivism, agnosticism, or indifferentism, affirming rather "that God himself has made known to mankind the way in which men are to serve Him" and that the "one true religion subsists in the Catholic and apostolic Church" (1; 162–3). Indeed, far from embracing a religious subjectivism, the declaration affirms that its doctrine of religious freedom "has to do with immunity from coercion in civil society" and "leaves untouched traditional Catholic doctrine on the moral duty of men and societies toward the one true religion and the one Church of Christ" (1; 165). Nor does the declaration ground religious freedom in the subjective rights of conscience—in the idea that, as Murray puts it, "I have the right to do what my conscience tells me to do, simply because my conscience tells me to do it."[10]

In contrast, in articulating the foundations of religious freedom, the declaration avows its intention "to develop the doctrine of recent Popes on the inviolable rights of the human person and on the constitutional order of society" (1; 165). The right to religious liberty, the declaration avows, is rooted in "the very dignity of the human person, as this dignity is known . . . by reason itself" (1; 162–63). "It is in accordance with . . . [men's] dignity as persons . . . ," says the declaration, "that all men should be at once impelled by nature and also bound by a moral obligation to seek the truth, especially religious truth," and, once the truth is found, "to order their whole lives in accord" with its dictates. Truth, however, must be sought in a manner consistent with our dignity as persons—"as beings endowed with reason and free will and therefore privileged to bear personal responsibility"—and, once discovered, it must be adhered to by an act of "personal assent." Men "cannot discharge these obligations, in a manner in keeping with their own nature, unless they enjoy immunity from external coercion as well as psychological freedom" (2–3; 167–70). "It follows," the declaration continues, that a person "is not to be forced to act in a manner contrary to his conscience" or "to be restrained from acting in accordance with his conscience" (3; 168–70).

The very responsibilities inherent in the nature of the human person, in short, thus mandate a zone of personal freedom within which man can confront these responsibilities: "every man" has "the right to seek truth in matters religious" because "every man has the duty" to seek, and order his life in accordance with, "religious truth." Religious freedom is rooted in the objective fact of man's dignity as a person: "The right to religious liberty has its foundation, not in the subjective disposition of the person, but in his very nature" (2; 168).

The Role of the Government

The declaration briefly considers the responsibilities imposed on government by the right of religious freedom:

> The common welfare of society consists in the entirety of those conditions of social life under which men enjoy the possibility of achieving their own perfection in a certain fullness of measure and also with some relative ease. Hence this welfare consists chiefly in the protection of the rights and in the performance of the duties, of the human person. (6; 173)

Since the "protection and promotion of the inviolable rights of man ranks among the essential duties of government," it follows that government must "safeguard . . . the religious freedom of all its citizens" (6; 174). More than that:

> Government is also to help create conditions favorable to the fostering of religious life, in order that the people may be truly enabled to exercise their religious rights and to fulfill their religious duties, and also in order that society itself may profit by the moral qualities of justice and peace which have their origin in men's faithfulness to God and to His holy will.

In fulfilling this function, government must "see to it that the equality of citizens before the law, which is itself an element of the common welfare, is never violated for religious reasons, whether openly or covertly" (6; 175).

Because it is exercised in human society, however, the right of religious freedom "is subject to certain regulatory norms." Among the basic responsibilities of government is the protection of the public order, a responsibility composed of three elements: "the effective safeguard of the rights of all citizens," the guaranteeing of

"genuine public peace," and the "guardianship of public morality."
Hence, government may restrict the free exercise of religion when
it issues in "abuses" that threaten public order (7; 176–77).

Religious Freedom and the Gospel

The declaration examines religious freedom in the light of Christian revelation, and concludes that the Church, in recognizing this
right, "is being faithful to the truth of the Gospel" (12; 184),
which discloses both "the dignity of the human person in its full
dimensions" and "the respect which Christ showed towards the
freedom with which man is to fulfill his duty of belief on the Word
of God" (9; 179).

This right is fully compatible with "the freedom of the Church,"
which is "the fundamental principle" governing "relations between
the Church and governments." This freedom is rooted in "the
divine mandate" given to the Church by Christ to preach the
gospel, and encompasses "the full measure of freedom which her
care for the salvation of men requires." Wherever religious freedom
is "given sincere and practical application, there the Church suc-
ceeds in achieving a stable situation of right as well as of fact and
the independence which is necessary for the fulfillment of her divine
mission" (13; 185–86).

SIGNIFICANCE OF THE DECLARATION

If the declaration had done no more than state the Church's belief
in the existence of a human right to religious freedom, that alone
would have justified Paul VI's estimation of its importance. The
significance of *Dignitatis Humanae*, however, extends well beyond
this. To begin with, it offers the broad outlines of an approach to
the proper relationship of religion and public life that differs in
both spirit and substance from the theory that in recent years has
come to order America's public argument and shape its public life.

The dominant theory today espouses what might be called the
"privatization" of religion.[11] While individuals must be left free to
profess religious beliefs if they so choose, the proponents of
privatization demand that such beliefs be relegated to the private

sphere. Under no circumstances can they be allowed to impinge on the community's public life. Neither religion itself nor religiously grounded values, in this view, has any legitimate role in public life; for either to enter the public square is subversive of both the rights of other citizens and the integrity of political life. Government, in this view, must not aid a particular religion, aid religion in general, or prefer religion over irreligion. The result is what Richard John Neuhaus has aptly termed "the naked public square": the creation of a society whose public discourse and public life rigorously exclude all "particularist religious and moral belief."[12]

In recent years, the theory of religious liberty has had a far-reaching effect on the American body politic. Organizations such as the American Civil Liberties Union have led an effort to refashion American public life so it will conform to the demands of this conception of religious liberty. A host of seminal Supreme Court decisions—concerning such matters as religious displays on public property, prayer or religious instruction in public schools, and prayer at school-related functions such as commencements—bear witness to the influence this theory has had on our public law. It is responsible, moreover, for the view widespread among our cultural elites that efforts to protect pre-born human life, secure public aid for religiously affiliated schools, or establish school choice are illegitimate because they violate the fundamental principles governing church-state relations.

Freedom "for" Religion

The declaration's theory of religious freedom entails none of these consequences. Far from mandating a governmental posture of indifference, even hostility, to religion, the declaration insists that religious liberty, correctly understood, requires government to "take account of the religious life of the people and favor it" (3; 170). Public life, in other words, must accommodate the religious convictions and spiritual life of the community. From the perspective of the declaration, demands for the privatization of religion amount to nothing less than a violation of the principle of religious freedom: "It comes within the meaning of religious freedom, that religious bodies should not be prohibited from undertaking to show the special value of their doctrine in what concerns the organization of society and the inspiration of the whole of human activity" (5; 172).

The declaration's understanding of the nature of religious liberty thus differs fundamentally from the theory ascendant today. The latter sees religious freedom as freedom *from* religion—hence as dictating a public order from which religion and religiously grounded values are excluded; the declaration views religious freedom as freedom *for* religion—hence as mandating the establishment of a public order open to religion and religiously based values. What *Dignitatis Humanae* offers us, to begin with, is an alternative to the dominant view of the proper relation of church and state, and thus to the constitutional theory and public policy rooted in this view.

The Declaration and Constitutional Democracy

More than just this, however, the declaration voiced its emphatic approval of the widespread contemporary demand that "constitutional limits should be set to the powers of government in order that there may be no encroachment on the rightful freedom of the person and of associations." Such demands, it says, are "in accord with justice and truth" (1; 162–63). Thus, while not renouncing the Church's traditional neutrality on political systems, it displays what Francis Canavan has termed "a bias" towards constitutional government, toward government that is both "limited in its powers and . . . responsible to those it governs."[13] In this respect it invites comparison with *Gaudium et Spes*, which, while declaring that the Church is not committed to any political, economic, or social system, simultaneously criticizes political systems that hinder civil and religious freedom, are dictatorial, or display contempt for human rights. What issues from these documents is described by Murray as "a political commitment, however discreet, to constitutional government"[14]—a preferential option, as it were, for the juridical state.

The idea that the dignity of the person demands an environment of freedom where human beings may personally confront the demands of truth and goodness, and the closely related idea of a limited state, were pregnant with implications for the whole structure of rightly constituted political order. By containing in embryonic form the affirmation that constitutional democracy is the form of government most in keeping with the dignity of the human person, the declaration's personalist theory of religious freedom laid the intellectual foundation for the Catholic human-rights revolution.

COMPETING CONCEPTS OF DEMOCRACY

Dignitatis Humanae established a two-part agenda for a far-reaching redefinition of the role of the Church in world affairs. First, the Church was to assume the role of patroness of human dignity and defender of human rights before governments around the globe. This part of the agenda set by the declaration has been largely realized. As the events of the last several decades attest, the Church has emerged an effective advocate of human rights, a friend of democracy, and a foe of authoritarian and totalitarian regimes.

The second aspect was theoretical. The declaration fully elaborates neither the theory of religious freedom it embraces, nor the philosophy of democratic government implicit in that theory. Rather, it limits itself to suggesting the broad lines of argument that would inform such a theory, leaving its systematic elaboration to the future.[15] Unfortunately, this aspect of its agenda remains largely unrealized. Although before Vatican II a host of Catholic scholars—especially Murray, Jacques Maritain, and Yves Simon—made impressive contributions to the development of a philosophy of democratic government rooted in the Catholic understanding of man and society, from the close of the Council until quite recently little new work has been done in this area.

The completion of this task ought to be a priority of the first order. While democracy has been triumphant in theory, and has recently been ascendant in practice, there is still a pressing need to formulate a *philosophy* of democracy, rooted in the teaching of *Dignitatis Humanae*. For as the declaration observes, "not a few can be found who seem inclined to use the name of freedom as the pretext for refusing to submit to authority and for making light of the duty of obedience." In the face of this disturbing fact, it urges "those who are charged with the task of educating others" to do their utmost to "form men who will be lovers of true freedom":

"who will respect the moral order and be obedient to lawful authority," whose decisions will be made "in the light of truth," and whose actions will be governed by "a sense of responsibility" (8; 178). The declaration thus distinguishes between a true and a false freedom, implying that if the former is a great blessing, the latter can—and in the contemporary context does—constitute a threat.

There is no single notion of democracy. Rather, there are various theories, rooted in different understandings of politics and animated by divergent conceptions of the nature and destiny of man. Although similar in their institutional and procedural frameworks, the democracies created by these conflicting philosophies differ greatly in their spirit and substance. In the face of the democratic revolution that is sweeping the world today, the key question becomes: Which conception of democracy is animating this revolution?

This is no academic question. History attests that democracy is a rare and delicate form of government that has eventuated more often in anarchy or tyranny than in the regime of ordered freedom it promises. Democratic institutions, as John H. Hallowell has warned, "are a means to freedom . . . but they are not identical with freedom itself." In the end, "it is the way in which they are conceived and the way in which they are used that will ultimately determine their efficacy as instruments of freedom."[16] Not all versions of democracy are equally capable of advancing the cause of the freedom and dignity of the human person, or of providing a secure foundation for a vigorous democratic polity. "The fatality that has worked against . . . modern democracies," Maritain observed, is "the false philosophy of life" they have enshrined at the center of their public life.[17] The direction taken by the democratic experiments of today will depend largely upon what philosophy undergirds them.

Preconditions of Democracy

To achieve stability and vitality, democratic institutions require certain conditions. That democracy has preconditions is not a new notion. The American Founders, for instance, considered it axiomatic that a successful democratic society—one that effectively secures freedom, order, justice, and the common good—presupposes a particular kind of citizenry. In *The Federalist Papers*, James Madison wrote:

> As there exists a certain degree of depravity in mankind which requires a certain degree of circumspection and distrust: so there are other qualities in human nature, which justify a certain portion of esteem and confidence. Republican government presupposes the existence of these qualities in a higher degree than any other form.[18]

Why should democracy presuppose for its proper operation such a virtuous people? In authoritarian regimes, order is imposed from the top down, through force and fear. Eschewing such methods, a free society relies on the willingness of individuals and groups to cooperate freely to secure the common good, and to use the freedom given them in a responsible fashion. A vigorous democracy thus presupposes what Daniel Bell terms *civitas*, a "spontaneous willingness to obey the law, to respect the rights of others, to forgo temptations of private enrichment at the expense of the public weal—in short, to honor the 'city' of which one is a member."[19]

To appreciate the importance of *civitas* to the health of a democratic society it is necessary only to reflect upon its importance to democratic decision-making. Compromise is essential to the functioning of a democratic polity. But whether or not compromise takes place will depend largely on the attitude the citizens take toward public affairs, on whether they acknowledge a standard higher than their own self-interest. If politics is reduced to a mere clash of wills, self-interest dictates that groups intensify their demands and refuse to take no for an answer. Under such conditions, R. Bruce Douglass has written, the process of give-and-take

> would probably break down, and even if somehow that were avoided, the likelihood of truly workable policies being adopted on a consistent basis would be very small. At best government would limp along from one ill-designed compromise to the next; at worst, it would be paralyzed. It simply would not function.[20]

Inasmuch, furthermore, as political decisions would be reduced to nothing more than amoral compromises registering the relative strengths of the contending parties, it is difficult to see how such a political system could long sustain its moral authority and the active support of the citizenry.

The Sacredness of the Human Person

There is, however, a deeper sense in which a virtuous people is essential to democracy. The moral foundation of democracy is found in the affirmation of an order of rights and justice that transcends the positive laws of the state, one to which states, majorities, and individuals alike are held accountable. This affirmation is rooted in a particular understanding of the nature of a human being. At the heart of democracy is found an exaltation of the worth and value of the individual person. Democracy finds its inspiration in the affirmation that, as Maritain put it, "a single human soul is of more worth than the whole universe of bodies and material goods" and thus that "society exists for each person and is subordinate thereto."[21] The source of the "absolute dignity of the individual human being," writes Maritain,

> is rooted in the fact that as a person, a human being bears the image of God. The worth of the person, his liberty, his rights arise from the order of naturally sacred things which bear upon them the imprint of the Father of Being and which have in him the goal of their movement. A person possesses absolute dignity because he is in direct relationship with the Absolute, in which alone he can find his complete fulfillment. His spiritual fatherland consists of the entire order of things which have absolute value and which reflect, in some way, an Absolute superior to the world and which draw our life towards this Absolute.[22]

This affirmation of the sacredness of the human being is the ultimate inspiration of democratic institutions and practices. As Murray has written, it is this affirmation that ultimately inspired the American democratic experiment:

> This truth [i.e., the sacredness of the human person] is embodied in the American Declaration of Independence. The Constitution and the whole fabric of political and social life that it inspired were to institutionalize this truth in multiple ways. The Great Experiment [of American democracy] was a Great Hope precisely because it was an effort to set at the center of organized social

life the idea of man in his sacredness, in his panoply of human rights, with his endowment of spiritual freedom, as a being created by God, who must make his own creations serve purposes defined by God.[23]

This vision constitutes the very soul of democracy. Obviously, however, the laws and policies emanating from democratic institutions need not be, and often have not been, consistent with this vision. In a democratic society, a people governs itself. This means, in the final analysis, that the laws will reflect the convictions, the moral values, the character of the citizens. Thus, whether a particular democratic society serves the cause of the sacredness of the human person will depend on the character of its citizens, on their internalization of the moral substance and spiritual vision that properly lie at the heart of democracy. Only to the extent that this vision is a living reality in the hearts and minds of citizens will it be a living reality in their laws and public life. Do they know and obey the order of justice and rights? Do they understand the sacredness of man, and the imperatives this sacredness imposes on them both individually and collectively? If not, then, although democracy may exist in the sense of a set of procedures, democracy as an ethos is dead; and democratic institutions, rather than serving the cause of man's sacredness (and hence freedom), will only be instruments for the construction of new forms of servitude and injustice. Indeed, it is doubtful whether the institutions and procedures will long endure among a people who do not accept the affirmations that are their foundation and very reason for existing.

Whether or not a particular society's citizens constitute a virtuous people will depend on whether they acknowledge, and are faithful to, a set of moral norms that transcend their own subjective interests and desires, as well as the minimal moral standards enforced by positive law and the formalities of democratic procedures. It will depend on whether they wholeheartedly accept the moral affirmations that a free society requires for vitality and stability. A vigorous democratic polity thus has as its precondition a people who recognize, and whose actions are inwardly governed by, the imperatives issuing from these affirmations. If, historically, democracy has been a rare and fragile form of government, this is due in large part to the demands it makes on the moral character of the citizenry.

LIBERAL INDIVIDUALISM AND AMERICA'S CULTURE WAR

The relevance of these rather abstract considerations to the topic at hand will be more apparent if we turn our attention to the state of the world's oldest and most successful democratic experiment. The United States is in the midst of a full-fledged culture war. At stake in this *Kulturkampf* is nothing less than America's self-definition, our understanding of the moral and political principles that are to guide and inform our institutions.[24] The precipitating event in this culture war has been the rise of a new philosophy of democratic government that is close to establishing itself as the reigning orthodoxy, the public philosophy, of contemporary America. Our culture war is between the proponents and the opponents of this new philosophy of democratic government and the vision of man and the universe on which it rests.

This new model of democracy and the worldview on which it rests are rooted in the liberal individualist tradition in political thought. From its very inception in the seventeenth century, liberalism was a highly individualistic doctrine, taking its bearings from the individual conceived of as a sovereign will. Yet as Hallowell demonstrated in his classic *The Decline of Liberalism as an Ideology*, the full implications of this individualism were obscured by the countervailing belief of early liberals, like John Locke and Hugo Grotius, in the existence of an objective moral order, discoverable by reason, that transcended the subjective will of the individual.

This "integral liberalism," in Hallowell's terminology, was from the beginning a highly unstable doctrine because it juxtaposed two conflicting principles: the autonomy of the individual will, and the idea of a higher moral law. Over time, a number of factors, most notably the internal dynamic of liberalism's own rationalism and nominalism, acted to erode its belief in an objective moral order. The history of liberalism is thus the story of the triumph of the individual's subjective will over the objective moral order, of the individualism that lies at the heart of liberalism over the elements that had initially acted to restrain it.[25]

From this triumph emerges the new theory of democracy we are discussing. Its starting point is a particular understanding of human nature. As Michael Sandel observes, it conceives of human beings as "free and independent selves unclaimed by moral ties antecedent to choice." The self is thereby "installed as sovereign, cast as the author of the only obligations that constrain."[26] Man, in this view, is essentially a sovereign will.

From this idea of man its proponents develop a theory of politics. Three ideas are at the heart of the theory. First, a radical individualism: all social institutions and relations must be understood as nothing more than the purely conventional product of free choice on the part of naturally autonomous individuals; social relations are artificial, external, and contractual rather than being rooted in man's nature as a social being. Second, a thoroughgoing subjectivism, what Stanley C. Brubaker terms a "dogmatic doubt that we can ever know what is good for man and woman or that there even is such a thing as the human good."[27] Third, in the absence of a substantive theory of the good, the elevation of individual choice to the status of the highest good; the result is what Francis Canavan has described as "an unrelenting subordination of all allegedly objective goods to the subjective good of individual choice."[28]

This view finds institutional expression in a "neutral" state. Far from basing law and public policy on a particular conception of the good life, such a state—in the name of affording all lifestyles and belief systems equal treatment—seeks to establish a "neutral" framework of public order within which each individual is free to pursue his or her own vision of the good life. This freedom is limited only by the freedom of other individuals to do the same; the ends to which this freedom is put are not a legitimate public concern.

Inasmuch as such a regime is committed to public neutrality, no group must be allowed to impose its particular conception of the good life on others. All such beliefs must be checked at the gate of the public square; they cannot be allowed to impinge on the making of public policy. Thus the public square must be hermetically sealed against religious traditions that encompass a substantive vision of the good life.

The Rise of "Anomic" Democracy

The rise of this new liberalism has been paralleled by a number of disturbing developments in American public life. Politically, we have witnessed a decline in public-spiritedness and the loss of any overarching sense of community or of a common good to which private interests must be subordinated. The result has been the rise of what has been called "anomic" democracy: the fragmenting of the body politic into a plethora of aggressive interest groups whose ever-escalating and conflicting demands on the government have produced the phenomenon we call gridlock.[29] This political paralysis has combined with the perception that laws and public policies are a product of cynical deals between self-seeking groups to create a crisis of public confidence in our institutions. Simultaneously, there has emerged a "rights mania," wherein individuals and groups claim an ever-expanding array of hitherto unknown rights that supposedly "trump" the claims of the common good or of public morality. The result has been the progressive disabling of key social and political institutions.[30] We seem to be experiencing the disturbing phenomenon described by William Ernest Hocking as "the impotence of the state": an ever-expanding state is incapable of effectively using the far-reaching powers it has assumed to achieve the goals for which these powers were granted.[31]

Culturally, over the past few decades a moral and spiritual void has developed at the center of American life, manifesting itself in a corrosive individualism, a widespread moral relativism, a soulless hedonism, a shallow materialism, and a pervasive pursuit of immediate gratification. One thinks immediately here of Allan Bloom's portrait of American life, his characterization of our emergent cultural ethos as nihilism American-style.[32] More and more, we appear to be free-falling in a moral vacuum, approaching what Will Herberg once described as "a non-moral, normless culture."[33] To an increasing number of Americans, the very idea of an objective moral order transcending their subjective desires lies beyond their range of experience. The social consequences of this new ethos are immense: a wholesale unraveling of the social fabric, the most dramatic sign of which is the disintegration of the American family.

It has become increasingly apparent that these disturbing developments are the product of the transformation of American life under the impact of the liberal individualist view of man and society. These developments are particularly ominous because they seem to signal the erosion of the moral and cultural preconditions of a viable democratic polity. We are today forced to inquire whether our commitment to liberal individualism is making us incapable of sustaining constitutional democracy, and whether liberal individualism might actually subvert the culture on which a free society depends.

Liberalism's Moral Failure

How contemporary liberalism subverts what George F. Will has aptly termed "the intangible prerequisites of free government" is not hard to see.[34] A viable democracy, as we have seen, requires a people who acknowledge and freely embrace the moral principles on which a free society depends. Contemporary liberalism subverts the foundations of democratic government because the thorough-going subjectivism toward which liberalism inexorably tends precludes in principle the affirmation of these moral principles. The culture of unbridled individualism and subjectivism fostered by liberalism is hardly a fertile soil for cultivation of the character on which democracy depends.

The rise of anomic democracy itself attests to the erosion of *civitas*. Even more ominous than its subversion of *civitas*, however, is the inability of liberalism to affirm the moral absolutes that are the moral foundation of a free society. As many of its own theoreticians now admit, contemporary liberal theory has proved incapable of providing any kind of persuasive grounding for the rights it affirms.[35] This failure is due, not to the timidity or lack of ingenuity of contemporary liberal theorists, but to the very epistemological and metaphysical premises that inform liberalism. As Thomas A. Spragens, Jr., and Alisdair MacIntyre, among others, have shown, these premises inevitably issue in a corrosive skepticism and, finally, in an utter nihilism.[36]

Liberal thinkers are left with the impossible task of trying to project the organizing principles of a free society from the starting point of an utter skepticism. Admittedly, some contemporary liberal thinkers do argue that since we cannot determine the "good," the freedom of all persons to live the way they choose must be respected. The problem with this argument is that it doesn't work: if there is no foundation for judgments of right and wrong independent of the subjective desires of the individual, then there is no compelling reason for the individual not to impose his will on others if it serves his own interest to do so.

The ultimate effect of liberalism's inability to provide the moral soil in which a free society is rooted is the erosion of the moral substance of democracy. This erosion manifests itself in an inability to answer what Irving Kristol terms "the ultimate subversive question: 'Why not?'"[37] Why shouldn't people be treated as means rather than ends? Why shouldn't the strong enslave the weak? Why shouldn't people use their freedom just as they choose to? In the spiritual universe of nihilistic relativism, there is no compelling answer to such questions. In such a universe, where it is impossible to affirm the moral absolutes that are the charter of a free society, it is, to say the least, doubtful whether democratic institutions can effectively serve the dignity of the human person, or, for that matter, whether those institutions themselves can long endure.

This concern might seem exaggerated. Yet it needs to be seen against the backdrop of one of the most striking and disturbing features of contemporary American life: our diminishing respect for the sanctity of human life. The signs of this are unmistakable: 1.5 million abortions a year; widespread acceptance of abortion on demand; a growing acceptance of the legitimacy of euthanasia; and the gradual return of eugenics. These developments are the direct and inevitable result of liberalism's inability to affirm the sacredness of human life, an inability rooted in the very philosophical premises that inform the liberal tradition. How can a society unable to affirm the sacredness of human life advance the cause of human dignity? How long can any rights be secure in such a society? How long can democracy endure in such a society?

A New Basis for Democracy

The ascendancy of liberal individualism has not gone unchallenged. Large segments of American society have refused to acquiesce in the far-reaching political and cultural revolution this model entails: hence today's culture war. But the opponents of the liberal model have been handicapped by their lack of a coherent theory of politics to put forward as an alternative. While offering a trenchant critique of liberalism, they have been unable to supply an intellectually compelling model of democratic government that could supplant liberalism and supply us with the new and better public philosophy we need.

Dignitatis Humanae lays the foundation for such a model. This new theory of democratic government could draw, not only on the Church's two millennia of reflection on the right ordering of society, but also on a tradition of philosophical inquiry untainted by the rationalism and immanentism of the Enlightenment, and on an anthropology of unrivaled richness and depth. It could therefore play an important role in providing a secure foundation for the many democratic experiments taking place in Central and Eastern Europe and Latin America, and in revitalizing the American democratic experiment itself.

A Personalist Orientation

What would be the hallmarks of this newly conceived democracy? What Maritain termed "personalist democracy" would begin by radically rejecting liberal individualism's reductionist understanding of a human being as essentially a sovereign will. It would be rooted instead in the idea of what Canavan terms "a universal human nature whose natural needs and tendencies are knowable to the mind."[38] At the same time, it would affirm that a human being is more than an individual exemplar of human nature: human beings are persons, beings endowed with intelligence and freedom, and are thus charged with the responsibility for, in Maritain's words, "making oneself the sufficient principle of one's own operations; in other words, . . . [of] perfecting oneself as an indivisible whole in the act one brings about."[39]

The implications of this are immense. Personalist democracy would insist that social and political institutions exist to serve the human person by fostering the integral development of the person. A democratic system committed to this development would be acutely aware of the ethical dimensions of political life. It would emphatically reject the liberal individualist notion of the neutral state, insisting that such a state is neither possible nor desirable— not possible because politics is an inherently moral enterprise and the making of law and public policy necessarily involves moral judgment; not desirable because, although the state may be limited in its scope, it nevertheless exists to serve the integral development of the person. Law thus has the moral function of creating a framework within which men can lead truly human lives—lives of reason in accordance with virtue.

While grounding public life in the objective moral truth of the dignity of the human being, personalist democracy would insist that this dignity demands a zone of freedom within which the person can confront his or her ineluctable responsibility. Politically, therefore, the personalism of *Dignitatis Humanae* would issue in a firm commitment to *constitutional democracy*. The state, it would insist, is not coextensive with society but is a limited order of action for limited purposes. Its structure must be defined by law, and its scope and power carefully specified and circumscribed by law. In the exercise of its powers, moreover, government must be regulated and directed by the society it exists to serve. Likewise, inasmuch as, in the words of John XXIII, "there is nothing human about a society welded together by force,"[40] personalist democracy is committed to what might be called the method of freedom: freedom becomes the political method of choice. In the concise formulation of *Dignitatis Humanae*: "Freedom [must] be respected as far as possible, and curtailed only when and in so far as necessary" (7; 178). Obviously, the principle of "subsidiarity" figures centrally in this context.

Sharing liberalism's concern for the rights of individuals, or, more properly, the rights of persons, personalist democracy would nevertheless refuse to follow liberalism into the abyss of subjectivism and individualism. In keeping with the declaration's distinction between true and false freedom, it would insist on the distinction between liberty and license. Similarly, it would maintain that because democracy is as much a spiritual and moral enterprise as a political one, the enterprise of self-government presupposes virtue. It would thus embrace Edmund Burke's postulate that "men are qualified for civil liberty in exact proportion to their disposition to put moral chains on their appetites." It would recognize that "men of intemperate minds cannot be free" because "their passions forge their fetters."[41]

Likewise, personalist democracy would reflect the declaration's recognition that man is a social creature. Instead of posing the political problem exclusively in terms of the individual and the state, it would insist both that the state is a natural institution, and that the development of the person requires a plurality of autonomous sub-political and supra-political groups whose well-being is essential to the happiness of persons and the health of the political community. Breaking out of what Mary Ann Glendon has termed the "familiar individual-state-market grid,"[42] it would insist that a society is not an atomistic collection of individuals but a community of communities. Government, far from undermining these communities in the name of the autonomy of the individual, must strengthen them, respect their rights, and create an environment in which they can flourish.

Making Room for Religion

Finally, a theory of democratic government grounded in the philosophy of the declaration would adopt a strikingly different posture towards religion and religiously based values from that assumed by liberalism's naked public square. Personalist democracy would maintain that the liberal state's posture of indifference and, in the final analysis, hostility towards religion is inappropriate and ultimately dangerous.

To begin with, personalist democracy would insist that such a posture is inconsistent with government's most basic responsibility: its obligation to protect the rights of its citizens and facilitate their performance of their duties. Furthermore, it would maintain that the public indifference toward religion demanded by liberalism fails to appreciate the vitally important contribution religion makes to the temporal welfare of the community, both by instilling in the citizenry the moral character on which democracy depends and by bearing witness to the transcendental dimension of the human person. By restricting the Church's freedom to take an active role in public life, the naked public square endangers democracy itself. Accordingly, while respecting the religious freedom of all citizens, personalist democracy would seek to foster religion and would welcome the active participation of all the community's religious groups in public life.

Toward the close of 1989, the *Wall Street Journal* solicited the expectations and hopes of a number of prominent Americans for the coming decade. "There will occur the spread of democratic societies," novelist Walker Percy predicted, "but of a certain sort: deeply informed by the values of the visual media, violence, pornography, standard network Brokaw-Rather ideology, Hollywood morality, and 10,000 Japanese car commercials. My hope is that we might do better."[43] The philosophy of democratic government whose foundations are laid by *Dignitatis Humanae* offers a chance for transforming Percy's hope into a reality.

7

Reforming International Development
Populorum Progressio (1967)

ROBERT ROYAL

THE development of people who are making very great efforts to free themselves from the hardship of hunger, poverty, endemic diseases, and ignorance, who are seeking a more bountiful share in the benefits flowing from civilization and demanding that greater value be set upon their qualities as human beings, and who are constantly giving their attention to greater growth is gladly and encouragingly viewed by the Catholic Church."[1] With this serpentine opening sentence to Paul VI's 1967 encyclical *Populorum Progressio*, which any composition teacher would regard with horror, the Vatican announced its rather passive ("is . . . viewed") and adverbially vague ("gladly and encouragingly") embarkation upon the muddy waters of modern international development.

La question du style is not insignificant in this, as in many other recent papal documents. (The uncertain trumpet sounded by the Vatican during the Nazi Holocaust, for example, failed to echo the heroic actions of Pius XII and other church officials in aiding European Jews.[2]) The language of *Rerum Novarum* (1891) and *Quadragesimo Anno* (1931), the two cornerstones of modern Catholic social teaching, is crisp in a way that is largely absent in the

---

Robert Royal is the vice president for research and the John M. Olin Fellow in Religion and Society at the Ethics and Public Policy Center.

later encyclicals. The drafters of the earlier texts were particularly careful because they thought someone might, at some point, ask them to form a government on their principles. Subsequent encyclicals, with no such possibility in view, exhibit a corresponding lack of meticulous attention to social problems. In the later texts, genuine moral urgency frequently jumps to quick political conclusions or even outright simplifications of complex social realities. The popes always have a serious social question in view. But as Aristotle observed, the burden of responsibility educates the good man in the ways of the statesman. Personal virtue without that reality test does not automatically translate into political virtue—or lucid political commentary.

Given the encyclical's murky language, it is not surprising that the first readers of the document construed it in contradictory ways. Conservative commentators charged that it promoted "warmed-over Marxism," a reading endorsed and extended by the French communist newspaper *L'Humanité*, which observed that the evils denounced by the encyclical were the same evils "Marxists have been calling attention to for more than a century." The eminent American theologian John Courtney Murray, however, regarded it as "the Church's definitive answer to Marxism." Newspaper columnist Mary McGrory reported that, according to White House aides, Lyndon Johnson claimed the encyclical vindicated his War on Poverty. To *Time* magazine, though, the pope's document "looked in some ways as if it had been drawn from a U.N. economic report." *Time* also noticed a papal quirk: Paul VI criticized the developed countries but directed only a few warnings toward communist nations about the inadequacy of materialism and atheism as social philosophies. Although there was widespread consensus that the pope had made a strong statement about the need for balanced world development, there was little agreement about the exact nature of his advice.

Almost as passionate as the disagreement about the encyclical's politics and economics was the controversy about paragraph 37, the section on population control. Alan Guttmacher of Planned Parenthood and Dr. John Rock, the inventor of oral contraceptives, immediately claimed the pope as an ally. Theological experts, however, saw little new in paragraph 37's badly garbled discussion of the respective roles of parents and the state in determining family size, a view confirmed a year later when Paul published *Humanae Vitae*, his encyclical condemning contraception.

Several Catholic journals, weary of all the squabbling, recommended that future encyclicals be officially issued in a modern language to minimize confusion. A Latin text could still be done, but the original-language text would be definitive. Paul VI, as everyone knew, had written the encyclical in French with the advice of French experts on development, several of whose names and works are cited in the footnotes. But even the French shows little of the fabled Gallic *clarté*. The problem lay elsewhere.[3]

Moral Language versus Social-Science Jargon

In *Populorum Progressio* the clear language of traditional Catholic moral teaching swims against strong currents of 1960s social-science jargon. Liberal Catholic critics accused the conservative Paul VI of taking his usual "one step forward, two steps back," but the pope had in fact tried to take two major steps forward. Paul underscored once again the importance of those elements of Catholic anthropology that bear directly on social and economic life, and then he tried to apply them to the current situation. If he did step backward, it was not because he adhered to Catholic principles but because he failed to bring the Church's views of the human person fully to bear on then-current developmentalist orthodoxies. This failure resulted in contradictory messages in his text. Several of these contradictions would be resolved in John Paul II's *Sollicitudo Rei Socialis* (1987), where the view of the human person as an active agent of change in the world profoundly transforms the Catholic discussion of development. And with *Centesimus Annus*, John Paul would extend that insight to include a "right of economic initiative" hinted at but never fully stated by any previous occupant of the Chair of Peter.

Yet bedrock Catholic teaching and a confidence in the Church's role in the world remained in Paul's texts despite occasional lapses into now-doubtful policy prescriptions. Perhaps in 1967 the mere sight of the Catholic Church, the pre-modern institution *par excellence*, preaching human progress stunned some readers to such a degree that they assumed the Church now viewed its social doctrine in progressive secular terms. The text does not easily lend itself to such an interpretation. For example, even addressing a thorny question like Western colonialism, the pope argues:

> Colonizing countries at times sought nothing but their own advantage, aggrandizement, and glory, and when they relinquished their rule, left those countries in an ill-balanced economy, based, for example, on the production of one kind of crop, the market price of which is subject to very great and sudden changes. Though it must be acknowledged that some harm has stemmed from *colonialism* from which other evils arose later, it is nevertheless necessary to give grateful recognition to the merits of colonizers who have conferred real benefits on not a few undeveloped lands by employing the skill of their scientists and technicians whose benefits still endure. (paragraph 7)

These benefits were not solely of a material nature either. Paul VI admits that the Catholic missionaries who accompanied the colonists were flawed like other men, and sometimes

> mingled the modes of life and thought characteristic of their own country with the true message of Christ. Nevertheless at the same time the missionaries not only cherished the institutions of these people but also developed them further in such a way that not a few are to be considered pioneers who have made very great contributions either to material or intellectual progress. To prove the point let it suffice to take the example of the holy man Charles de Foucauld who because of his charity merited the name *universal brother* and who composed a splendid dictionary of the Tuareg language. (12)

This pope was aware of, but did not wholly accept, the charge of "Eurocentrism" and cultural imperialism leveled both then and now against the Church.

Perhaps one reason Paul asserted the basically positive value of Western contacts with underdeveloped peoples was that he still believed, unlike many Catholics and other Christians today, that his church had a serious—in fact, a singular—role to play in human life and development. After acknowledging the supremacy of church and state, in their respective spheres, he concludes that the Church desires to assist all peoples "to attain to their greatest fulfillment and for this reason offers to them what she alone possesses, that is, a view of man and of human affairs in their totality" (13). Amid the euphoria in some media circles about the Catholic embrace of progress, this traditional Catholic claim to a unique universality was overlooked.

Human Responsibility and Weakness

Also missing from secular progressivism was the Catholic insistence on human responsibility and capacity for self-improvement. Unlike philosophical fatalists and social determinists of various stripes, the pope boldly rejects the argument that bad environments make people unable to live a fully human life: "each individual, whatever influence external circumstances have upon him, is the chief architect of his own fortune good or bad, and merely by exerting powers of his intellect and will every man can grow in humanity, enhance his value, and perfect himself" (15).[4]

Such a belief in the power of individuals, however, did not lead the pope to the view that culture does not matter, or to a facile "multiculturalism" of the sort that flourishes today, which holds that all cultures are equally worthy of attention in a pluralist society. Paul VI notes that some cultures foster the development he seeks, while others hinder it. At times, this leads to tensions, and then "social structures not corresponding to modern needs are almost shattered." Such fractures are regrettable, and a more organic development of culture and society in all parts of the world would better promote the common good. For the pope, however, the full development of persons depends on acceptance of the Catholic understanding of human nature and some elements of Western civilization.

Perhaps the most anti-progressive side to the document, though, is the old Catholic wariness about human weakness, which runs like a leitmotif throughout the policy recommendations. Reminders of our fallen nature erupt at crucial points, such as in the tart comment on the need for guarantees to lenders that recipients will make good use of loans, since, observes Paul, "idlers and parasites are not to be encouraged." But while such truths are essential to understanding any human situation, they were given short shrift in the basically secular development theories on which the pope relied in writing *Populorum Progressio*. Nor did anyone anticipate that development organizations themselves would generate numerous evils.

Misguided Policies

In 1967 it seemed self-evident to many people that government-to-government aid programs could be widely successful vehicles for development. The only things lacking were the will and the resources. No one foresaw the bureaucratic morass of the U.S. Agency for International Development, the counterproductive and debt-creating loans of the International Monetary Fund, and the disincentives from institutions like the World Bank. The eminent scholar and Nobel Prize–winner Gunnar Myrdal observed approvingly at the time that in developing countries "national economic planning is almost everywhere a universally acclaimed ideal."

Within the developed nations and in international-relief contexts today, however, there is far less confidence in the capacity of state institutions to encourage authentic development, and far more attention given to evidence of their tendency to choke off natural economic growth. The economic collapse of the Soviet system and the worldwide accumulation of foreign debt by developing countries have pointedly confirmed other indications of the dangers of state-controlled economic practices. When the World Bank met in the fall of 1990 to consider aid programs, the bank's own officials were touting privatization and entrepreneurship as a basic prerequisites to further developmental assistance.

Guided by its own principles, the Church could have predicted such development failures. The Vatican early embraced subsidiarity as a key principle of modern social theory.[5] Subsidiarity, simply defined, means that the smallest possible grouping in society (say a family, parish, school, union, or other association) should bear primary responsibility for an activity. These groups understand problems close to their origins and are in a good position to respond effectively. The national state is an agent of last resort because of its basic incapacity to deal with small-scale difficulties and because of the inherent danger in turning over too many social responsibilities to state power. Typically, the state deals with problems such as natural disasters and defense against aggressors.

State-to-state aid is warranted, therefore, only in an emergency and for a limited period. Using it as a permanent method for dealing with the economic life in a society ignores basic truths about human life in community and, over time, subverts the true order of reality, paving the way for real disorder. John Paul II, writing exactly twenty years later with this history of international aid in view, sounded a warning absent from Paul's text: developing nations first need initiative *within* if they are to have any hope of making proper use of help from without.[6] Taking note of this fact seems, even for many people sympathetic to markets and democracy, tantamount to falsely identifying Catholic social teaching with some sort of radical individualism. But all modern social encyclicals have made it clear that development requires both a sound institutional framework *and* properly formed personal and societal virtues. In *Centesimus Annus*, for example, John Paul approves of markets inscribed in a proper juridical order.

Populorum Progressio is right to point out that suffering persists in the world because of a lack of development, and that the developed world could help alleviate it. But the encyclical's economic recommendations inspire little confidence. They often seem reminiscent of the plea made by a Brazilian archbishop during a visit to São Paulo by West German chancellor Helmut Schmidt. Voicing the sentiments of a group of liberation theologists, the archbishop insisted that Volkswagen pay workers in its Brazilian division as much as it paid workers in its Stuttgart plant. This seemed like simple justice and a way to stop "exploitation of cheap labor in the Third World" by a profitable multinational corporation. Schmidt, hardly a defender of capitalism, replied: "Good idea! If that happens, São Paulo VW will shut its doors and return to Germany, which would help a lot in resolving my unemployment problems."[7] There has been no indication that this incident provoked the Brazilian hierarchy into reconsidering how international economics, admittedly a complicated subject, works in the world. Various Vatican and episcopal documents make similar recommendations to extract economic "justice" by uneconomic means.

Mistaken Moral Categories

Populorum Progressio condemned the neglect of poor nations by rich ones on traditional moral grounds. As every reader of the Bible knows, the rich have an obligation to share their abundance with the poor. But its moral condemnation falters because the encyclical does not acknowledge that the relationship of individual to individual is not identical to the relationship of state to state. While most individuals can quite accurately judge the effect their charity is having on recipients, for example, governments have much more difficulty assessing the effect of their aid on other countries. In fact, because of the complexities of economics, recipient governments themselves are not always able to tell whether aid programs have been harmful or beneficial.

Another serious obstacle to development undercuts even generous transfers from First World countries to Third World governments: few, if any, Third World governments show the respect for human rights and the proper juridical order recommended by popes from Leo XIII to the present. Corruption and waste are rampant among Third World elites and often lead to increased exploitation of the poor. Many First World activists, who are rightly suspicious of the motives and behavior of their own politicians, seem convinced that political leaders in developing nations belong to a different species than their First World counterparts. Nonetheless, the usefulness of bigger and more ambitious development programs now seems to be questioned by all who debate the larger cultural issue of what produces wealth and poverty.[8]

Populorum Progressio takes far too simple an approach to international economics. For example, Paul traces back through the documents of Vatican II and other points in the Catholic tradition the belief that God intended the goods of the earth to be shared by all, and that property owners have an obligation to use their property for the common good. While this principle is certainly true—and was even affirmed by such early proponents of modern political and economic rights as John Locke and, later, John Stuart Mill[9]—it is announced in a context that implies that the developed world is robbing the developing world by using a disproportionate share of the world's resources. According to the pope, even morally neutral technology needs to be restrained to prevent wider gaps from opening between rich and poor. Marxist and *marxisant* theorists have long relied on similar analyses, and continue to do so today after the intellectual, moral, and social collapse of socialism.

Yet such conclusions may be morally suspect. If one farmer discovers a technique that makes him more productive than his neighbor, for example, the inventor has not sinned but contributed to human welfare. Though the invention may make the second farm economically non-viable, the second farmer may now better serve the human community by devoting his time to some other productive enterprise. Whatever temporary dislocations such developments produce, restraining human creativity will, in the long run, lead to even greater human ills. In any case, regulation that props up the failing farm by reducing the efficiency of the successful one does not necessarily benefit anyone. Individuals and governments may wish to help those displaced by such developments as they adjust to new economic activities. But true advances in the capacity to grow food should be seen as the blessings they are. At least in the United States, technology and productivity have resulted in food surpluses that have saved people from starvation around the world; any serious attempt to fiddle with international economics must ensure that disincentives do not destroy that often unremarked safety net.

As to industrial production—a more complex issue—the ethical implications are usually construed in two ways. The first contends that the relatively few in the industrialized nations are unjustly consuming more than their fair share of resources. Paul's thinking is influenced by this view. The second regards the developed world as performing a service by *producing* goods from raw materials for the good of the human race (taking it as a given that, without other changes, the developing nations would not much benefit from greater access to raw materials). Even in his meandering opening sentence to the encyclical, the pope recognizes that developing nations want "a more bountiful share in the [material] benefits flowing from civilization." The first view of the industrialized world, however, leads to endorsing international regulation of production. The second suggests that the best thing the industrialized world can do for developing areas, besides preventing short-term starvation, is to teach them how to become more productive themselves.

What Works and What Doesn't

The main reason that regulation appeals to Paul VI and his development specialists is that profit, competition, and the free use of property are not, on their face, altruistic. Christian teaching urges us always to have others' needs in view. And since helping poor people requires some measure of altruism, we need international control of economic activity. While there is some truth to this view, most developing countries would benefit more from the removal of tariff barriers and increased domestic economic activity than they would from merely restraining the First World.

We should be cautious about advocating for weak, developing nations what has failed for stronger, more advanced countries. No planned economies have met the needs of their peoples in the developed world, much less in the developing world. Far from being merely savage survival-of-the-fittest mechanisms, profit and competition operating within proper legal systems accurately indicate how well an activity is being performed. If an enterprise consumes more than it produces, whether in materials or capital, it is a net loss to society. If an enterprise does not compete freely and therefore has no incentive to make its product better and more affordable, it is to that extent an economic drag on society. Both profit and competition are as necessary to the efficient functioning of an economy as exercise is to the continued health of the body. These are moral, not merely economic, considerations because the weakest and poorest suffer most from economic sluggishness. John Paul II, who has lived under a state-directed economy, has written: "The challenge of poverty is of such magnitude that to overcome it we must fully resort to the dynamism and creativity of private enterprise, to all its potential effectiveness, to its capacity for the efficient allocation of resources, and to the fullness of its renewing energies."

In the late 1960s, however, most developmentalists would have said along with Paul VI that "the initiatives of individuals and the fluctuation of competition will not assure the success of development. For it is not lawful to go to such lengths that the resources and power of the rich become even greater, and the distress of the needy be increased and the enslavement of the oppressed aggravated." The non sequitur in this passage of clotted prose shows that Paul has here listened to theorists who have not thoroughly analyzed the problem. Clearly, he has in mind the abuses of rich landowners or exploitive outsiders in some developing countries. Initiative and competition, however, are not inherently oppressive. On the contrary, in modern growth economies they have proven to be the very remedies for underdevelopment that Paul seeks. The problem in most countries throughout history has been that elites, usually allied with governments, have prevented the great masses of the population from obtaining the skills and capital, the protection of law and exemption from regulation, that make human enterprise the engine of growth.

Everywhere that developmental programs have been implemented, they have spawned elite and oppressive bureaucracies as socially deadening as anything in the former communist bloc. The sheer size of these bureaucracies is ominous. The U.S. government employs about 1.5 million people. By comparison Brazil, with only half of the U.S. population and no serious global responsibilities, supports 1.6 million federal employees. Worse still are Argentina, with more than 2 million bureaucrats out of a work force of 11 million, and Mexico, with 3.2 million federal workers. Paul VI mistakenly assumed that international programs would be more benevolent and effective than individuals and markets. Yet in Brazil, for example, by the estimate of the Brazilian government itself, only 3 per cent of the rural poor have ever received any benefit from the $1.5 billion poured into rural development programs for a decade. The rest of the money has gone to administrative salaries, waste, and corruption.[10]

Even where money does not disappear en route, formidable obstacles must be overcome in order to use aid effectively. Paul suggests that, with improved communication between donors and recipients, "the result could easily be achieved that the aid to be given would be equitably appointed not only to the generosity and wealth of donors, but also according to the real need for assistance and the ability of using aid on the part of the recipients." This sentiment, for all its roundabout qualifications, has proven to be false. Despite all the aid programs funded by America, Europe, and the Soviet Union, no developing country has "easily"—or even with difficulty—found itself with the right amount and type of aid.

In fact, where inefficient state-run enterprises and non-responsive ruling oligarchies are in place, massive amounts of aid rarely lead to development. The habits they induce in the populace, too, become an additional obstacle. Until recently, Western institutions were providing Kenya with about $1 billion a year in aid—more than the Kenyan government's budget. But theft, waste, and the inefficiency of Kenya's three hundred state-run enterprises have all but neutralized the potential effects of even a billion dollars. Kenyans refuse to pay taxes, having seen what happens to foreign money. Their country remains a basket case despite this lavish beneficence from the developed world. Aid organizations have begun to reduce their contributions to Kenya pending internal reform.

The unification of East and West Germany is another good case in point. Despite tens of billions of dollars available from the West, careful planning by one of the world's most successful economic powers, and a well-trained, if somewhat passive, work force in the East, the East's transition remains a problem. Besides the sheer complexity of the task, the infrastructure of the East is simply inadequate. East German factories are so inefficient compared to their counterparts in free societies that they are widely regarded as "socialist scrap heaps," fit only to provide material for the new structures that must be built.

A Lack of Charity?

For Paul VI and many developmentalists even today, however, the primary obstacles to development are selfishness or lack of concern on the potential donor's side. The pope is right that the well-off should show far more concern for the poor than they have. But his analysis mixes two distinct categories. The pope urges the citizen of a developed country to ask himself several questions: "Is he ready to pay more taxes so that the public authorities can more vigorously promote development? Is he ready to pay a higher price for imported goods so that the producers get a fairer return? Is he ready, if it is necessary and he be in the prime of life, to quit his native land to help emerging countries?" The last question confuses the first two *economic* questions with the *moral* demands of charity and solidarity. But lack of charity, or at least a lack of money, is not really the immediate problem confronting developing countries.

From 1956 to 1986, governments in the developed world transferred nearly *$2 trillion* (in constant 1989 dollars) to the developing nations. This figure does not include military aid, and already allows for financial withdrawals, profit repatriation, and loan payments.[11] Also not included are the billions of dollars churches and other charitable organizations have channeled into the developing world. This aid is quite considerable; Americans alone give about $12 billion yearly through private non-governmental institutions for work in developing nations, half of that figure through religious groups.[12] Though the intentions behind all these initiatives are admirable—and though assistance on such a scale could not help but do some good—the world situation $2 trillion later, as John Paul II has observed, "offers a rather negative impression."

Economic analysts in growing numbers have noticed the harmful effects of aid transfers to governments, and have begun to ask why this is so. In Latin America, Africa, and parts of Asia, well-intentioned aid by institutions like the World Bank has done much to increase the size of bureaucracies and state-owned enterprises, but precious little to stimulate private-sector initiative and independence, which are everywhere the real engines of development. The international "aid" programs have created an extensive network of non-viable economic projects roughly similar in international terms to the savings-and-loan debacle in the United States. In a sense, this should come as no surprise because the precise purpose of these programs was to support non-viable enterprises. Few analysts, however, have seen through the symptoms—crushing foreign debt—to the underlying malady: making loans that can never show a real return.

In the international arena, recipients of foreign aid are displaying characteristics of welfare dependency. After decades of assistance, not a single recipient of aid has moved from underdeveloped to developed status. But agencies charged with making or receiving loans in donor and recipient countries have a vested interest in assuring that their mutual programs appear not to fail. As a result, even the largest debtor nations (Mexico, Argentina, and Brazil), which clearly have not used aid successfully, require larger loans every year to prevent default on earlier loans and the discrediting of the entire aid apparatus. When the payments on these loans come due, the common folk, not the bureaucrats, must pay through austerity measures. Breaking this cycle would be the kindest gesture a caring people could make toward their poorer brothers and sisters.

A Better System

While the situation in every developing nation is different (so much so that the very terms "Third World" and "the South" refer to no common set of problems) and should be evaluated on its own terms, thinking about the world's poor in ways that we now think about America's poor may be helpful. In modern economies, even developing ones, human virtues and habits are a *sine qua non* of wealth creation. As Paul knew in 1967, missionaries who taught reading, writing, arithmetic, hygiene, and other useful skills were preparing native populations for eventual participation in greatly improved economies. These skills are necessary, though not sufficient, prerequisites to growth. The communist world, for example, wasted many potential advantages of its fairly high levels of education by not only failing to provide opportunities for human creativity and labor but by stifling many currents that existed. The great development task now in both the former Second World and the Third World is to establish institutions that foster and reward economic initiative as a God-given vehicle for the betterment of all. Some government-to-government assistance, like the U.S. aid to the former Soviet Union, may help during the transition. But far more significant will be the private investment that will inevitably arrive in any country once political and legal systems guarantee stability.

Paradoxically, in international development less is often more. One of the most effective aid operations in the past few years has been the systematic distribution of "micro-loans" by non-governmental agencies. In many places in the developing world, a loan of a hundred dollars or so may enable a enterprising person to start a bakery, open a repair shop, finance the purchase of equipment for manufacturing and assembly, or engage in a host of other endeavors crucial to a society's grassroots economic ferment. These loans are usually made in a non-bureaucratic way, often by religious groups, with the grantors carefully selecting grantees who they think are likely to use the aid productively. Most such loans bear fruit—and are also repaid in a timely fashion.[13]

Though small-scale measures may look too much like traditional "charity" to warrant serious consideration by professional developmentalists, to ignore such successes is to neglect some basic truths of human psychology. As the experience of Eastern Europe and other communist states has made abundantly clear, people do not work very hard at enterprises that are nominally owned by "the people" but in fact belong to the state. Nor do they care much for equipment, livestock, raw materials, and so forth that are provided by large bureaucratic enterprises. Even the managers of these enterprises have few incentives. By 1990, in the homeland of socialism, a committee created by Mikhail Gorbachev to recommend measures to prevent financial disaster put human truths and economic wisdom into a single statement:

> Humanity has not yet developed anything more efficient than a market economy. . . . The prerequisite to ensure effective functioning of the market [includes] *de jure* equality of all types of property, including private property. . . . Revenue from property should be recognized as lawful profit.[14]

The tragic paradox in the former Soviet Union is that the highest levels of government are now frantically trying to create decentralized economic activity through highly centralized decision-making.

Traditionally, the Catholic Church has been wary of unconditionally blessing private property and initiative because the Church associated them with "Protestant" individualism. The Catholic vision of the person and the community has regarded the two as interdependent. The Church has been right to emphasize this dimension, which has not been as absent from so-called capitalist societies as rhetoric extolling individualism may suggest. Capitalist democracies simply recognize the cooperative nature of markets, which is by and large what makes them so acceptable to large portions of their populations. Whatever imbalances or injustices markets may temporarily produce, moreover, are mostly corrected by the legal systems and social controls within these countries.

In recent years it has become increasingly clear that the state does not necessarily represent the interests of the community, and entrepreneurs do not represent merely the interests of individuals. Communities of entrepreneurs interact and serve one another's needs far more efficiently and even humanely than the gargantuan projects of centralized states. The poor in particular need a different path than that offered by state supports, however essential they may be in emergencies.

While cultural factors play an essential role in the achievement of economic success, predominantly Catholic countries have not displayed any insuperable cultural obstacles to development. It is also instructive that in the United States, despite all the talk about the Protestant work ethic, Catholics do better economically than their counterparts in any Protestant denomination. Among American religious groups, only Jews have a higher per capita income, and that reflects the demographic fact that they are an older population and older populations earn more. In Italy, Spain, and Portugal, under proper political conditions, Catholic virtues have fostered peace and prosperity.

The crucial components in the equation, however, are the conditions. The United States rewards enterprise and makes relatively secure the fruits of labor. While this may seem a natural condition to most residents of the First World, in the Third World, at least officially, it is rarely the case. Hernando de Soto's highly influential study *The Other Path* has revealed the plight of those who work very hard in places like Peru.[15] Since the legal system makes it difficult to start a business and the tax structure punishes productive enterprises, many of Peru's most dynamic citizens have been forced into the so-called "informal" economy. These are not people seeking merely to avoid regulation and taxes; they simply could not be productive under Peru's legal system. Given all the institutional handicaps, their productivity is impressive: they account for 60 per cent of Peru's gross domestic product; half of Lima's population live in houses built by the informal sector; 95 per cent of public transportation is "informal"; and the list goes on. In Peru, as elsewhere in the developing world, institutional reform would have immediate economic effects far more wide-ranging and far less fragile than those brought about by international aid.

The most essential reforms would aim at promoting political stability and the legal protection of private property. Real investment—i.e., investment that is expected to be productive and therefore profitable—can occur only where the danger of loss from social turmoil is minimal. Much has been written, for example, of the "immorality" of wealthy people in places like Latin America who export capital to Switzerland and the United States. Without question, this capital flight threatens every country in which it occurs with economic disaster. But the primary cause of capital flight is uncertainty about the political and economic decisions of Third World governments. While the rich in developing countries have serious social responsibilities, they are not under any divine command to go bankrupt pointlessly. Capital flows to Switzerland and the United States, particularly in times of crisis, because people know those countries are highly unlikely to confiscate property or demand exorbitant taxes, whatever the world situation. For all developing countries, guaranteeing investors a stable climate for the future is necessary to attract capital and entrepreneurs.

In all of *Populorum Progressio*, there is little suggestion that such institutional factors play a major role in development. No doubt, much of this is due to Paul's reliance on development experts in the 1960s who saw the needs of the Third World primarily in terms of income transfers. We now know that, absent internal reform in developing countries, such transfers are doomed to failure.

The Immediate Prospects

The historical verdict on socialism seems to be in. The socialist idea is already moribund and may not survive into the third millennium. But, like the death of God, the death of socialism may take unpredictable forms. Nietzsche was right about the death of a certain conception of God, just as euphoric Westerners are right about the demise of systematic socialism. Yet piecemeal forms of socialism and state direction persist, and may frustrate the very development so many people seem to favor. The irony is that central planning and redistribution, which have consistently failed wherever they have been tried at the national level, continue to be proposed as an international remedy. In countries like Mexico, however—countries that are finally beginning internal reform and opening to the outside world—the emphasis now is on removing obstacles to trade and growth rather than on extracting concessions from other governments that can have only marginal and temporary effects.

No one can argue baldly at present for state ownership of the means of production: the recent evidence runs too strongly against that error. But we have not yet exorcised the evil spirit that, as Nobel Prize–winning economist James Buchanan has described it, led us to believe "the romantic myth that politically organized authority could satisfy our needs more adequately than we might satisfy them ourselves through voluntary agreement, association and exchange." Myths die hard, and the particular myth of international development through worldwide regulation and redistribution seems destined to live on in new forms.

Since Paul VI made his attempt to contribute to world development, the Catholic Church, especially under John Paul II, has moved vigorously both to commend economic enterprise and to encourage the creation of proper institutional frameworks that register the lessons of recent experience. *Populorum Progressio* was a noble beginning, but Paul could not know all the things we now know about the problems and promises of development. The collapse of socialism does not mean that we should take a laissez-faire attitude toward peoples who still need various kinds of assistance to improve their future. Rather, we need to recognize, as John Paul II has done, that Catholic anthropology, taken in its fullness, demands vigorous if far different approaches to promoting a humane global economy. In the coming century it would be a great achievement for modern Catholic social teaching—as well as a fitting tribute to Paul's generous spirit—to bring its accumulated wisdom about the human person and human society to bear on the deep human problems of peoples who need to be liberated from poverty, political oppression, and several developmental myths.

8

Beyond Economics, Beyond Revolution
Octogesima Adveniens (1971)

JAMES FINN

Like *Quadragesimo Anno* and *Centesimus Annus*, Pope Paul VI's apostolic letter *Octogesima Adveniens* ("On the Eightieth Anniversary") is related by its very title to the first encyclical to consider the "social question," *Rerum Novarum* of 1891.

Although it is sometimes slighted in discussion of the social teachings of the Catholic Church, *Octogesima Adveniens* (1971) occupies a special place in that tradition. The particular teachings of all historical documents are subject to the vicissitudes wrought by changes in the conditions they address; *Octogesima Adveniens* is no exception. But it has been less touched by time than many of the social encyclicals. Indeed, it addresses national and international issues that will demand attention during and beyond the last decade of the twentieth century.

The special place of *Octogesima Adveniens* becomes clear when we look at it in relation to some of the other major church documents that discuss social issues. After *Rerum Novarum* there was a gap of forty years before the next major document, *Quadragesimo Anno*

James Finn is senior editor of *Freedom Review*, which is published by Freedom House. He is author and editor of numerous books and articles, including *Private Virtue and Public Policy: Catholic Social Thought and National Life*, a collection of essays on Catholic social teaching and the economy.

(1931), and another thirty before John XXIII produced *Mater et Magistra* (1961). Then, in a great burst of creative energy, five more documents followed in the next ten years, the last of which was *Octogesima Adveniens* in 1971. (It would be another ten years before John Paul II issued *Laborem Exercens*, the next link in the tradition, to be followed a decade later by *Centesimus Annus*.) This document should be read, then, in the context of this intense and ongoing effort, taken up most enthusiastically by Vatican II, to bring the Church's teachings on social justice to bear on pressing problems of the modern world.

In the time-honored fashion of papal encyclicals, all the social-justice documents produced during this brief period (1961–71) pay full obeisance to *Rerum Novarum* and stress the line of continuity even as they silently jettison some dated analyses of social justice. But many shifts in emphasis are noticeable. The mostly static conception of the world evident in the older documents has given way to a vision of dramatic flux; the triumphalistic tone has been muted; and the gap between the Church and the world has narrowed. The documents have shifted their emphasis from workers in the northern industrialized countries to increasingly concrete worldwide concerns, from the model of a monarchical church to that of the Church as a servant of humanity, and from the idea of a laity dutifully following papal initiatives to the notion of laity and clergy as co-innovators in the social order. These changes are everywhere evident in *Octogesima Adveniens*.

Two particular features of this document and its author, Paul VI, should be noted. First, unlike other documents of the social tradition, *Octogesima Adveniens* was not an encyclical addressed to all "the faithful," but was, rather, an open letter to Cardinal Maurice Roy, then president of the Council on the Laity and of the Pontifical Commission on Justice and Peace. It was Paul VI who established the commission, in order, as he said, "to bring the People of God to full awareness of its role at the present time," to promote the development of people, and to encourage "international social justice." These same purposes run through the letter to Cardinal Roy and the encyclical *Populorum Progressio*, which preceded it.

Second, it is useful to recall that Paul VI was the first modern pope to leave the confines of the Vatican to visit countries abroad.[1]

He mentions his travels early on in *Octogesima Adveniens* in the context of asserting that authentic apostles of the gospel emerge in all countries, under all conditions, and among all races, nations, and cultures:

> We have had the opportunity to meet these people, to admire them and to give them our encouragement in the course of our recent journeys. We have gone into the crowds and have heard their appeals, cries of distress and at the same time cries of hope. Under these circumstances we have seen in a new perspective the grave problems of our time. (*Octogesima Adveniens*, paragraph 2)

It is with these grave problems, as illuminated by his travels, that Paul VI's apostolic letter is concerned.

The travels of Paul VI and of the even more peripatetic John Paul II are important, not only in themselves, but as a symbol of the modern Church's efforts to understand the particular circumstances in which people live, and to address the social, economic, and political issues that touch their daily lives. To appreciate the full force of the changes the Church has been undergoing in this century, one has only to recall Pius XII, almost ethereal in his ascetic appearance, addressing in his elevated but highly abstract manner the harsh realities confronting the Church during the period of World War II. It is certainly a far cry from John Paul II, going from continent to continent, subjecting himself to rain and freezing cold, blazing sun and swirling dust, surrounded by people of different colors and different cultures. Paul VI is the transition figure in this transformation of the ministry of the Bishop of Rome. He is the first pope to assert, as he did more than once, that "today . . . the principal fact that we must all recognize is that the social question has become worldwide" (5).

The Church and the Modern World

Because it casts so wide a net, *Octogesima Adveniens* appears at first glance to be a sprawling document that heads off in many different directions simultaneously. Yet one concept unites its apparently disparate concerns. In *Populorum Progressio* Paul VI focused on an economy that "is in the service of man." Here he asserts that, though economic activity is necessary, "the need is felt to pass from economics to politics. . . . each man feels that in the social and economic field, both national and international, the ultimate decision rests with political power" (46). It is with that appreciation of political power in mind that Paul VI considers the many grave problems of our time: political power, its proper use, and its potential for abuse. This is the document's binding theme.

Paul VI begins his apostolic letter by saying that the eightieth anniversary of *Rerum Novarum* prompts him "to extend the teaching of our predecessors in response to the new needs of a changing world" (1). He lists and considers briefly many of these new needs and the social problems they engender. He notes the role that science and technology plays in altering the conditions in which humanity must make its way. The attitudes of people are also changing as, with greater education, they aspire to equality and the opportunity to participate in making the decisions that shape their lives. He then criticizes and strongly rejects ideologies and movements that acknowledge our problems but block, rather than advance, the liberation they promise. The letter concludes by recalling *Populorum Progressio* and its insistent message that "lay people should take up as their own proper task the renewal of the temporal order. . . . to take the initiative freely and to infuse a Christian spirit into the mentality, customs, laws and structures of the community in which they live" (48). *Octogesima Adveniens* is thus nothing if not a direct call to action: Catholics must face the same problems as their countrymen and, in light of the Church's social teaching, attempt to resolve them.

Among the troubling new social issues to which Paul VI calls attention are those associated with urbanization, its disruption of traditional structures of family and neighborhood, and the new forms of loneliness and alienation to which it gives rise; the increasing separation of youth from proper adult authority, education for freedom, and long-held beliefs and values; the growing independence of women and their right "to participate in cultural, economic, social and political life"; continuing racial discrimination; the need of workers to adapt to changing modes of work, as well as their right to emigrate in search of better working conditions; the expanding ability of the media to transmit news and information worldwide almost instantly and, thus, to transform mentalities, organizations, and even entire societies; and, not least, the ill-considered exploitation of the environment that could threaten humanity itself.

Paul VI follows this list with a brief but pregnant paragraph in which he asserts that aspirations to equality and participation arise in these new conditions even as science and technology continue to change the conditions themselves. Nor has the pace of change slowed since *Octogesima Adveniens*. The small silicon chip has markedly altered the workplace, for example; as computers and facsimile machines enhance productivity, modes of work change, making obsolete older machines and the skills required to use them. In many instances new methods of production reduce the need for unskilled workers and place an even higher premium on education.

The media have a definite—if not always clearly defined—influence on the "internationalization" of the problems the pope mentions. In the decades since *Octogesima Adveniens*, television has not only strengthened its hold, powerfully projecting the values and attitudes it chooses to emphasize; it has become more specialized, allowing a wider range of choice for consumers, notably young people. This places a special obligation on those who provide what is chosen. Viewers can learn about, and be moved by, catastrophes, natural and man-made, in countries around the world. People in poor countries are increasingly exposed to the high living standards, and even extravagances, of people in richer countries, allowing them to make comparisons that were formerly unavailable to them. Such changes brought about by science and technology show no sign of slowing down. The world will continue to be presented with new opportunities and new problems, and with the prospect of what Paul VI dared to call "an original mode of knowledge and a new civilization" (20).

To the extent that people are becoming better informed and better educated, their desire and demand for equality and participation has grown. These impulses create pressure for the recognition of human rights and their protection through the rule of law. But legislation, while certainly necessary, is not sufficient to establish proper relationships of equality and justice. These must be bolstered through other agencies.

It is not for the State or even for political parties, which would be closed unto themselves, to try to impose an ideology by means that would lead to a dictatorship over minds, the worst kind of all. It is for cultural and religious groupings, in the freedom of acceptance which they presume, to develop in the social body, disinterestedly and in their own ways, those ultimate convictions on the nature, origin and end of man and society. (25)

Then Paul VI evaluates with care and precision the principal alternatives that have been presented to us in the late twentieth century. And it is here that recent history has most clearly overtaken this letter, even as it confirms the analysis the letter provides.

Quoting liberally from *Pacem in Terris*, Paul VI points out those aspects of Marxism that allowed some Christians to idealize it and, in various degrees and ways, to join forces with it. But the pope goes on to note that Marxist ideology, analysis, and praxis inevitably lead to a "totalitarian and violent society." Here, Pope Paul strikes a more sober note than *Pacem in Terris* and *Populorum Progressio*, both of which carefully refrained from affixing a label to any revolutionary group or movement. Perhaps influenced by the radicalisms of the late 1960s, Paul VI explicitly names and rejects Marxist ideology, which denies all transcendence to man, as false and damaging. At the same time he also rejects those liberal ideologies that deny any limitations can rightly be placed on individual freedom in the name of a common good.

In their faith and in the teachings of the Church, Christians, says Paul VI, have the resources to discern the limitations of various ideologies, among which he names "bureaucratic socialism, technocratic capitalism and authoritarian democracy" (37). It is because of the evident deficiencies of these systems that people look to utopias, which have escapist appeal but which can, at their best, suggest previously unglimpsed possibilities.

The validity of Paul VI's analysis has since been answered in the historical order by the definitive collapse of the Soviet Union and the communist regimes of Eastern Europe. In the conceptual order it has been answered, at least in its economic aspects, by *Centesimus Annus*, with its new and remarkably sympathetic analysis of a market, or free, economy.

Political and Economic Lessons

These, then, are the issues addressed by the apostolic letter and the ecclesiological context in which the document was written. The Church is not morally disarmed by the severity of the world's problems. Drawing on its rich resources, it can challenge excessive concentrations of power on the social, cultural, and even political levels. In so doing, it confronts the ultimate limitations of economics. That is why there is a need to pass from economics to politics.

Pope Paul VI noted that the thrust of the modern quest for equality and participation was toward some form of democratic society, but that no existing political-economic model was completely satisfactory: an irrefutable observation. With this in mind, and in light of the tasks the pope assigned to the political order, we can survey the contemporary international scene, where great changes are taking place.

It may be well to recall what, in Catholic social doctrine, the state is for and how it is modified by a democratic polity. First of all, the state provides order in human affairs through juridical structures, which authoritatively settle the differences that inevitably arise in human communities. The conflicts that we observe in, for example, Somalia, the former Yugoslavia, Russia, and India do not, as some analysts argue, point to a decline in the state. Rather, they underline the importance of the state, which remains the principal agent in international affairs.

The collapse of communism has shaken the social foundations on which a number of regimes have rested. Contrary to what some have suggested, that collapse has not left a vacuum into which different forms of democracy can flow unimpeded. It has left, instead, a legacy of degradation that permeates all aspects of life— the environment, the political and economic systems, the social and spiritual realms. The last of these may prove most critical. For while the peoples of Eastern and Central Europe must surely attend to the creation or rebuilding of sound political and economic systems, those systems will be unstable unless they are based on an underlying moral order. Without such a moral order, efforts at democratization will fail.

This is precisely what Václav Havel argued when, as president of

Czechoslovakia, he addressed a joint session of the U.S. Congress on February 21, 1990. Referring to what the people of his country were forced to endure under communism, he said:

This specific experience I speak of has given me one great certainty: that consciousness precedes being, and not the other way around, as the Marxists claim. For this reason, the salvation of our world can be found only in the human heart, in the power of humans to reflect, in human meekness and responsibility. Without a global revolution in the sphere of human consciousness, nothing will change for the better in the sphere of our being as humans, and the catastrophe towards which the world is headed—be it ecological, social, demographic, or a general breakdown of civilization—will be unavoidable.

The sentiment and tone of Havel's statement are reminiscent not only of the essays he wrote during his imprisonment under the communists but also of *Octogesima Adveniens*. For if the phrase "consciousness precedes being" is understood to apply to the political economy (the context in which Havel used it), his statement has clear analogues in the apostolic letter, which speaks of modern conditions that "put the very future of man in jeopardy," and which must be considered "in the wider context of a new civilization."

The damage communism wrought on the environment is glaring: land, air, and water were routinely and recklessly poisoned, and life expectancy in Eastern Europe was drastically lowered. The corruption of the social and spiritual order is more subtle, but no less pernicious. Communism deliberately eroded the social ties that bind people in common understanding. Its rulers systematically introduced fear and mutual distrust into the society.

The struggles we now observe in the former Soviet bloc reflect the people's efforts to restructure the social and economic orders so that new and improved states might arise. If these states move in the direction promoted by Paul VI, one that allows the growing aspirations of people to be more fully realized, they will move toward democracy. For it is democracy—which is based upon consent, voluntarism, and popular participation—that depends upon and grounds its moral legitimacy in the sovereignty of the people. As Quentin Quade has said, "The democratic nations, in their roots and their natures, are assertions about human nature itself, and about the value of individuals."[2] Thus societies that have cast off totalitarian or authoritarian regimes and now claim to favor democracy must reconstitute themselves in their moral self-understanding.

The desire for equality and participation is, of course, not limited to countries of the collapsed communist empire; it is felt in countries that have long described themselves as democratic and others that would claim that designation today. As the noted political scientist Samuel Huntington has observed: "Between 1974 and 1990, at least thirty countries made transitions to democracy."[3] This shift confirms what Paul VI said about the aspirations of people in his apostolic letter of 1971.

Prerequisites for Democracy

But this heartening change in the political climate should not blind us to some harsh realities. Democracy is demanding and its secure establishment a true achievement. As the peoples in Eastern Europe and Russia are learning at great cost, there must be pre-political conditions for democracy to take root. Democracy must be nurtured by certain habits of the citizenry and by a variety of voluntary organizations if it is to perform as expected.

Regrettably, there is no common understanding of the meaning of democracy. (John Paul II offered a usable working definition in *Centesimus Annus*: "The Church values the democratic system inasmuch as it ensures the participation of citizens in making political choices, guarantees to the governed the possibility both of electing and holding accountable those who govern them, and of replacing them through peaceful means when appropriate" [46].) Nor is there a clear understanding of how the political order is related to the economy. This remains true even though it has been substantiated that the correlation between democracy and free market economies is high.[4]

The difficulties of agreeing on the meaning of the term "democratic" become clear if we look at some Latin American countries that are usually described as such. In February 1990 Violeta Chamorro was elected president of Nicaragua in a free and fair election. But the Sandinistas, whom the electorate threw out of political power, still retain control of significant sectors of the society, thus thwarting the expressed will of the people. In El Salvador, the judiciary, far from being independent, is subject to political control; one of the principal criteria for a democracy is, thereby, abrogated. In Mexico the institutionalized revolutionary party (PRI) has retained unbroken control of the federal government for more than six decades, often stifling voices of opposition. Brazil emerged from military rule in 1985, but not from corruption and a high degree of control by a small group of the nation's elite—labor, big business, and regional interests. Though these countries may, perhaps, be considered democracies, they still suffer from serious political deficiencies.

Those deficiencies are offset, however, by encouraging signs that lend support to Paul VI's belief in the power of people's democratic aspirations. In an unofficial 1993 plebiscite, the residents of Mexico City voted overwhelmingly for the right to elect their own government instead of accepting politically appointed officials.[5] In Brazil, President Fernando Collor de Mello was officially charged with corruption and, under public pressure and the threat of impeachment, resigned. He thereby earned the distinction of being the first Latin American president in history to be removed by constitutional procedures. These are signs of a changing political culture.[6] Polls show that people want to rid their governments of corruption, but they do not want to do it by returning to dictatorship. They are pushing toward sound democracies.

The Cultural Dimension

Functioning democracies have functioning economic systems; thus democracies are among the wealthiest countries in the world. Preeminent among these countries in the post–Cold War world is the United States. What obligations to the rest of the world does America's wealth and power place upon it?

The primary agents for change within other countries must be their own people. The United States, however, for its own welfare as well as that of other countries—and particularly those that would pattern themselves on democratic principles and practices—must play a large role in international affairs. By precept and example, and with various kinds of material and technological aid, we can help poorer countries restructure their political and economic systems. Substantial efforts to do so are presently being made.

But, as a number of encyclicals on the social question have insisted, a society cannot be measured only in terms of the material benefits it makes available to itself and to others, however valuable they are. All countries and all societies must be measured in both their material and spiritual dimensions. What value does a society put upon the human person? How does it treat the poorest and most vulnerable? What does it teach other societies about the dignity of each human being? How does a country transmit those understandings to other people, other countries?

In America, the answers to these questions raised by Paul VI will depend in part upon the workings of the U.S. government. But they will depend even more upon social and civic institutions—the churches and synagogues, families, neighborhoods, and voluntary associations—that have traditionally educated our society in the habits, or virtues, of loyalty, honesty, temperate behavior, responsibility, self-control, compassion, and love.

Measuring shifts in the quality of our national life is no easy business, but it is not wholly beyond our ability to make informed judgments. Traditional family life is under assault in the United States, and some of the alternatives to it are not performing well.[7] The changes over the last thirty years in the incidence of crime, children born out of wedlock, abortion, single-parent families, teen-age suicides, divorce, children in poverty, and the prison population are disheartening. A country fully aware of its moral obligations would not choose to export the values or practices that contributed to its own cultural decline. But much of the understanding of our culture will be transmitted by what Paul VI called "a new power" wielded by "the media of social communications."

> One cannot but ask about those who really hold this power . . . the effect of their activity on the exercise of individual liberty, both in the political and ideological spheres and in social, economic and cultural life. The men who hold this power have a grave moral responsibility with respect to the truth of the information that they spread, the needs and the reactions that they generate and the values which they put forward. (20)

American culture is vigorous and vibrant; it is undoubtedly attractive to others around the world. Willy-nilly, we will communicate who and what we are, exporting both our questionable and beneficial cultural values along with our political and economic values and our technology. Thus not only are the political, economic, and cultural aspects of our national life mingled; our domestic concerns and our international responsibilities are inextricably intertwined. For our own sake and for that of others, we need to remedy the deep flaws in our society.[8] What happens here shapes ideas and behaviors elsewhere, for good and for ill.

Justice and Real-World Political Systems

In the same year that *Octogesima Adveniens* was written, the Synod of Bishops produced "Justice in the World," a document that Paul VI endorsed and made public. It states that "action on behalf of justice and participation in the transformation of the world fully appear to us as a constitutive dimension of the preaching of the gospel, or, in other words, of the Church's mission for the redemption of the human race and its liberation from every oppressive situation" (6). That is, the Christian who strives to achieve justice for himself and others is acting in full accordance with the gospel; he is, indeed, proclaiming the good news by his very actions. This is a variation of Paul VI's statements that "politics are a demanding manner of living the Christian commitment to the service of others" (46) and that men and women today demand "a greater sharing in responsibility and decision making" (47).

The current turning point in the world's history presents a rare opportunity to introduce the sort of active participation and decision-making that *Octogesima Adveniens* recognizes as being so fundamental. There is a chance to encourage initiative, risk-taking, imagination, and mutual trust in areas where these qualities have long been squelched or undervalued. Encyclicals that followed this apostolic letter show how these qualities can affect both the political order and the economic order.

Those who look to the Church's social doctrine as a guide to a specific political-economic agenda should pause to evaluate the encyclicals' critique of various regimes and systems. The Church's social doctrine is quite modest. That modesty is nowhere more evident than in *Octogesima Adveniens*. Recognizing the wide diversity of conditions in which Christians and others live, the document warns that "it is difficult for us to offer a unified message and to put forward a solution which has universal validity" (4). Guided by the Church's fundamental conviction about the dignity and value of every human life—a conviction that is the basis of Catholic social teaching—particular Christian communities need to analyze their own situations and to reflect, judge, and act upon them.

On this basis Christians and non-Christians, believers and non-believers, can join in constructing societies in which each person can strive for a more profound understanding of what it means to be fully human, and in which each citizen can be an active participant in the social order.

In attempting to build the future without a sense of the transcendent, communism misread human nature and thus foundered. Its system to model and reshape human nature into "the New Man" could not contain what it could not comprehend and fell apart. That disintegration was initially observed in political and economic arenas. But if the newly forming economies and political structures of those countries emerging from totalitarianism are to be secure, they must be built on a public moral order that embodies the principles of equality and participation.

Equality and political liberty are frequently at odds, of course, and, as Paul VI stated, different countries and situations will vary in the ways they concretely implement these principles. But only those economic and political structures that fully appreciate the dignity of the human person and that respect the aspirations of every individual to shape his or her own life will long endure. That lasting theme of modern Catholic social teaching was given a particularly sharp political edge in *Octogesima Adveniens*—the lessons of which remain highly relevant today.

Depending on their role, vocation, and circumstances, men and women will have varying degrees of responsibility and obligation within their communities. But all Christians are called on to act in the light of the gospel—to treat every individual with dignity and to respect every individual's inalienable rights. In the realm of human rights, such assertions have succeeded in subverting cruel and totalitarian structures. And these values can unite Christians with other people of good will to reclaim decayed areas of society, to bring aid and relief to the poorest and most vulnerable people among us, and to help restructure failed political and economic systems. This formidable agenda demands the most responsible use of political power, which *Octogesima Adveniens* seeks to guide.

9

Work: The Human Environment
Laborem Exercens (1981)

ROBERT A. DESTRO

L aborem Exercens ("On Human Work," 1981), Pope John Paul II's commemoration of the ninetieth anniversary of the publication of *Rerum Novarum* (1891), is an insightful commentary on the nature of the human spirit. It continues and expands the Church's reflections on the "social question" by shifting the focus from where it traditionally was, on the relationship of capital and labor, to work as the integrative force that shapes an individual's identity, character, and dignity.[1] *Centesimus Annus* (1991), "The One Hundredth Year," marks the passage of a century of the Church's discourse with the world concerning the moral dimensions of the workplace. In tone and emphasis, the two later encyclicals bear the indelible stamp of the Polish working man, now the pope, who wrote them. Read together, they underscore his continuing efforts to challenge the mistaken notion that human existence can be hermetically divided between the "practical things" of the world and the "spiritual things" of the Kingdom of God.

Laborem Exercens appeared on September 14, 1981, nearly four

Robert A. Destro is associate professor of law at the Columbus School of Law at The Catholic University of America in Washington, D.C., where he also serves as director of its Law and Religion program. From 1983 to 1989, he served as a commissioner on the U.S. Commission on Civil Rights.

163

months after its intended publication date. John Paul II's convalescence from an assassination attempt, widely rumored to have been the work of Eastern-bloc governments fearful of his influence on the emerging trade-union movement in Poland, prevented him from finishing the encyclical by the May 15 anniversary of *Rerum Novarum*.[2] *Centesimus Annus* was published on May 1, 1991, and could not have been more timely. Though it can be read as an extended commentary on the death of communism, its real function is to remind those left standing at the grave that they are obliged not only to inter the corpse but also to see to the physical and moral welfare of the millions of family members left behind.[3]

The essential thrust and direction of both encyclicals stand out clearly. John Paul II intends to speak plainly, now and in the future, to *all* who work—from common laborers in the field and unskilled workers on the shop floor, to institutional investors, bankers, bureaucrats, and politicians whose decisions shape the direction of the world's economy—about their respective places at the "great workbench." And *Centesimus Annus* emphasizes that each person *has* a place there: "the obligation to earn one's bread by the sweat of one's brow also presumes the right to do so" (paragraph 42).

The goal of *Laborem Exercens* was to aid the Church in its mission "to form a spirituality of work which will help all people to come closer, through work, to God, the creator and redeemer, to participate in his salvific plan for man and the world, and to deepen their friendship with Christ" (paragraph 111). Rather than viewing work as merely the "objective" or tangible result of human endeavor, it considers work in its "subjective" sense—that is, as "a fundamental dimension of man's existence" (12). The Church thus joins ranks with those, like David Meakin, who have explored the reasons early man is called *Homo faber*, the toolmaker. Man produces not just to satisfy his needs; he works and creates for the sake of creation.[4]

> Work—and not least manual work—is an integral part of our humanity and our intelligence. It dictates not only our relationship to nature, to our environment, but thereby also the working and scope of our consciousness itself, for consciousness is born of that active confrontation with nature.[5]

By focusing on the spiritual dimensions of work and its role in God's salvific plan, *Laborem Exercens* serves as an important reminder that the "social question" is, in its entirety, a moral and ethical one. The encyclical discusses the *ethical* and *human* dimensions of work without specific references to either Western-style capitalism, which turns work into a commodity, or Marxist-Leninist socialism. As a result, it is able to criticize the failure of economic systems across the political spectrum (East, West, and Third World). And precisely because these encyclicals do *not* offer a set of political or economic prescriptions, but rather examine the common good of the people whose work provides the foundation of the world economy, their many significant insights should be considered carefully by those making economic policy.

The Social and Spiritual Dimensions of Work

The main theme of both *Laborem Exercens* and *Centesimus Annus* is that, in work, humankind shares a common social and spiritual mandate. We are "to subject to [ourselves] the earth and all that it contains, and to govern the world with justice and holiness. . . . Thus, by the subjection of all things to man, the name of God would be wonderful in all the earth" (*Laborem Exercens* [*LE*], 112, quoting *Gaudium et Spes*, paragraph 64). Since this is God's design for us and we act in his image when working, any analysis of moral questions affecting work must proceed from the premise that work is a good thing for man, not simply the wages of sin. To work is both a right *and* a duty.[6]

Perhaps because such an approach is firmly rooted in the Bible, it also makes eminent practical sense. Whether or not one believes in a creator, the material and human resources necessary for work *are* gifts, passed down through successive generations. An ethical perspective tempers the human right to discover and exploit the gifts of nature by subjecting our birthright to its correlative social duty: to act justly and, thereby, to further the common good.

Centesimus Annus expands upon the relationship of human right and social duty elaborated in *Laborem Exercens,* and places the "social question" first highlighted by Leo XIII into a broader social and ethical "ecological question." This latter term is both interesting and significant. Though often used as a synonym for "environment," "ecology" is defined generally as "the study or science of the relationships between organisms and their environments."[7] By shifting the focus on the "social question" from inanimate "conditions" to the dignity of persons and the ethics of their actions in work relationships, Pope John Paul brought a fresh perspective to what had become a moralistic debate that seemed, at times, to be strangely out of touch with lived experience.

Thus, where *Laborem Exercens* underscores the social nature of work and the fact that intangible "human resources" (such as education and knowledge) are the foundation upon which human inventiveness, artistry, and creativity depend (53–54), *Centesimus Annus* elaborates and reflects upon the degree to which labor is an extremely important human activity in society and culture. Emphasizing that both dimensions of work involve others, *Centesimus Annus* stresses the point made in *Laborem Exercens*: that it is impossible for any person, nation, or culture to speak of complete self-sufficiency. We are mutually dependent, not only on our contemporaries, but on those who have come before.[8] "In a sense, man finds [these resources] already prepared, ready for him to discover them and to use them correctly in the productive process" (*LE*, 54). We depend on God and one another and must act—if we are to further God's plan—in a manner consistent with "the moral obligation of work understood in its wide sense" (*LE*, 73, 78–80).

Whatever we bring to the "great workbench," then, is instrumental only. Its function is not, in the view of the Church, to maximize profit to the point of injustice, or to serve the ends of what John Paul calls the "rigid capitalism" of those who claim an exclusive dominion over the means of production (*LE*, 66). Rather, capital, properly understood as a collection of tangibles and intangibles, is one of the tools we utilize, individually and collectively, "to realize [our] humanity, to fulfill the calling to be a person that is [ours] by reason of [our] very humanity" (*LE*, 23).

That biblical—and, some would contend, Marxist—premise informs every point in both encyclicals: the identity of labor and capital (defined in human terms) and the resultant priority of labor over capital (defined as things); the philosophical and operational similarities among capitalist, socialist, and Marxist economic systems; the right of labor to form unions and associations as a basic human right; moral limits on the right to use private property; and the public obligation to acknowledge the importance of, and compensate justly, work for which there is no clear "market price," but which is essential to the life and development of family and community (e.g., the value of a mother's labor, or a father's presence, in the home).

The path from *Rerum Novarum* is thus nicely drawn through the historical topography. Up to and through *Quadragesimo Anno*, the primary theme of Catholic social teaching was "the impact of industrialization on the dignity and rights of workers" in the early and adolescent phases of the Industrial Revolution. Given the nature of early technology and the problems it created, the focus of these encyclicals was *local*: on workers within their respective industries and nations (*LE*, 6, 8).

The next phase, which ran from Pius XII through Paul VI, focused on questions of distribution of the fruits of industrialization, on "economic justice among nations, . . . international social justice."[9] Paul VI, responding to the increasingly global dimensions of the world economy, was the first to highlight some of the transnational issues that will dominate the twenty-first century—the obligations and behavior of the multinational corporation, world hunger, and environmental concerns—in his apostolic letter *Octogesima Adveniens*. *Laborem Exercens* continues that trend at an even higher level of generality in its reflection on the social and spiritual nature of work and its role in God's design.

Now, one hundred years after Pope Leo addressed the "new things," *Centesimus Annus* reminds us that, despite all that is new in the world, the ethical dimensions of human behavior—and the promise of redemption—have not changed one bit. Seen in context, *Laborem Exercens* can best be described as an "update" and expansion of the Church's response to the industrial and technological revolutions, while *Centesimus Annus* is a reflection upon the moral problems facing a world that is only now entering a "post-War" *and post-industrial* period (*Centesimus Annus* [*CA*], 28).

The key to both encyclicals is to be found in their *approach* to questions of capital and labor. Though *Laborem Exercens* may not have convinced everyone that Christian ethics is a suitable lens through which to view the operations of every economic system on earth, the collapse of communism and the emergence of vast trading blocs and electronic "superhighways" should leave them with little doubt that *Centesimus Annus* is an important economic blueprint in its own right. The pope also expressly states, of course, that "the Church has no models to present" (*CA*, 43), and strongly criticizes the failings of each economic system. *Centesimus Annus* makes it abundantly clear, moreover, that specific suggestions should be viewed only "within the framework of different historical situations, [and] through the efforts of all those who responsibly confront concrete problems in all their social, economic, political and cultural aspects."

This, too, is an important teaching; for it sheds considerable light on the pope's thinking concerning the respective roles of laity and clergy. It is the vocation of the *laity* to deal with the specifics of "concrete problems in all their social, economic, political and cultural aspects, as these interact with one another."[10] It is the duty of the Church to "offer her social teaching as an *indispensable and ideal orientation*" for the resolution of practical problems (*CA*, 43). Thus, just as the relevance of unions and the need for other forms of worker solidarity and collective action will vary according to the situation in each local or regional labor market, the wisdom and utility of any specific "operational" suggestion, including those made by the pope himself about the role of international organizations, is opened both to good-faith difference of opinion and to empirical investigation. In the final analysis, both *Laborem Exercens* and *Centesimus Annus* propose an ethical *outlook*, not a specific plan of action.

Integrating the Workplace and the World

Though many commentators have found in *Laborem Exercens* a ringing criticism of capitalism and a vindication of what Gregory Baum has called "the recent shift to the left in Church teaching,"[11] the real culprit the pope identifies there and in *Centesimus Annus* is materialism—the dialectical materialism of Marxists and the practical materialism, or consumerism, of just about everyone else. In John Paul II's view, materialism is not so much a reflective philosophical stance as simply "a particular way of evaluating things . . . on the grounds of a certain hierarchy of goods based on the greater *immediate* attractiveness of what is material" (*LE*, 61; emphasis added). As applied to labor, this "error of economism" takes the form of considering human labor solely according to its "economic purpose" (*LE*, 60).

What the pope calls "economism" might be described more accurately as economic tunnel vision. Whatever it is called, it is a serious error that was, and continues to be, made not only by governments but also by representatives of labor and management. Economics is not bookkeeping. Rather, it is the study of human behavior in the marketplace, and history demonstrates all too clearly that common laborers can be as materialistic and self-centered as the captains of their respective industries.

American labor unions provide a valuable lesson. No longer able to deliver large wage and benefit increases to their members because of various market forces and global competition, unions in the United States have suffered a precipitous drop in their membership—from 35 per cent of the non-agricultural labor force in the mid-1950s to about 15 per cent in 1993.[12] To stave off corresponding losses in political influence and in their ability to affect the wage-and-benefit packages offered by non-union employers—as well as for their very survival—unions must now inquire deeply into the purpose of their existence.[13] Lawsuits challenging the right of unions to compel their members to support political agendas unrelated to bargaining, representation, or professional issues make even more urgent questions about the duty and right to work.[14] As John Paul himself points out:

> The role of unions is not to "play politics" in the sense that the expression is commonly understood today. Unions do not have the character of political parties struggling for power; they should not be subject to the decision of political parties or have too close links with them. In fact, in such a situation, they easily lose contact with their specific role, which is to secure the just rights of workers within the framework of the common good of the whole of society; instead they become an instrument used for other purposes. (*LE*, 98)

If unions are to survive and prosper, they must rediscover the human dimension of the solidarity that the pope values so highly in the labor-union movement. Issuing discount-rate credit cards to their members may be a small step in the larger task of meeting the human needs of trade unionists, but it is a step in the right direction: back to the original conception of unions as sources of solidarity, support, and mutual benefit.[15] Also needed is a moral dimension—a *raison d'être* rooted in concern for the individual dignity and freedom of each individual worker—to counteract the tendency of both unions and managers to equate self-interest with the common good.[16]

Centesimus Annus builds on these points by encouraging management to raise its consciousness as well. Ethical stewardship of managerial responsibility requires a reasoned balance between the need to demonstrate a short-term profit and concern for the long-term viability of a company within the global economy. *Laborem Exercens* and *Centesimus Annus* clearly urge that this balance be achieved through more humanistic, justice-oriented, and economically responsible approaches to company operations and employee relations. To date, however, the threat of legislation or legal action has been a more effective spur in the United States.

The transition to a different model of corporate governance and labor relations has been a difficult one, and it is far from over. Despite Adam Smith's still timely warning about the peril of leaving a worker "no occasion to exercise his invention in finding out expedients for removing difficulties,"[17] the fixation on short-term performance, widely decried in business publications as the cause of much economic dislocation, remains. In the end, only international competition, particularly from foreign (especially Japanese) multinationals, compounded by the ever-present threat of bankruptcy or hostile takeover, seems to have provided the impetus for a more enlightened use of human-capital resources. *Laborem Exercens* and *Centesimus Annus* make the same point, though from a moral perspective: materialism is capitalism's worst enemy.

The Identity of Capital and Labor

Among the most intriguing, and provocative, points raised by *Laborem Exercens* is the *identity* of capital and labor from a human perspective. In this view, "capital" is material; people claim it and put it to work. Described by some commentators as essentially Marxist in its origins (because Marx viewed capital as "congealed labor"), the attempt in *Laborem Exercens* to transcend the historical antagonism between management and labor can be seen as suggesting a "third way" between capitalism and Marxism.

There is a grave difficulty with this analysis, however. In *Laborem Exercens* the pope rejects "rigid capitalism," communist centralism, and the essentially socialist claim that what might be termed "democratic collectivism" provides a meaningful alternative to individual and institutional greed. But that rejection is rooted in a worldview stuck in the late nineteenth century. By the time he came to write *Centesimus Annus*, John Paul's own perspective concerning the world in the late twentieth century had changed. He sees that the world is different in ways that have moral meaning, but reaffirms the eternal relevance and verity of the message of Jesus Christ.

Microprocessors and software underscore the ephemeral nature of the concepts of "ownership" and knowledge. It makes no difference whether an ownership claim relates to tangible assets like machines or factories, or to intangible assets like capital stock, debt, credit, or information. "Ownership," as opposed to mere possession, is a claim of right or priority due respect by others. Increasingly, the only records of such claims are electronic or digital images stored on magnetic or optical media. One cannot "own" or control such images any more than one can "own" knowledge itself: fortunes can be made or lost, debts created or extinguished, and ownership claims seriously compromised by the push of a button or an electric power surge. Small wonder that computer-related crime—including the theft (piracy) or destruction of digitized information—is currently one of the most common forms of larceny.

Today, as is the case in common law over the centuries, the best evidence of ownership is the exercise of dominion over and the use of one's goods in a creative process—a process that, inevitably, depends to some degree on the work and creativity of others. "Rigid capitalism," as described in *Laborem Exercens*, turns out to be, in the end, as chimerical as "pure" Marxism. The marketplace—people acting in pursuit of their respective political, social, and economic goals—will not long tolerate either one.

The moral issues for the late twentieth century are thus correctly identified: *who* shall have access to the marketplace of knowledge, ideas, and work—and on what conditions? *Centesimus Annus* notes the reality of today's marketplace:

> Whereas at one time the decisive factor of production was *the land*, and later capital—understood as a total complex of the instruments of production—today the decisive factor is increasingly *man himself*, that is, his knowledge, especially his scientific knowledge, his capacity for interrelated and compact organization, as well as his ability to perceive the needs of others and to satisfy them. (32)

There are, to be sure, larger-than-life "captains of industry," multinational corporations, and governments that, individually and collectively, manipulate markets to maximize profits at the expense of the common good. But the pope rightly sees that the problems looming ahead in the third millennium are primarily ethical in nature. The great human and economic costs we will endure if we do not undertake to use our talents to bring everyone with ability to the "great workbench" has less to do with ownership than it does with a failure of stewardship.

Thus the distinction in *Laborem Exercens* between "those who do the work without being the owners of the means of production, and . . . those who act as entrepreneurs and who own these means or represent the owner" (63), more accurately describes the situation in the West one hundred years ago than it does today. It also correctly captures the vision of socialist centralism and of what passes for an economic system in much of the Third World. At least in the contemporary United States, however, the capitalist owners of the means of production include workers with direct stock holdings in their companies, and company and union pension funds owning millions of dollars of "capital" in trust for the benefit of workers and their families.

Not surprisingly, these pension funds are legally bound to maximize return on investment by the terms of their agreements with the workers themselves; their duty is to work for the good of the collective enterprise, but nowhere is it written that they must inevitably engage in exploitation of others to do so. Of course, such "prudent investor" rules greatly magnify the difficulty for pension managers whose portfolios include substantial holdings in profitable multinational companies doing business in repressive regimes or abusing their employees or the environment at home or abroad. But this simply underscores the point that broad-based ownership of the means of production will not, by itself, suffice to make the international economy just. Taking moral responsibility for what one owns or manages is also necessary—and it is also good for business.

The case of small businesses having fifteen employees or fewer is a good illustration of the weakness of the alleged dichotomy between capital and labor. As the primary source of job creation in capitalist economies, such businesses are so small that the physical, emotional, and professional proximity of the "capitalist" to the persons who are "the work force" virtually obliterates the distinction between them. Responsibility is undertaken because the survival of the business, if not that of the family of the entrepreneur, depends on it. Those who work in such businesses know it "in their bones." The near-routine exemption of "small business" from otherwise onerous workplace regulations demonstrates, albeit imperfectly, that the United States government knows it too. Both the recently adopted Americans With Disabilities Act and the Family and Medical Leave Act of 1993 contain exemptions for "small business."[18]

This does not mean, however, that small businesses (including professional-service companies such as small law firms or grocery stores) are immune from the siren song of materialism and its attendant abuses, or that the solidarity that comes from the sense of shared endeavor and challenge will overcome bad economic or management practices. What it does mean is that institutions and economies that "work" to their fullest potential do so because they are committed to a vision of the common good of the enterprise, as defined by the management or ownership and agreed to by those who participate in it. In short, it is the capitalists (whether individuals or millions of shareholders), managers, workers, consumers, and market regulators who together, in the words of a long-running commercial for an investor-owned Ohio electric utility, "are the company." To the extent that mechanisms exist for contact and dispute resolution among these divergent groups, each of which may have a different sense of "the good," the only missing ingredient is a common, humanistic ethic of work. By maintaining the focus on the human dimension, *Laborem Exercens* goes a long way toward suggesting one.

The Human Dimension of the Worker and Workplace

Though John Paul II is elaborating a moral argument for the dignity of labor in *Laborem Exercens*, his experience as a working man imparts an internal cohesiveness, tone, and force to the text. This gives the encyclical an even higher degree of credibility than other papal statements enjoy.

Because it is a document concerning ethics—a letter formally addressed to the Church and directed to working people and governments rather than owners and managers—*Laborem Exercens* is not full of concrete suggestions for change. But it does include proposals of a more general nature that make good sense morally and economically: just wages, benefits, and labor-management relations (including non-discrimination in the workplace); education and training adequate to meet the needs of individuals to participate in the *existing* economy; child and family welfare as a legitimate concern of both business and government; the need for the economy to utilize the skills of persons with disabilities and immigrants who want little more than an opportunity to work to better themselves and their families.

How to implement these proposals is left, as it should be, to the discretion of those who are charged with the practical responsibility of making economic judgments. As the pope notes in another context, "It is not for the Church to analyze scientifically the consequences that these changes may have on human society" (*LE*, 6). But only a fool would ignore the economic imperatives they reflect.

The commentary that followed *Laborem Exercens*, including the U.S. Catholic bishops' pastoral letter on the American economy and the critical analysis that attended it, makes it clear that the Church speaks most effectively when it speaks in ethical terms, makes general suggestions, and invites lay reflection on the practical problem of translating exhortation into concrete change across the spectrum of human economic undertaking: capital, labor, management, and consumer (who is, after all, one who labors as well).

Church institutions, particularly its universities, have a special obligation to demonstrate, in empirical terms accessible to anyone with a sense of profit and loss, that an ethical approach to business will improve the "bottom line." Business ethics has, in recent years, become a "hot" topic. Though *Laborem Exercens* may not have focused on this dimension of the Church's mission, concentrating instead on its message to the East, it did suggest a different direction for the West, and *Centesimus Annus* confirms that course. Church institutions, to the extent that their endowments are healthy, can no longer remain comfortable in the conformist mainstream of "concerned" social criticism. The Church is on a mission to evangelize the capitalists themselves.

Evangelization of the world economy is, in fact, the central purpose and starting point of *Centesimus Annus*. In this encyclical John Paul makes it clear that the Church is not simply a far-off, moralistic observer of intolerable "conditions" in the workplace and economy but a "citizen" (*CA*, 5) with the right and obligation to elaborate the moral underpinnings of its vision of the common good. He recognizes that "different cultures are basically different ways of facing the question of the meaning of personal existence," and that evangelization efforts aimed specifically at the world of work will, over the long term, contribute significantly to "the culture of the various nations" (*CA*, 24).

This important insight should remind both clergy and laity (particularly in the United States) that *religious* education is, and always has been, part of the foundation of the democratic vision of the common good. Just as the evangelization of the young has lasting ramifications, the Church's attempt to evangelize the workplace will cast new light on the all-important human components of our economy. "It is on this level that *the Church's specific and decisive contribution to true culture* is to be found" (*CA*, 51).

Global Trends

Laborem Exercens and *Centesimus Annus* accurately read the trend lines in economic and social policy that are now apparent to all. The prime sticking points in the negotiations under the General Agreement on Tariffs and Trade (GATT), for example, have been agricultural subsidies that insulate farmers in developed countries from competition from poor farmers in the Third World; tariff and other barriers that protect home markets and domestic workers from foreign competition; and the refusal of Third World countries to respect the intellectual property rights of computer and software developers in the West. No one seems willing to budge unless others first make a tangible showing of good faith, and both the European Community and the United States are angry about Japan's slow pace on the issue of market access.[19] At bottom, the impasse in the GATT process has been brought about by a lack of trust and an unwillingness to face the cold, hard facts of life in a global economy.

Though the human component of these political and economic struggles is most critical, it receives the least attention. Discussions of the "global" economy focus on market shares and the instantaneous transfers of capital and information over vast distances, but there is considerable movement of people as well. Immigration and falling birth rates are remaking the ethnic and cultural face of North America and Western Europe, where economies would sputter and fail without the cushion provided by the new arrivals and "guest" migrant workers. When "economic refugees" are often needed to keep an economy afloat, it is hard to see why they are described as refugees at all. A *truly* global economy demands free movement of individuals as well as of their capital and ideas. And yet both the United States and the countries of the European Community have resisted meaningful immigration reform, preferring instead to utilize the labor of "guests" (in the EC) and "illegal aliens" (in the United States) without coming to grips with the practical and cultural problems of integrating the new arrivals.

The results have been disastrous in direct proportion to the shortsightedness of the policies that produced them. Even while "multiculturalism" and cross-cultural "sensitivity" are discussed earnestly in the halls of academe, there seems to be little real appreciation of either individual cultures or the impact that *genuine* "multiculturalism"—the one brought about by massive demographic shifts—can have on a society and its values. Germany is beset with race riots aimed at foreigners; inter-ethnic tension and violence in Los Angeles, touched off by the police beating of Rodney King, made news around the world in 1992; New York City's parents recently sacked a school-board chairman because his cultural sensitivities were so finely attuned to "politically correct" opinion that he forgot ordinary people have culture, values, and ethics too; and the United States Supreme Court is being forced to decide whether President Clinton can legally continue to round up starving Haitians at sea—well before they reach the U.S. mainland—and return them to a truly hellish political, economic, and cultural climate.

Some contemporary developments, however, are more positive. Policy-makers are beginning to realize that educational and other human-capital development assistance may allow persons with disabilities to become productive members of society, rather than wards of a paternalistic and uncaring government bureaucracy that seems only too willing to suggest death is preferable to a life without sufficiently high "quality."[20] Workplace policy is also changing to accommodate family needs that go beyond those brought about by births, adoptions, serious illness, or death.

The pope is quite correct that "a given culture reveals its overall understanding of life through the choices it makes" (*CA*, 36), and the choices made by contemporary Western culture and politics can best be described as muddled, if not contradictory. Bioethics issues, family and social-welfare policy, the content and ethical orientation of education, and the role of religion in public life generate enormous controversy across the political spectrum in the United States and elsewhere. Only a few years ago debates over access to day care and "early childhood education" served as proxies for an ongoing debate over women's participation in the labor market as wage-earners, as well as for a larger cultural battle over the respective roles of the state and the family in the acculturation and moral development of children. Today there is no need to hide behind proxies; the culture war has broken out into the open, and people are taking sides.[21] Not surprisingly, the Church itself is playing a central role and, as a result, increasingly finds itself under direct and sustained attack.

The Church's Perspective

The ideological fault lines dividing people on these and other issues have been apparent for years. They center on liberty and justice, and it is, ultimately, to these issues that *Laborem Exercens* and *Centesimus Annus* speak. Joseph Pichler has pointed out that "liberty is a touchstone of both capitalism and *Laborem Exercens*. In its fullest meaning, the pursuit of self-interest, which [the pope] define[s] as encompassing moral, aesthetic and social concerns, is synonymous with self-determination."[22]

Centesimus Annus makes this point in no uncertain terms:

> An understanding of human freedom which detaches it from obedience to the truth, and consequently from the duty to respect the rights of others [is fraught with socio-economic consequences]. The essence of freedom . . . becomes self-love carried to the point of contempt for God and neighbor, a self-love which leads to an unbridled affirmation of self-interest and which refuses to be limited by any demand of justice. (17)

Whether the issue is immigration, massive population flows from the countryside to teeming cities that are both opulent and squalid, the determination of wage rates for a given industry, access to the worldwide information and knowledge "market," or any of labor's other pressing problems identified in *Laborem Exercens*, justice requires not only a supportive environment for human liberty and the development of individual potential but a recognition that human relationships are reciprocal, and that for every claim of "right" there is a corresponding duty, either to oneself or to others. This, in the final analysis, is why John Paul throws his weight as the Vicar of Christ behind "democracy"; for of all political systems, it alone makes government "accountable."

One of the more noteworthy concepts developed by the pope in *Laborem Exercens* is the distinction between the "direct" and the "indirect" employer (77–81), "for when we speak of the obligation of work and of the rights of the worker that correspond to [the moral obligation of work understood in its wide, human sense], we think in the first place of the relationship between the employer . . . and the worker" (74).

> The concept of indirect employer includes both persons and institutions of various kinds and also collective labor contracts and the principles of conduct which are laid down by these persons and institutions and which determine the whole socio-economic system or are its result. . . . The indirect employer

substantially determines one or other facet of the labor relationship, thus conditioning the conduct of the direct employer when the latter determines in concrete terms the actual work contract and labor relations. This is not to absolve the direct employer from his own responsibility, but only to draw attention to the whole network of influences that condition his conduct. (*LE, 77*)

Though some commentators have interpreted this concept as a quite radical indictment of developed countries and their economic systems, its main thrust is more basic: in a global economy one cannot evade moral responsibility for the welfare of workers in other countries by the simple expedient of pointing the finger at the local plantation or sweatshop owner. If one enjoys the fruits of others' labor, one must assume some degree of moral responsibility for their welfare. Only rarely does this message seem to get through.[23] *Centesimus Annus*, however, provides us with the powerful concept of "human ecology" that, if understood in the sense in which John Paul uses it, makes the point quite nicely.

Thinking About the "Moral Environment"

Environmental questions are, in the United States at least, rarely debated in human, much less moral, terms. In common parlance, environmental issues are about *mother* nature, not *human* nature. To some, "nature" unspoiled by man is good, while "development" is evil; to others, "nature" (viewed as "things" such as trees and owls) is expendable and "jobs" are the top priority. In John Paul's view, however, the problem is not "nature versus development" but human arrogance and sin. "Man thinks that he can make arbitrary use of the earth," subjecting it without restraint to his will, "as though it did not have its own requisites and a prior God-given purpose" (*CA*, 37). In fact, the pope takes care to distinguish "development" of the fruits of nature, which is good, from acts that "betray" our trust as stewards of nature's resources.

This is an important distinction—and one often missed in the impassioned battles between proponents of "the environment" and proponents of "jobs." Human beings are both part of the natural order and its temporal stewards; the foundation of what has been termed "environmentalism," then, is really morality and ethics. Given the limits of human knowledge concerning the natural environment, and the now quaint but still fervently held belief that man can use the natural environment for his own benefit without regard for consequences, it is not surprising that nature is "more tyrannized than governed by man," and that nature itself will likely provoke "a rebellion." But so too will "environmentalism" that does not take into account the human costs of devotion to a nature unsullied by human contact. John Paul puts the problem into perspective by mentioning the dire consequences that follow whenever "man sets himself up in place of God."

The human environment also requires attention. Preserving the natural habitats of the various animal species threatened with extinction is an important part of our stewardship role, but so too is safeguarding *"the moral conditions for an authentic 'human ecology'"* (*CA*, 38). Nurturing the "moral infrastructure" of society is an essential element in solving the "ecological" problem. Morality and ethics, not law, are the foundational "elements [that] can help or hinder [men and women] living in accordance with the truth."

Decisions affecting urbanization, joblessness, economic dislocation, and the moral conditions under which people live, work, and raise their children "create a human environment [which] can give rise to specific structures of sin [and] which impede the full realization of those who are in any way oppressed by them" (*CA*, 38). These, too, are crucial "environmental issues." By focusing on human dignity, which "is by no means receiving the attention it deserves"—especially when compared to the high visibility of movements organized to preserve animal habitats and green space—the pope emphasizes that we are *persons*, not simply objects or means of production. Our lives are affected not only by decisions made in the workplace but also by those who live in, and are responsible for, the larger human ecosystem in which we live and work.

As *Centesimus Annus* profoundly observes, "Besides the earth, man's principal resource is *man himself*" (32). In one stroke the pope knits together the discrete categories so often utilized for analyzing economic and social questions—including those affecting the environment. Economics, says John Paul, is "in fact . . . only one aspect and one dimension of the whole of human activity. If economic life is absolutized, if the production and consumption of goods become the center of social life and society's only value," workers will clearly be under great pressure to "produce" everything but a God-centered life devoted to family and community. In a social milieu ostensibly committed to "freedom of choice," it has become economically impossible for many parents to assign top priority to family. In fact, the very act of *having* children is deemed by some to be antisocial.

In this respect, the pope's observations are right on target. Our cultural environment subjects us to "intolerable pressures" that inevitably become a "new form of oppression." Chief among these pressures is advertising's incessant manipulation of public tastes, which subordinates values to instincts. Our "entire socio-cultural system" has been weakened "by ignoring the ethical and religious dimension" of human existence (*CA*, 39), and such neglect has given rise to antisocial behavior and attitudes manifest in drug use, senseless violence, and grave disparities between the opportunities available to rich and poor. A society and culture that loses sight of the necessary relationship among the human persons who comprise it "ends up . . . alienating and oppressing" them by sacrificing the conditions that foster "authentic human growth" on the altar of consumption (*CA*, 39).

What Is to Be Done?

The more difficult part of John Paul's analysis is the age-old question of what is to be done, given the realities of human self-interest and its protection in the name of national and regional sovereignty. The pope correctly notes that the state itself is the primary example of the "indirect" employer, "for it is the state that must conduct a just labor policy" (*LE*, 78). Beyond the state, though, is the international economic and political system, and here the going, both politically and practically, gets a bit rough.

The global economy is interdependent, and focusing on profit alone dooms at least some of the world's poor to exploitation. What is less clear, however, is that international organizations "have fresh contributions to offer" (*LE*, 81). Without a common practical or philosophical reason to cooperate, self-interest takes over in international organizations just as it does within states. Even attempts to work out mutually beneficial trade policies among advanced nations like the United States, Japan, Canada, and members of the European Community, are fraught with emotion and financial and political risks. And European unity still remains a dream: the United Kingdom is not yet on board, and Denmark's participation is reluctant at best. The North American Free Trade Agreement (NAFTA), so essential for the development of Mexico, is viewed with disdain in Canada and with fear in the United States. When the worldview or "particular way of evaluating things" (*LE*, 61) is radically different, cooperation is nearly impossible.

In the United States, for example, trade policy has always been a controversial political issue, even though we live and prosper as a nation under the world's most liberal free-trade agreement: the Constitution of the United States (art. I, §§8–10; art. IV §§1, 2; art. VI). Although they are not at all well known, the Constitution's Commerce (art. I, §8, cl. 3), Tariff and Duty (art. I, §9, cl. 5; §10, cl. 2–3), Interstate Privileges and Immunities (art. IV, §2), and Supremacy (art. VI, cl. 2) clauses guarantee some of the most important freedoms Americans enjoy. And they have been vigorously enforced by the Supreme Court of the United States since the early 1800s on the assumption that "the entire Constitution was 'framed upon the theory that the peoples of the several states must sink or swim together, and that in the long run prosperity and salvation are in union and not division.' "[24] American citizens are thus free to trade, travel, and live in whatever locale best suits their personal, economic, or family needs. Yet only rarely do Americans even consider that there may be a "trade deficit" between, for example, the midwestern and the southwestern regions of the country. Such imbalances, while relevant at the local level, are deemed irrelevant (though not in human or political terms) at the constitutional level. We take the notion of a common economic bond so much for granted that we question it only when those involved live in other countries.

In fits and starts, the European Community and the North American Free Trade Agreement are moving the First World in this same general direction, but they are doing so without taking the suggestions of *Laborem Exercens* to heart. Whereas the Western Europeans and North Americans are forming community trading blocs with the power to exclude others, both *Laborem Exercens* and *Centesimus Annus* envision a *universal* community, connected by human rather than economic, regional, or national ties. Though small components of John Paul's global perspective have influenced the discussion of NAFTA, a more selfless concern for the natural and human environment in Mexico would surely further reduce the protectionist edge to the debate.[25] To gain attention for the human dimension, however, the Church will have to take an active, evangelistic role in the debate. Similarly misguided priorities have arisen in the former Soviet Union as control of trade and natural resources has devolved from the federation to the republics. Capital not being stolen outright is fleeing the country, and this trend will not be reversed by emphasizing economic growth and material gain alone. Economic reform will fail unless it enhances the freedom and ability of *individuals* to participate in the economic life of the community. Exclusivity claims by labor unions both at home and abroad will fail for the same reason.

Focus on the Human Subject

If there is one practical warning contained in *Laborem Exercens*, it is that dehumanizing work leads to disaster. Pope John Paul II has been intimately familiar with the manner in which Marxist command economies treat most workers as the functional equivalent of slaves, and others as *zeks*—real slaves like Solzhenitsyn's fictional Ivan Denisovich. To the extent that capitalist and Third World countries allow managers and bureaucrats to treat workers as fungible commodities, to be used and discarded when spent or injured, they do not differ much from communist states, except, perhaps, for the rate of pay or the comfort of the working environment. In recent years a number of persons have been prosecuted and convicted in the United States for holding desperately poor, foreign agricultural workers as slaves. And Haiti is, in fact, a country of slaves.

The pope's warning, of course, is intended to maintain the focus where it should be: on the necessity of keeping the person at the center of the equation. In a globally competitive, modern, technological society that operates at speeds hitherto unknown in human history, this is no easy task. Advances in technology so integrate operator and machine that the machine (which monitors the work done) can become the functional equivalent of the plantation overseer or labor-camp sentry unless management accepts its moral obligation to act in a manner consistent with the human dignity of the worker. Speed and pressure take their toll on capitalists and "professionals" as well: "burn out" and stress management are common topics in nearly every trade and professional journal.

Viewed in this light, payment of a just wage does not necessarily reduce the pain when unreasonable physical, emotional, or mental demands are placed on workers. Money, in and of itself, simply does not cure the disease of dehumanization—notwithstanding John Paul's assertions that "the key problem of social ethics in this case is that of just remuneration for work done" (*LE*, 89). No amount of money will compensate for the damage done by an employer who does not take into account the total welfare of both worker and customer. As the growing appetite of government for funds illustrates, the "total package of benefits" is the true measure of justice in the workplace. Were it not so, the United States government would not be spending so much time trying to figure out how to measure—and tax—its value.

The Legacy of Laborem Exercens

Pope John Paul II, who helped conceive Poland's Solidarity trade union and who views the role of unions as no less than "to defend the existential interests of workers in all sectors in which their rights are concerned" (*LE*, 95), has clearly had a profound impact on contemporary history, in Poland and elsewhere. Yet the nature of his impact and his encyclicals remain subject to dispute. *Laborem Exercens* was described by some American commentators as suggesting a "third way" between capitalism and Marxism,[26] as rejecting "the notion of the absolute right to private property,"[27] and as heralding "a new era of social teaching" ripe with possibilities for those eager to provide "detailed moral norms for the transnational [economic] level."[28] The Catholic bishops of the United States understood *Laborem Exercens* in those terms and took up that challenge in their 1986 pastoral letter on the U.S. economy, "Economic Justice for All."[29]

The stated goal of *Laborem Exercens*, however, was considerably more modest. It was simply to sketch out a moral *approach* to the problems of workers to "guide . . . authentic progress by man and society," and to "condemn" situations that violate human dignity (*LE*, 5). Viewed in light of *Centesimus Annus*, such a general approach is clearly preferable to the more detailed one proposed by the American bishops' pastoral. It is, moreover, the only vision that will be taken seriously enough to have a long-term impact on human ecology.

Quentin de la Bedoyere has noted that papal teaching is "primarily deductive, starting from the data of revelation or abstract reflection on the nature of man and leading to the practical applications which do justice to the initial principles. Its ultimate criterion is to establish what is right." By contrast, "management theorists have used an inductive approach observing man at work and drawing from general principles. Their ultimate criterion has been what produces the best results." If both have been on the right track for the last one hundred years, "the conclusions of both should be in fundamental agreement."[30]

Nearly twelve years after its publication and four years after the implosion of communism in Eastern and Central Europe, the relevance of *Laborem Exercens* remains undiminished, both as a statement of moral principle and as a commentary on the illegitimacy of economic policies that treat work and workers simply as so much "merchandise" to be traded in an impersonal and impartial "marketplace." Its focus on the human dimension of work captures the essence of the "social question" inherent in labor-capital issues, and transforms it into a series of practical and philosophical inquiries (much like Douglas McGregor's "Theory Y"[31]) for those who design market, management, investment, and labor policy. It makes no difference whether the would-be reformer's goal is to increase a given company's productivity, to inhibit labor unrest, to throw off the economic and social oppression of Marxist command economies, to decrease the abject poverty of the Third World, or to avoid the all too frequent abuses of the Western-style "labor market." The nature of the people who *are* those economic "systems" remains a constant. And it is to this "constant" that *Centesimus Annus* is directed.

When the Church becomes a critic or advocate of specific policy options, however, it becomes open to (and often deserves) criticism not applicable to either *Laborem Exercens* or *Centesimus Annus*. First, the message will not be transcendent; it will be "old news"—or irrelevant—by the time it is published. More importantly, legitimate moral criticism of specific programs must be based on some knowledge of their goals and *actual* operating record before abstract alternatives are advanced. Ecclesiastical judgments about the "morality" of specific programs will not be taken seriously by those most in need of guidance—sometimes including the most fervent of the "reformers"—unless those judgments are morally, socially, *and* economically credible.

This is why *Laborem Exercens* is best read as an important chapter in the Church's broader ministry to opinion leaders: management, educators, and investors. Though it was written to inspire, encourage, and support solidarity among workers, its real—and most enduring—message is for all those charged with the duty of managing their own work and the work of others: i.e., all of us. In *Laborem Exercens* John Paul suggests (like McGregor), not "a way of managing" an economy, "but a way of being a manager—a fundamental attitude toward human beings and not merely a technique." Unlike the U.S. Catholic bishops, he does not advance any set of practical guidelines for resolving specific management or moral dilemmas.

To the extent that those who work in or manage enterprises, people, or government (including those who shepherd the institutional and human resources of the Church) act as if people are inherently unmotivated and antagonistic toward work, injustices will abound. To the extent that *Laborem Exercens* is heeded, however, injustices will decrease as the marketplace becomes more "human," more competitive—and, eventually, more profitable for all who participate. For the yearning for fair competition, at a fair price, is also in the nature of man. This is the essential message of *Laborem Exercens* and the evangelistic goal sketched out for the Church in *Centesimus Annus*.

10

The Turn Toward Enterprise
Sollicitudo Rei Socialis (1987)

WILLIAM McGURN

F EW sights are so charged with promise as an Asian sunrise. Just a few hundred yards from the commercial heart of the East's financial center, dawn illuminates a harbor little altered by more than a hundred years of spectacular economic expansion. Trading ships from all corners of the earth rest peacefully in its waters; tiny wooden fishing boats thread their way to and fro; off in the distance, the mountaintops of China fade into the morning mist. The Chinese called this place "Fragrant Harbor," or Hong Kong.

Today the city is a far cry from "the barren rock with hardly a house upon it" contemptuously dismissed by Lord Palmerston back in 1840, when the British first acquired Hong Kong as a spoil of their victory over imperial China in the First Opium War. In contrast to the picturesque languor of much of the rest of the developing world, modern Hong Kong is an energetic jumble of high-rise apartment blocks, super-size shopping malls, and five-star hotels. Everywhere it sweats with commerce: street hawkers crowd each alleyway with all manner of wares; taxis, ferries, subways, limousines, buses, jetfoils, trains, and planes carry the colony's 5.9 million people hither and yon; jackhammers pound and bamboo

---

William McGurn is senior editor of the *Far Eastern Economic Review* in Hong Kong.

scaffolding marks the birth of new buildings whose outlines are just rising from the ground. And all this is but a fraction of the dynamic energy behind what is to the economist but a dry statistic: the world's eleventh-largest trading entity and its busiest port.

There was not a great deal to recommend the newly acquired British possession back in 1840 because then, as now, Hong Kong had no natural resources and an inhospitable climate. Today, with one of the most densely packed populations on earth, it remains dependent on communist China for food and even water. Yet Hong Kong has prospered, to the point where its residents enjoy the highest per capita income in Asia next to Japan (and an arguably higher standard of living if one takes account of purchasing power and the distortions created by an inflated yen). Indeed, per capita income in the crown colony has just surpassed Mother England's. Hong Kong is a development success story, perhaps *the* development success story.

For precisely this reason Hong Kong is an especially advantageous point from which to review Catholic social teaching on economics. The task has acquired a special urgency in light of the breakup of the Soviet bloc, the emergence of China and India as economic powers, and the desire of impoverished peoples, from Africa and the Americas to Asia and beyond, for some relief from the perpetual dependency and destitution to which they have hitherto been consigned. What kind of world will ultimately emerge in the twenty-first century is not yet clear, though the stubbornness of original sin has already chastened those who thought the mere collapse of an evil would guarantee the triumph of the good. Amid the tumult of the emerging new order, the Church alternately reminds us that human nature remains imperfect and that a God who created us in his likeness has made despair the one unpardonable sin.

In this regard *Sollicitudo Rei Socialis*, issued in December 1987, represented the first tentative steps in stressing man's God-given creativity as the foundation for a new direction in Catholic social teaching. Like Paul VI before him in *Populorum Progressio*, John Paul II has been alarmed by the seemingly intractable problems plaguing development in the Third World, even more so now that the dominant development strategy has proved such a resounding flop. *Populorum* was very much a document of its time, suggesting as it did that all that stood between poverty and progress was a helping hand from the West. The subsequent two decades saw an international initiative marshalling unprecedented amounts of aid for development—the multilateral equivalent of Lyndon Johnson's Great Society—but it accomplished virtually nothing. In many cases it only made the situation worse, by saddling would-be beneficiaries with staggering levels of foreign debt. *Sollicitudo* thus addressed a world all too conscious of its failures.

CRAFTING A THEORY OF DEVELOPMENT

Within the Church's own frame of reference, *Sollicitudo* was written both to mark the anniversary of *Populorum Progressio* and to flesh out the more positive vision behind the 1984 and 1986 Instructions on liberation theology issued by the Congregation for the Doctrine of the Faith. All these are constituent parts of a coherent whole that has as much relevance for the developed world as for the undeveloped: setting out the boundaries of the permissible, showing the relevance of classical social teaching to the task today, and above all insisting that development must not be regarded solely in material terms.

According to the former Rome correspondent for the *New York Times*, Robert Suro, *Sollicitudo* had its origins in 1987 during the pope's trip to Chile. The solemn Mass in the capital city of Santiago drew almost a million of the faithful to see their spiritual leader. Unfortunately, what ought to have been a day of joy turned ugly when anti-government protesters clashed with police in a riot that went on for the length of the service and injured hundreds of innocents. Instead of incense and church bells, tear gas and gunshots filled the air. "When the long liturgy ended at nightfall," wrote Suro, "John Paul seemed unwilling to leave. He repeatedly paused to stare at the violence unfolding before him even as aides tried to usher him off the altar toward a heavily guarded motorcade."[1]

Certainly the conflict between radical anti-government protesters and the police of an authoritarian regime parallels *Sollicitudo*'s view of violence as emanating from "the division of the world into ideological blocs" (*Sollicitudo Rei Socialis*, paragraph 10), a somewhat crude division between a North that knows how to make money but whose soul has been suffocated and a South whose people lack even the most fundamental bodily essentials but are strong in spirit. Such a situation cries out for an alternative that avoids these two traps, for that elusive golden mean that embraces the people's legitimate thirst for social justice while rejecting the liberation theologians' means. "True development cannot consist in the simple accumulation of wealth and in the greater availability of goods and services," the pope writes in *Sollicitudo*, "if this is gained at the expense of the development of the masses, and without due consideration for the social, cultural, and spiritual dimensions of the human being" (9). Characteristically, John Paul has tried to do this in a spirit of charity, with an emphasis on culling truths from each side rather than merely condemning error.

A Continuum of Views

With these concerns in mind, John Paul issued what would be his most comprehensive statement on economic life until *Centesimus Annus* in 1991. Although the sections of *Sollicitudo* dealing with his equal criticisms of "Marxist collectivism" and "liberal capitalism" dominated discussions of the encyclical (especially in the press), such criticism was neither the most significant nor the most original aspect of the letter. To the contrary, what was most striking about this encyclical was the intimation of an empirical approach hitherto absent from most such papal documents—the value put on entrepreneurship, the concern over increasing world protectionism, and the recognition of the havoc wrought by floating exchange rates. At the time it was unclear whether these views represented a fundamental shift in Rome's approach, or whether they would recede into interesting but ultimately irrelevant footnotes. The publication of *Centesimus Annus* suggests the former.

Even many Catholics find it difficult to sift the enduring from the heavily time-conditioned in the key documents of Catholic social teaching. For there exists an inevitable tension between transmitting timeless truths about God and man and the neverending changes in world circumstances that require the Church to apply these truths anew, often in apparent contradiction to what has gone before. Similarly, John Paul's 1987 letter had two objectives, laid out at the very beginning of the encyclical: "on the one hand, to pay homage to this historic document of Paul VI [*Populorum Progressio*] and to its teaching; on the other hand, following in the footsteps of my esteemed predecessors in the See of Peter, to reaffirm the continuity of social doctrine as well as its constant renewal" (3).

This latter point is critical to understanding any church document. Newspapers, alas, are predisposed by their nature to emphasize how encyclicals differ from their predecessors, in much the same way that they would report the differences between, say, the Bush and Clinton administrations. This already skews the coverage, given that church teaching is a continuum, with each pope complementing—not overriding—what has come before. The core truths are the same but require different adaptations and emphases to fit particular times and places. And the Church claims no infallibility in the details that these adaptations and emphases entail.

Posing the Key Issues

In light of the fall of the Berlin Wall two years after *Sollicitudo* was published, the letter's reference to "the eve of the third Christian millennium" is particularly worth noting (4). This recurrent theme in John Paul's theology is not only a literal reference to the approach of the year 2000; it is also a metaphor for a rebirth of faith that the pope sees over the horizon. Indeed, the collapse of the USSR has been accompanied by revivalism among all religious faiths that gives little sign of abating. Even twisted manifestations of religiosity—I think of the Hindu destruction of the mosque at Ayodhya in India, the continued rise of militant Islam, and the festering of liberation theology—suggest that two centuries into the Enlightenment the world has come to recognize what is only dawning on intellectuals: the rationalist experiment is not enough to satisfy deep human longings.

John Paul takes that experiment head on by beginning his own letter with a short discussion of *Populorum Progressio*, emphasizing Paul VI's point that development must be distinguished from rank materialism, and that better-off nations have an obligation to share their wealth with the less fortunate. This said, John Paul then compares the world as he found it with the one to which Paul VI aspired, ruefully concluding that it "offers a rather negative impression" (13). Among the negatives he cites are the then-division of the world into ideological blocs, the "leveling down" (15) that replaced development in all too many Third World states, the impersonal "economic, financial, and social mechanisms" (16) that exploit the masses of people, and the "tendency toward imperialism" (22) in both capitalist and Marxist countries. These factors have, in turn, spawned other problems, most of which are still with us: an arms race, state-imposed population control, insufficient supplies of food, and so on.

Only after he has given the lay of the land does John Paul set forth his own ideas of how things ought to be, the central theme of which is that goods exist to serve man and not vice versa. The right to property, while strong, is by no means absolute; society, he points out, sometimes has needs that override this right (as when, for example, the resources of the earth, meant for all, are wrongly confined to a few). By virtue of the fact that all goods have a moral dimension, so all development must have a moral dimension.

Sollicitudo thus examines the obstacles to development through a moral lens. The pope's own preferred term here is "structures of sin" (36), one of which had been the aforementioned division of the world into rival blocs. Others include "the all-consuming desire for profit" (37), "the thirst for power" (37), and the lack of international solidarity. In other words, in *Sollicitudo Rei Socialis* John Paul hopes to encourage the experts to look up from their five-year plans and to recognize that development is fundamentally tied up with solidarity, the love and service of one's neighbor.

Given the radical transformation of world politics in 1989 (a transformation reflected in *Centesimus Annus*), perhaps the most enduring teaching in *Sollicitudo* is the pope's insistence that many of the shortcomings plaguing the world today derive from "a too narrow idea of development, that is, a mainly economic one" (15). Interestingly enough, a few years earlier the U.S. Agency for International Development had reached virtually the same conclusion in its so-called Woods Report, which noted that not a single recipient of U.S. assistance had moved from undeveloped to developed status in the two decades since that aid had started—a stunning indictment of the development-through-aid orthodoxy.[2] Indeed, the case can be made that aid actually enervates recipient nations, particularly when one compares, say, the track record of Manila against that of Hong Kong, Singapore, Seoul, and Taipei, each of which has managed to achieve spectacular economic growth despite challenges far more severe than anything faced by the Philippines.

Yet despite its caveat about narrow conceptions of development, the general approach of *Sollicitudo* suggested that Catholic thought on development continues to have more in common with what has failed in the past than with what has succeeded. The blame for this cannot be placed solely, or even primarily, on John Paul. Two years before the publication of *Sollicitudo*, Joseph P. Martino neatly summed up the difficulty papal encyclicals have always had in tackling this subject:

> Their major strength is that they give first priority to the moral order. They begin with perennial Catholic teachings on the moral goals people ought to pursue. Their major weakness is that they try to prescribe how society should be organized in order to achieve these goals, but without exhibiting sufficient understanding of why people behave the way they do.

CAPITALISM RECONSIDERED

This criticism would be stood on its head by *Centesimus Annus*, not simply for what it said but *how* it said it: proceeding from the astonishing events of 1989 and the pope's own experience in Poland, the 1991 encyclical imparted to the larger understandings in *Sollicitudo* a force and vigor sometimes difficult to discern in its 1987 predecessor.

Indeed, the reaction to *Centesimus Annus* within the Church suggests that the pope's dramatic shift in emphasis has yet to be appreciated by many within the fold. The charitable explanation is that these people—the U.S. Catholic Conference, for example— simply have not caught on; certainly the political priorities evident in their approaches to such issues as poverty and development reflect few of the themes of *Centesimus*. Perhaps this is not too surprising, for many of these same groups failed to detect the foundations of *Centesimus* in *Sollicitudo*. When John Paul talks about those with "a too narrow view of development"(15), he has to worry about those in his own church. In the past many of these churchmen have embraced an essentially managerial approach to wealth that ignores the infusion of human creativity and faith that bring wealth into being in the first place. Unfortunately, *Sollicitudo* itself, like the documents that preceded it, lacks a fully developed spiritual conception of wealth to match its conception of poverty. From the vantage point of history, however, we can see that it planted the seed.

The main stumbling block to such a conception of wealth is the Church's past analysis of the world not so much from an anti-capitalist perspective as a *pre*-capitalist one. Thus, while John Paul is able to draw a vivid portrait of the failures behind collectivist systems, his descriptions of capitalism (until *Centesimus*) were thin, even stereotypic. Marxism may have proved itself a practical disaster in our century, but its basic assumptions about labor, capital, and people seem to have triumphed in every aspect of development economics. Coupled with Rome's unhappy experience with the virulent anti-clericalism of Continental liberalism in the last century, these assumptions continue to lead some church figures to reach conclusions that are hard to square with the classic Catholic social principles of subsidiarity, individual dignity, and the common good. It was the special disappointment of *Sollicitudo* that it dealt with these sturdy Catholic principles in only the most abstract and glancing manner.

Today, as the world gropes for an order that will replace the artificial divide of the Cold War, it is incumbent on church leaders to study, not simply the theoretical underpinnings of capitalism, but capitalist societies themselves in the same, dramatic way the pope has addressed communist societies. For example, the millions of small, individual actions that occur every hour in a place like Hong Kong might seem random and disorderly to the casual observer. Yet it is not a matter of chance that in Hong Kong there is food on the shelves, abundant water (though the territory has no water supply of its own), and no shortage of commodities (despite an absence of natural resources). In her history of the territory,

British author Jan Morris put it this way: "In a small Chinese shop on Cheung Chau [island] I once bought myself a packet of candies made in Athens, and even as I opened it I marvelled at the chain of logistics that had brought it from the shadow of the Acropolis to be chewed by me on the corner of Tung Wan road."[3] While not the outcome of any specific human plan, the obvious ease with which capitalism literally delivers the goods demonstrates that a capitalist system is not the chaotic process it appears to be at first glance.

Capitalism Misunderstood

Much like other documents in the tradition, *Sollicitudo* fails to take adequate account of the efficiency of capitalist production of goods and services. Indeed, until recently Catholic social teaching failed even to wonder whether this unquestioned ability to generate wealth might be attributed to something more than mere greed. Capitalism is rarely spoken of in poetic terms, yet it is an almost mystical process by which man infuses the inert materials of the earth with his intelligence and creativity, and through cooperation with others in enterprise—each of whom reaps some share of his effort—gives this hitherto worthless matter utility and value. To make worth of matter, man adds to it his idea of what it might become.

This concept of wealth as fundamentally spiritual lies at the heart of the capitalist revolution, both yesterday and today. At the dawn of the nineteenth century, the new capitalists had trouble getting parliaments and princes to accept manufactured goods as a source of wealth in their accounting; the prevailing wisdom, against which Adam Smith had written his famous work, was that national wealth consisted of vast tracts of land and hordes of gold. Today we smile at the naiveté of such assumptions, but our own are not much better. Communists and socialists, for example, accepted the idea of manufactures but never appreciated the animating spirit that gave them life. The result was the pathetic Soviet effort that has left a landscape littered with mute testimonials to industrial idolatry: gargantuan steel mills, huge truck factories, sprawling power plants, heavy machinery, large bulldozers, and so forth.

Nor have even the developed nations necessarily advanced much beyond materialist conceptions of capitalism. As former Citibank chairman Walter Wriston notes, the accepted definitions of capital and trade today betray a staggering crudity. "On the accountants' ledgers the intellectual capital a company acquires tends to be treated as an expense, not as a real asset," he writes. "[I]t is not carried on the capital accounts along with the shiny new company car or the aging brick factory building, though neither contributes as much to the enterprise's productive capacity."[4] And while the old assets remain fixed and inflexible—the factory, the machinery, etc.—Wriston points out that intellectual capital is highly mobile and can move over borders and bypass customs officers.

In *Sollicitudo*, unfortunately, John Paul reduces the great engine of capitalism simply to "the all-consuming desire for profit" (37). The pope does defend the "right of economic initiative" (15), a phrase repeated several times in *Sollicitudo* and pursued more fully in *Centesimus*; obviously, this was no throwaway line, particularly in light of John Paul's experience in communist Poland. But this abstract concept would have been much more illuminating had it been fleshed out with the actual experience of real, live entrepreneurs.

In Hong Kong, entrepreneurs are as likely to be barefoot and in T-shirts as they are to resemble Donald Trump. They are likely to take you through their factories, talk proudly about the number of people they employ, and pause over the minutest aspects of their enterprise to explain precisely how everything fits together. Even the lowliest entrepreneur is as proud of what he makes as an artist is of his paintings, and with good reason. It is not difficult to imagine John Paul on such a tour, caught up in the enthusiasm of the idea made real. But by taking these finished goods and services as the starting point of its analysis, *Sollicitudo* begins too late and is working from only half the story—and not even the most important half at that.

Capitalism and History

This is a mistake that is possible only in societies where the spectacular success of the market has allowed people to take their historically unprecedented high standard of living for granted. The triumphs of capitalism blinded even Marx, who believed that history had arrived, or would soon arrive, at the point where material progress had been maximized and the equitable redistribution of its fruits could finally begin. Marx consequently regarded capitalism as a necessary step in development, which is why he predicted that communism would begin in the most advanced economies, Germany and England, rather than in the least, Russia and China.

To his credit, though, and in contrast to the last of his followers today, Marx at least understood the inherent dynamism of capitalism as a force in human history. His writings are almost lyrical in their descriptions of how capitalism broke down Europe's feudal barriers, sweeping aside a system based on privilege and replacing it with one based on merit. There was conflict, yes, between the old and the new, but a conflict unlike any other in that it advanced the public good as it gave more and more people ever greater control over their own lives and destinies. This link between economic and political liberty, implicit even in Marx, is only hinted at in *Sollicitudo*.

Is it any wonder, then, that traditionally Catholic nations have lagged behind, politically as well as economically? The four dragons of Asia (Hong Kong, Singapore, Taiwan, and South Korea) have all achieved world-class economic status in scarcely more than a generation, with Malaysia and Thailand close behind (and Vietnam threatening to outdo every one of them once the shackles of the Hanoi regime are broken). In the midst of the most dynamic economic center on earth, the Catholic Philippines remains the "sick man of Asia," lurching from government to government while more than half its people live in unspeakable poverty—all this despite an elite largely educated at America's leading universities, a plethora of natural resources, a hard-working and English-speaking labor force, and billions upon billions of dollars in foreign aid over the past three decades. There are indeed "structures of sin" in the Philippines, but they do not come from the outside, and they are not limited to greed.

THE CRIME OF WEALTH

The implicit charge that the developed world has become wealthy at the expense of the undeveloped world, a theme of the liberation theologians, is undoubtedly the most troubling suggestion raised in *Sollicitudo*. John Paul does not say this directly, but he does hint at it strongly in a number of places. For instance, he speaks of "the unequal distribution of the means of subsistence originally meant for everybody" (9), and asserts that "the abundance of goods and services available in some parts of the world, particularly the developed North, is matched in the South by an unacceptable delay [in distribution]" (14). And he notes that "peoples excluded from the fair distribution of goods originally destined for all could ask themselves: why not respond with violence to those who first treat us with violence?" (10).

What links all these statements is the assumption that wealth is inert, something that is out there ripe for the picking, and that the problem is simply that some nations are seizing more than their fair share. The implication becomes even clearer when considered in light of the pope's statement that "in a world ruled by concern for the common good of all humanity . . . instead of the quest for individual profit, peace would be possible as the result of a 'more perfect justice among the people' " (10).

Considered as an aspiration for a world ordered by Christian charity, the pope's statement is something of a tautology. But as a guide to setting up social structures designed to take into account man's fallen nature, it is no answer at all. Free-market economists are the first to point out that it is not from the benevolence of the baker that we expect our bread. Accordingly, they see among the beauties of the market system its ability to function without a legion of saints at the helm. It is, in fact, *designed* for sinners—to channel energies into serving the public good even when that may not be the personal intent, as well as to limit the harmful effects of individual shortcomings and weaknesses. To return to the example of Hong Kong: Hong Kong developed not because people put aside their own interests for the common good but because, in an environment of freedom, creativity—and, as a result, choice—blossomed. In Hong Kong too (as in all other capitalist nations) wages are rising, giving the lie to the Malthusian position that wages fall in a capitalist society because of competition among workers who have only their labor to sell.

The Personal versus Public Realms

It is especially in the area of individual competition that Catholic social teaching most often parts company with market theory. That this disagreement has become so entrenched is particularly regrettable in that it is arguably a misapplication of personal criteria to the public sphere (an error traditionally associated with fundamentalist Protestantism). Catholic teaching quite rightly takes the family as the essential unit of society; it encourages brothers, sisters, and parents to sacrifice for one another and expects order to emanate downward from a loving father and mother. The Catholic vocabulary reverberates with family metaphors ("Holy Father," "Reverend Mother," "Bride of Christ"). Not so capitalism. It reorders society from the bottom up rather than the top down, elevating conflict from a personal irritant into a public principle.

The honored place accorded conflict within a market society is frequently misunderstood. It is often thought to sanction a dog-eat-dog ethos by which the poor necessarily come up short against the rich, clever, and well-connected. In *Sollicitudo* this classic negative assessment of the market reveals itself in John Paul's "solid conviction that what is hindering full development is that desire for profit" (38). The not unreasonable argument here seems to be that competition would be fine if we were all blessed with equal advantages, but since some folks obviously and undeservedly enjoy more advantages than others, the game is stacked. Or, as George Orwell put it, the problem with competition is that somebody wins. In a family, by contrast, parents compensate for the different talents and abilities of their children. Because socialist or corporatist systems claim to do this at a public level, they have traditionally and naturally attracted those who take their religious commitments seriously.

The mistake here is of applying right principles to the wrong arena. Society is not a family made up of children looking to their parents for comfort and sustenance; society is a collection of adults. The social order, as Catholic teaching has always maintained, has its own rules and interests, and in the economic, no less than the political, realm it is best regulated by the principle of competition, the social meaning of which transcends the literal division of people into winners and losers.

Even the most moral and pious individuals acknowledge this distinction in their everyday lives. We don't, for example, choose a restaurant because of the chef's piety; we choose it because it offers the best food, prices, atmosphere, and location. When we receive good service from an establishment, we don't conclude that the proprietor is a virtuous human being. We simply conclude that he is a smart businessman and, moreover, think no less of him for this. We realize that the qualities we look for in our social intercourse have more in common with manners than with morals. Social virtues are not any less important, but they are important in their own way. They require their own definitions and a set of virtues that complement rather than compete with private ones.

Sollicitudo might have mined this vein, but instead it confined its notion of conflict to a fixed-pie view in which one bloc wins at another bloc's expense (in this case, the North and South blocs rather than the old East and West blocs). The animating spirit of capitalism is thus missed, and symptoms are mistaken for causes. (It is useful to remember, too, that competition on a personal scale is not unique to capitalist societies; what is distinctive about capitalism is that it channels conflict into public service. True, this is not the "love of neighbor" *Sollicitudo* sets up as the ideal, but in terms of its consequences it has the same *effect*: it forces even the crassest businessman to ponder new ways of attracting customers.)

The Flip Side of Competition

The irony is that while the Church has been wary of embracing competition in the economic realm, it has readily endorsed it in the political—to wit, democracy. In a democracy, politicians are not expected to be driven by that solidarity the pope speaks of in *Sollicitudo*. Instead, they compete with one another for votes, a process that is usually accompanied by conflict and always by clear winners and losers. Democracy contains no notion of an "intrinsic right" to hold office, merely the right of citizens to offer themselves as candidates. If a Michael Jackson grasping at his crotch before a television audience of millions discredits capitalism, then the often disgusting and not infrequently appalling excesses and antics of politicians the world over ought to discredit democracy. The reason they do not is that we recognize that an oft-regrettable amount of excess is the price we must pay for freedom and the greater good it serves.

Sollicitudo would have been a more compelling document had John Paul considered capitalism in this *social* context, instead of concentrating on the personal intentions and motivations of its participants. For capitalism is to economics what democracy is to politics: a choice arrangement that empowers those on the bottom, be they consumers or voters. Occasionally we are repelled by the choices individuals make; but we trust that, as a whole, prudence generally emerges triumphant. Perhaps most important, capitalist choices can be revoked at any time, which gives capitalist societies unparalleled flexibility and stability. Indeed, the emergence of Compaq, Apple, and Microsoft did in the end what legions of anti-trust lawyers and dozens of bureaucrats could not do: bring down what had been hitherto considered an invincible IBM. And when IBM did collapse, the reason was no mystery. Customers now found better deals elsewhere.

Given the practical successes of capitalist economies, the healthy, incarnational character of the Catholic imagination, and the dramatic flowering of the best of *Sollicitudo* in *Centesimus Annus*, market societies might well serve as the model for the next phase of Catholic teaching. After all, for a social teaching to be at all plausible, it must "work" in some real sense of the word, and the various non-market approaches have so far all proved wretched failures.

Moreover, it requires no sleight of hand to turn the Church's indictment of capitalism into its vindication. That rich nations get richer demonstrates that the creation of wealth feeds upon itself, is exponential. Hong Kong did not develop because its neighbors took a kindly, genteel attitude toward it; on the contrary, its development took off after a U.N.-imposed boycott of China (because of its invasion of Korea) deprived Hong Kong of its largest market and forced it to reach out and compete internationally. The colony also benefited immensely from the hundreds of thousands of refugees who poured out of China, people who were deemed grave liabilities by development specialists (e.g., the United Nations

High Commissioner for Refugees) but who have done much to make Hong Kong what it is today.

By the same token, the Philippines did not fail to develop because other Asian countries were successful at its expense. The most critical obstacle to economic development there is a constitution that walls off whole segments of the economy from foreign competition while permitting an absurd level of tariffs and overregulation. Indeed, Philippine attempts at autarky remain a classic example of perverse unintended consequences. Although the constitution was written to ward off foreign manipulation, its real effect has been to prop up Philippine monopolies at the expense of the Filipino people by preventing foreign firms from coming in and offering better-quality goods and services, better-paying jobs, and a higher degree of choice for all.

SOURCES OF WEALTH

Another challenge to development orthodoxies also requires our attention. Colonialism is almost always cited as a classic example of exploitation; but in fact most Third World countries were far wealthier as colonies than they are today as independent states. Burma, for example, was perhaps the wealthiest place in all Asia until its own home-grown despot, Ne Win, reversed all the economic progress of the British overlords and instituted a devastating socialism. India experienced a similar phenomenon. And the fact remains that in many (if not most) of these places, ordinary people would probably prefer a prosperous colonial order to rule by their own. The reason is not that they entertain any silly notion that their Western conquerors were driven by sentiments of "solidarity." But they recognize that the social order these foreigners brought—chiefly, the rule of law—was and is far superior to local despotism.

In today's world, of course, colonialism is not a real possibility, if only for reasons of national pride. But this only points out a tension in development theory—a tension that has sometimes shaped Catholic social teaching. If Western nations are not to have the power to determine the economic and political structures of the Third World, why is the West to be held accountable for the Third World's poverty? If we concede that colonialism is incompatible with national dignity, we must also insist that responsibility is the corollary of independence. In *Sollicitudo* and later in *Centesimus*, John Paul has acknowledged the Third World's complicity in its own impoverishment. But he has yet to accord that sorry fact its proper weight. However bad the policies of foreign countries may be—and in closing markets, for example, the United States is no innocent—a country's prosperity, or lack of it, ultimately depends on what it does to itself.

A Christian-inspired approach to development has much to contribute here, not least because economic growth depends on such old-fashioned virtues as hard work, thrift, integrity, and so forth that only religion has historically been able to cultivate. But the Church must also pay close attention to the actual workings of economic systems. To read *Sollicitudo*, and even more so *Populorum Progressio*, one would never know that places like Hong Kong, Taiwan, and South Korea exist. Although *Centesimus* represents a welcome turn toward empirical evidence, its practical and historical analysis focuses heavily on the failure of communism and devotes little sustained attention to the triumphs of capitalism, not only in the United States and Western Europe, but in the areas of the Far East to which it has been transplanted. If Thomas Aquinas could find truths about man in Aristotle, the Church should not be embarrassed by learning about development from Hong Kong.

For far too long, development specialists and church leaders have focused on poverty. But a genuine theory of development must reverse the question: instead of looking at what makes people poor, we must begin to ask what makes them rich. This is no less important to the "North," in John Paul's terms, than to the "South." Capitalism curiously nurtures within its success vices that, left unchecked by other institutions such as church and family, carry the seeds of the system's destruction. The ironies are almost diabolical. It is in capitalist lands that the family appears most threatened—not by poverty, but by riches. This, in turn, threatens to undermine the very virtues by which wealth is acquired.

This is perhaps the chief fear of the newly industrialized states of East Asia today. Although most church documents deem Europe a secure part of the thriving capitalist world, the countries of Asia, far more conservative in outlook, view social and economic developments in Europe with alarm. "Mother countries" such as Great Britain are seen as molting giants, hoping to forestall their rate of decline through currency games and protectionism. In short, Asia sees Europe (and, to a lesser extent, the United States) as decadent. What Asians also see, and what most Europeans and Americans do not, is that this decadence threatens the prosperity that spawned it. In *Centesimus* the pope has discussed the disastrous economic effects of protectionism on developing countries. But he might also, and with great profit, turn his attention to the enervating moral effects of protectionism on those in the developed world who try to retreat behind its walls.

For one great lesson of the last forty years is that development is impossible without freedom, but the fruitful exercise of "public" freedom requires a steady cultivation of private virtues. In his recent work on the contribution of religion and ethnicity to development, Joel Kotkin noted that while these factors color the shape and form development will take, the economic success of different peoples, and especially *sustained* economic success, is ultimately accessible to all: "Clearly identifiable values—such as strong ethnic identity, a belief in self-help, hard work, thrift, education and the family—have proved universally successful in all these different groups; stripped of the burdens of Cold War ideology and racism, the relationship between such values and group success is simply too self-evident to ignore."[5] The task for the social order is to create structures that enable these virtues to blossom.

This, of course, was implicit in Lord Acton's classic definition of liberty not as the ability to do what one pleased but as the freedom to do what one ought. In the former Soviet bloc the exercise of genuine, substantive freedom helped destroy communism and its grotesqueries; in the West our growing attachment to mere procedural freedoms is causing liberty to degenerate into license. The hard golden mean, not the mushy middle, is the provenance of Catholic social teaching. In *Sollicitudo* the outlines of such a mean became perceptible. Had the encyclical not been distracted by discredited development theories, and had it paid more attention to the relationship between development and genuine, substantive freedom, it might have given the world that spiritual definition of wealth without which such grim harvests continue to be reaped.

But God displays his wonder through imperfect vessels, and *Sollici-tudo*'s importance will almost surely be seen, in time, to lie less in this or that bit of analysis than in its first brief flashes of illumination of the path to the most lustrous of papal documents, *Centesimus Annus*.

11

The Virtues of Freedom
Centesimus Annus (1991)

GEORGE WEIGEL

THE appearance of Pope John Paul II's 1991 social encyclical was a landmark event in contemporary religious thought about human freedom and its embodiment in culture, economics, and politics. Issued to honor the centenary of *Rerum Novarum, Centesimus Annus* ("The Hundredth Year") offers both a look back at the *res novae*, the "new things" that seized the attention of Leo XIII, and a look ahead at what we might call the "new new things," the new facts of public life, at the end of the twentieth century and the turn of the third Christian millennium. Like other papal documents, *Centesimus Annus* reaffirms the classic themes of Catholic social thought. But it is John Paul II's creative extension of the tradition that makes *Centesimus Annus* a singularly bold document: one that reconfigures the boundaries of the Catholic debate over the right ordering of culture, economics, and politics for the foreseeable future.

Centesimus Annus is not, however, a matter of Catholic inside baseball. Like several of its predecessors, the encyclical addresses itself to "all men and women of good will." Moreover, scholars and religious leaders outside the formal boundaries of Roman Catholicism have been showing an increasing interest in modern Catholic

---

George Weigel is president of the Ethics and Public Policy Center.

social teaching as perhaps the most well-developed and coherent set of Christian reference points for conducting the argument about how Americans should order their lives, loves, and loyalties in society today. (Curiously enough, John Paul II has sometimes been more appreciated as a witness to Christian orthodoxy outside his church than within it: as a prominent Southern Baptist once put it to a group of Catholic colleagues, "Down where I come from, people are saying, 'You folks finally got yourself a pope who knows how to pope.' ")

Indeed, *Centesimus Annus* should be of special interest to citizens of the United States. For better and for worse—and usually for both—the United States is the test-bed for modernity, and for whatever-it-is that's going to come after modernity. The United States is the world's only superpower, and it is a superpower whose moral *raison d'être* is freedom. As a nation "conceived in liberty," and as the leader of the party of freedom in world politics, the United States might well pay careful attention to what the most influential moral leader in the contemporary world has to say about the many dimensions of freedom, and about the intimate relationship between freedom and truth, particularly the "truth about man" that has been such a prominent theme in the teaching of John Paul II.

Speaking in Miami in September 1987, the pope described the United States in these terms:

> Among the many admirable values of this nation there is one that stands out in particular. It is freedom. The concept of freedom is part of the very fabric of this nation as a political community of free people. Freedom is a great gift, a great blessing of God.
>
> From the beginning of America, freedom was directed to forming a well-ordered society and to promoting its peaceful life. Freedom was channeled to the fullness of human life, to the preservation of human dignity, and to the safeguarding of all human rights. An experience of ordered freedom is truly a part of the cherished story of this land.
>
> This is the freedom that America is called to live and guard and to transmit. She is called to exercise it in such a way that it will also benefit the cause of freedom in other nations and among

other peoples. The only true freedom, the only freedom that can truly satisfy, is the freedom to do what we ought as human beings created by God according to his plan. It is the freedom to live the truth of what we are and who we are before God, the truth of our identity as children of God, as brothers and sisters in a common humanity. That is why Jesus Christ linked truth and freedom together, stating solemnly, "You will know the truth and the truth will set you free" (John 8:32). All people are called to recognize the liberating truth of the sovereignty of God over them as individuals and as nations.

So much for the image of John-Paul-the-Polish-authoritarian so assiduously propounded by much of the prestige press (and by the party of dissent in American Catholicism). The truth of the matter is precisely the opposite: were there to be a nickname for this remarkable Bishop of Rome, he might well be called the "Pope of Freedom."

What John Paul II means by "freedom," of course, is not precisely what America's cultural elites have had in mind since the fevered "liberations" of the 1960s. And so an argument is engaged: What is this freedom that is a "great gift, a great blessing of God"? How is it to be lived by free men and women, in free societies that must protect individual liberty while concurrently advancing the common good?

Enter *Centesimus Annus.*

THE TRUTH ABOUT MAN

Viewed most comprehensively, *Centesimus Annus* is a profound meditation on human nature, on man's quest for a freedom that will truly satisfy the deepest yearnings of the human heart. John Paul II does not regard that human search for true freedom as something aberrant. Quite the contrary: the quest for freedom is "built in" to the very nature of man's way of being in the world, and "built in" precisely by a God whom we are to find, and worship, in freedom.

The "Problem" of Freedom

Centesimus Annus begins with a review of the teaching of Leo XIII in *Rerum Novarum*. For there, in 1891, the Church began to grapple with the new problem of freedom that had been created by the upheavals of the Industrial Revolution (in economics) and the French Revolution (in politics). "Traditional society was passing away and another was beginning to be formed—one which brought the hope of new freedoms but also the threat of new forms of injustice and servitude" (*Centesimus Annus*, paragraph 4). That threat was particularly grave when modernity ignored "the essential bond between human freedom and truth" (4). Leo XIII understood, his successor argues, that a "freedom which refused to be bound to the truth would fall into arbitrariness and end up submitting itself to the vilest of passions, to the point of self-destruction" (4). In the last decade of this bloodiest of centuries, it is difficult to suggest that Leo XIII was prematurely pessimistic about certain aspects of the modern quest for freedom.

From Leo XIII on, Catholic social teaching's "answer" to the "problem" of freedom has begun with a moral reflection on man himself, and an insistence on the dignity and worth of each individual human being as a creature endowed with intelligence and will, and thus made "in the image and likeness of God." Therefore the beginning of the answer to the rapaciousness of Manchesterian liberalism in economics was "the dignity of the worker . . . [and] the dignity of work" (6). And the beginning of the answer to the massive repression and injustice of twentieth-century tyrannies was Leo XIII's insistence on the "necessary limits to the State's intervention" in human affairs (8). Why are those limits "necessary"? Because "the individual, the family, and society are prior to the State, and . . . the State exists in order to protect their rights and not stifle them" (11).

The Catholic human-rights revolution of the late twentieth century thus owes a debt of gratitude to the last pope of the nineteenth century, Leo XIII, for it was Leo who first posed Christian personalism as the alternative to socialist collectivism (which subsumed human personality into the mass) and to radical individualism (which locked human personality into a self-made prison of solipsism). John Paul II, from the moment he took office in October 1978, has been a vigorous proponent of basic human rights, particularly the fundamental right of religious freedom. This pattern continues in *Centesimus Annus*, in which the pope decries the situation in those countries "which covertly, or even openly, deny to citizens of faiths other than that of the majority the full exercise of their civil and religious rights, preventing them from taking part in the cultural process, and restricting both the Church's right to preach the Gospel and the right of those who hear this preaching to accept it" (29).

"Rights": Deepening the Debate

For that reason, it is all the more striking that the human-rights language is a bit more muted in *Centesimus Annus* than in John Paul's earlier encyclicals—and far more muted than it was in Pope John XXIII's *Pacem in Terris*. John Paul II had not suddenly become less interested in the problems of human rights. Rather, he seemed determined to deepen (and, in some respects, to discipline) the debate over "rights" by linking rights to obligations and to truth.

On this latter point, John Paul argues forcefully that conscience is not a kind of moral free agent, in which an "autonomous self" declares something to be right because it is right "for me." No, conscience is "bound to the truth" (29). And the truth about man is not to be confused with "an appeal to the appetites and inclinations toward immediate gratification," an appeal that is "utilitarian" in character and does not reflect "the hierarchy of the true values of human existence" (29).

Nor are "rights" simply a matter of our immunities from the coercive power of others, important as such immunities are. Rights exist so that we can fulfill our obligations. Thus a man should be free economically so that he can enter into more cooperative relationships with others and meet his obligations to work in order to "provide for the needs of his family, his community, his nation, and ultimately all humanity" (43). Ownership, too, has its obligations: "Just as the person fully realizes himself in the free gift of self, so too ownership morally satisfies itself in the creation, at the proper time and in the proper way, of opportunities for work and human growth for all" (43).

By hearkening back to the Christian personalism of Leo XIII, while at the same time "thickening" the concept of "rights" in the Catholic tradition, John Paul II, in *Centesimus Annus*, provides a powerful example of Christian anthropology at its finest. But this is no abstract philosophical exercise. For having set the proper framework for thinking about public life, the pope immediately brings his analysis of the "truth about man" to bear on the Revolution of 1989 in Central and Eastern Europe.

REVOLUTION OF THE SPIRIT

The fundamental error of socialism is anthropological in nature. Socialism considers the individual person simply as an element, a molecule within the social organism, so that the good of the individual is completely subordinated to the functioning of the socio-economic mechanism. Socialism likewise maintains that the good of the individual can be realized without reference to his free choice, to the unique and exclusive responsibility he exercises in the face of good or evil. Man is thus reduced to a series of social relationships, and the concept of the person as the . . . subject of moral decision disappears, the very subject whose decisions build the social order.

From this mistaken conception of the person there arise both a distortion of law . . . and an opposition to private property. A person who is deprived of something he can call "his own," and of the possibility of earning a living through his own initiative, comes to depend on the social machine and on those who control it. This makes it much more difficult for him to recognize his dignity as a person, and hinders progress toward the building up of an authentic human community.

—*Centesimus Annus*, 13

Western political scientists and international-relations specialists have had a hard time figuring out what happened in Central and Eastern Europe in 1989. "Delayed modernization" seems to be the preferred answer from the ivory tower: the economic systems of the communist world couldn't compete, and the only way to change them was to get rid of the political regimes that had imposed collectivism in the first place. It is, in truth, a deliciously Marxist "answer" to the utter collapse of Marxism—and a worrisome indication of how deeply quasi-Marxist themes have sunk into the collective unconscious of the new knowledge class.

Pope John Paul II, for one, is not persuaded.

Centesimus Annus is well worth careful study for its marvelous third chapter alone. For in "The Year 1989," the pope offers a succinct, pointed, and persuasive analysis of the roots of the Revolution of 1989. The fundamental problem with communism or "Real Socialism" was not its economic decrepitude. Rather, communism failed because it denied "the truth about man." Communism's failures were first and foremost moral failures. "The God That Failed" was a false god whose acolytes led societies and economies into terminal crisis.

Yalta Revisited

Pope John Paul begins his historical analysis of "1989" in 1945, with the Yalta Agreements. "Yalta," in fact, has loomed very large indeed in the vision of the Polish pontiff. The Second World War, "which should have re-established freedom and restored the right of nations, ended without having attained these goals"—indeed, it ended with "the spread of Communist totalitarianism over more than half of Europe and over other parts of the world" (19). "Yalta," in other words, was more than a political decision; it was a moral catastrophe and a betrayal of the sacrifices of the war, a betrayal rooted in incomprehension of the nature of Marxist-Leninist totalitarianism. A failure of moral intuition led to a failure of politics.

And thus the first truth about Central and Eastern Europe is that the "Yalta arrangement" could not be regarded as merely a historical datum with which one had to deal. Dealing had to be done (not for nothing did Pope John Paul grow up under the tutelage of Cardinal Stefan Wyszyński of Warsaw, a tenacious prelate who gained the Church crucial breathing room in the 1950s). But there should be no illusions. The only "dealing" that would contribute to a genuine peace would be based on the conviction that no peace worthy of the name could be built on the foundations of Yalta.

As it began, so would it end. The origins of this bizarre and "suffocating" empire found their parallels, forty-four years later, in the ways in which the empire fell.

The moral catastrophe of Yalta was attacked at its roots by "the Church's commitment to defend and promote human rights," by a confrontation with Stalin's empire at the level of ethics, history, and culture. Communism, and particularly communist atheism, the pope says time and time again, was "an act against man" (22). And the antidote to the false humanism of Marxism-Leninism came from a truly Christian humanism in which men and women once again learned the human dignity that was theirs by birthright.

1979: A Return to Poland

That understanding had never been completely snuffed out in Central and Eastern Europe. But there was fear, the glue that held the Yalta imperial system together. Breaking the fever of fear was thus the crucial first step in addressing the calamity of Yalta.

And it seems, in retrospect, that the people of the region—first in Poland, and then elsewhere—began to face down their fear during John Paul II's first, dramatic return to Poland in June 1979. His message during that extraordinary pilgrimage was decidedly "pre-political": it was a message about ethics, culture, and history devoted to explicating "the truth about man" that Poles knew in their bones—which was precisely the truth that their regime had denied for two generations. It was not a message about "politics" in the narrow sense of the struggle for power. But it was high-octane "politics" in the more venerable sense of the term: "politics" as the ongoing argument about the good person, the good society, and the structure of freedom. And that upper-case Politics led, over time, to the distinctive lower-case politics of the Revolution of 1989, the revolution that reversed Yalta.

John Paul II believes that, among the "many factors involved in the fall of [these] oppressive regimes, some deserve special mention." The first point at which "the truth about man" intersected with lower-case politics was on the question of the rights of workers. And the pope does not hesitate to drive home the full irony of the situation:

It cannot be forgotten that the fundamental crisis of systems claiming to express the rule and indeed the dictatorship of the working class began with the great upheavals which took place in Poland in the name of solidarity. It was the throngs of working people which foreswore the ideology which presumed to speak in their name. On the basis of a hard, lived experience of work and of oppression, it was they who recovered and, in a sense, rediscovered the content and principles of the Church's social doctrine. (23)

That reappropriation of "the truth about man" led to another of the distinctive elements of the Revolution of 1989: its nonviolence. Tactical considerations surely played a role in the choice for nonviolence by what we used to call "dissidents": the bad guys had all the guns, and the good guys knew it. But it is hard to explain why the mass of the people remained nonviolent—particularly given the glorification of armed revolt in Polish history and culture—unless one understands that a moral revolution, a revolution of conscience, preceded the political revolution of '89.

Truth and Revolution

The pope was fully aware that the economic systems of Central and Eastern Europe were in a shambles by the mid-1980s, and that this shambles played its role in the collapse of Stalin's empire. But John Paul also argues that the economic disaster of command economies was not a "technical problem" alone, but rather "a consequence of the violation of the human rights to private initiative, to ownership of property, and to freedom in the economic sector" (24). Marxist economics, just like Leninist politics, refused to acknowledge "the truth about man."

State atheism in the Eastern bloc also carried the seeds of its own destruction, according to John Paul. The "spiritual void" the state created by building a world without windows "deprived the younger generation of direction and in many cases led them, in the irrepressible search for personal identity and for the meaning of life, to rediscover the religious roots of their national cultures, and to rediscover the person of Christ himself as the existentially adequate response to the desire in every human heart for goodness, truth, and life" (24). The communists, as noted above, had thought that they could "uproot the need for God from the human heart." What they learned was that "it is not possible to succeed in this without throwing the heart into turmoil" (24).

And communism onto the ash heap of history.

John Paul II's discussion of the Revolution of 1989 is carefully crafted, and makes no claims for the Church's role as agent of the Revolution that would strike any fair-minded reader as implausible or excessive. Nor was the Holy See unaware of the many other factors that conspired to produce the peaceful demolition of Stalin's empire: the Helsinki process, which publicly indicted communist regimes for their human-rights violations and created a powerful network of human-rights activists on both sides of the Iron Curtain; the fact of Mikhail Gorbachev; and the Strategic Defense Initiative (SDI), which any number of Vatican officials consider, privately, to have been decisive in forcing a change in Soviet policy.

But in *Centesimus Annus*, John Paul II was determined to teach a more comprehensive truth about the Revolution of 1989: that a revolution of the spirit, built on the sure foundation of "the truth about man," preceded the transfer of power from communist to democratic hands. The Revolution of 1989, viewed through this wide-angle lens, began in 1979. It was a revolution in which people learned first to throw off fear, and only then to throw off their chains—nonviolently. It was a revolution of conservation, in which people reclaimed their moral, cultural, and historical identities. It was, in short, a revolution from "the bottom up," the bottom being the historic ethical and cultural self-understandings of individuals and nations.

The Free Economy

Not only is it wrong from the ethical point of view to disregard human nature, which is made for freedom, but in practice it is impossible to do so. Where society is so organized as to reduce arbitrarily or even suppress the sphere in which freedom is legitimately exercised, the result is that the life of society becomes progressively disorganized and goes into decline.

Moreover, man, who was created for freedom, bears within himself the wound of original sin, which constantly draws him toward evil and puts him in need of redemption. Not only is this doctrine an integral part of Christian revelation; it also has great hermeneutical value insofar as it helps one to understand human reality. Man tends towards good, but he is also capable of evil. He can transcend his immediate interest and still remain bound to it.

The social order will be all the more stable, the more it takes this fact into account and does not place in opposition personal interest and the interests of society as a whole, but rather seeks to bring them into a fruitful harmony. In fact, when self-interest is violently suppressed, it is replaced by a burdensome system of bureaucratic control which dries up the wellsprings of initiative and creativity. When people think they possess the secret of a perfect social organization which makes evil impossible, they also think that they can use any means, including violence and deceit, in order to bring that organization into being. Politics then becomes a "secular religion" which operates under the illusion of creating paradise in this world. But no political society . . . can ever be confused with the Kingdom of God.

—*Centesimus Annus,* 25

Pope John Paul II does not hesitate to draw out the implications of his Christian anthropology of human freedom, and his analysis of the dynamics of the Revolution of 1989, in the field of economics. In fact, *Centesimus Annus* contains the most striking papal endorsement of the "free economy" in a century. The endorsement comes in the form of the answer to a pressing question:

Can it be said that, after the failure of Communism, capitalism is the victorious social system, and that capitalism should be the goal of the countries now making efforts to rebuild their economy and society? Is this the model which ought to be proposed to the countries of the Third World which are searching for the path to true economic and civil progress?

The answer is obviously complex. If by "capitalism" is meant an economic system which recognizes the fundamental and positive role of business, the market, private property, and the resulting responsibility for the means of production, as well as free human creativity in the economic sector, then the answer is certainly in the affirmative, even though it would perhaps be more appropriate to speak of a "business economy," "market economy," or simply "free economy." But if by "capitalism" is meant a system in which freedom in the economic sector is not circumscribed within a strong juridical framework which places it at the service of human freedom in its totality, and which sees it as a particular aspect of that freedom, the core of which is ethical and religious, then the reply is certainly negative. (42)

In other words, if by "capitalism" is meant what the West at its best means by capitalism—a tripartite system in which democratic politics and a vibrant moral culture discipline and temper the free market—then that is the system the pope urges the new democracies and the Third World to adopt, because that is the system most likely to sustain a human freedom that is truly liberating.

Some Striking Points

The defenders of the liberal status quo quickly insisted that this endorsement carries a lot of conditions with it. Of course it does; no surprises there. Nor would any thoughtful defender of the market deny the need for its careful regulation by law, culture, and public morality. What is new about *Centesimus Annus* comes in passages like these:

■ "The modern business economy has positive aspects. Its basis is human freedom exercised in the economic field, just as it is exercised in many other fields" (32).

■ "It is precisely the ability to foresee both the needs of others and the combinations of productive factors most adapted to satisfying those needs that constitutes another important source of wealth in modern society. Besides, many goods cannot be adequately produced through the work of an isolated individual; they require the cooperation of many people in working towards a common goal. Organizing such a productive effort, planning its duration in time, making sure that it corresponds in a positive way to the demands which it must satisfy, and taking the necessary risks—all this too is a source of wealth in today's society. In this way, the role of disciplined and creative human work and, as an essential part of that work, initiative and entrepreneurial ability becomes increasingly evident and decisive" (32).

■ "Another task of the State is that of overseeing and directing the exercise of human rights in the economic sector. However, primary responsibility in this area belongs not to the State but to individuals and to the various groups and associations which make up society. The State could not directly ensure the right to work for all its citizens unless it controlled every aspect of economic life and restricted the free initiative of individuals" (48).

■ "Indeed, besides the earth, man's principal resource is man himself" (32).

Centesimus Annus thus marks a decisive break with the curious materialism that had characterized aspects of modern Catholic social teaching since Leo XIII. Wealth-creation today, John Paul II readily acknowledges, has more to do with human creativity and imagination, and with political and economic systems capable of unleashing that creativity and imagination, than with "resources" *per se*. And that, John Paul II seems to suggest, is one of the "signs of the times" to which Catholic social thought must be attentive.

An Empirical View of the "Option"

In fact, one of the most distinctive characteristics of *Centesimus Annus* is its empirical sensitivity. John Paul II has clearly thought carefully about what does and what doesn't work in exercising a "preferential option for the poor" in the new democracies, in the Third World, and in impoverished parts of the developed world. The "preferential option," the pope seems to suggest, is a formal principle: its content should be determined, not on the basis of ideological orthodoxy (that is what was rejected in the Revolution of 1989), but by empirical facts. And so far as John Paul is concerned, the evidence is in. What works best for the poor is democratic polities and properly regulated market economies. Why? Because democracy and the market are the systems that best cohere with human nature, with human freedom, with "the truth about man."

It will take some time for this new departure in Catholic social thought to be digested by those committed to what the pope calls the "impossible compromise between Marxism and Christianity" (26), as well as by those who continue to search for a chimerical Catholic "third way" between capitalism and socialism. (At a meeting in Rome, for example, shortly after the encyclical was published, I was informed by the dean of the social-science faculty at the Pontifical Gregorian University that "Capitalism A [i.e., the capitalism the pope endorses in the paragraph cited above] exists only in textbooks." I privately suggested to the dean, a Latin American Jesuit, that if he really believed that, he had no business running a faculty of social science.) But the text of *Centesimus Annus* itself is plain: the authoritative teaching of the Catholic Church is that a properly regulated market, disciplined by politics, law, and culture, is best for poor people. It works. And it gives the poor an "option" to exercise their freedom as economic actors that is available in no other system.

CULTURE WARS

It is not possible to understand man on the basis of economics alone, nor to define him simply on the basis of class membership. Man is understood in a more complete way when he is situated within the sphere of culture through his language, history, and the position he takes toward the fundamental events of life, such as birth, love, work, and death. At the heart of every culture lies the attitude man takes to the greatest mystery: the mystery of God. Different cultures are basically different ways of facing the question of the meaning of personal existence. When this question is eliminated, the cultural and moral life of nations is corrupted.

—*Centesimus Annus*, 24

The truth of the matter is that, in *Centesimus Annus*, John Paul II is rather more concerned about the "culture" leg of the politics-economics-culture triad than he is about the argument between market economists and those still defending state-centered schemes of development. The latter debate has been settled. The real issue remains the ability of a culture to provide the market with the moral framework it needs to serve the cause of integral human development.

Once again, "1989" is on the pope's mind. Can the new democracies develop societies that provide for the free exercise of human creativity in the workplace, in politics, and in the many fields of culture, without becoming libertine in their public moral life? Will "consumerism"—that is, consumption as an ideology, not as a natural part of what dissidents used to call a "normal society"—replace Marxism-Leninism as the new form of bondage east of the Elbe River?

The pope is not persuaded by libertarian arguments. "Of itself," he writes, "the economic system does not possess criteria for correctly distinguishing new and higher forms of satisfying human needs from artificial new needs which hinder the formation of a mature personality." And so the market cannot be left on its own, so to speak. "A great deal of educational and cultural work is urgently needed" (36), so that the market's remarkable capacity to generate wealth is bent toward ends that are congruent with "the truth about man"—which is not, John Paul continually urges, an economic truth alone (or even primarily).

In fact, the pope seems convinced that consumerism-the-ideology ought to be blamed, not on the market system, but on the moral-cultural system's failures to discipline the market:

These criticisms [of consumerism in its hedonistic form] are directed not so much against an economic system as against an ethical and cultural system. . . . If economic life is absolutized, if the production and consumption of goods become the center of social life and society's only value . . . the reason is to be found not so much in the economic system itself as in the fact that the entire socio-cultural system, by ignoring the ethical and religious dimension, has been weakened, and ends by limiting itself to the production of goods and services alone. (39)

But *Centesimus Annus* can by no means be taken as a dreary exercise in papal scolding. John Paul II knows that the things of this world are important, and that material goods can enhance man's capacity for living a freedom worthy of a being made in the image and likeness of God. "It is not wrong to want to live better," according to the pope. "What is wrong is a style of life which is presumed to be better when it is directed toward 'having' rather than 'being,' and which wants to have more, not in order to be more but in order to spend life in enjoyment as an end in itself" (36).

Reconstructing Civil Society

So what is to be done? John Paul II is highly critical of the excesses of the welfare state, which he styles the "social assistance state." Here, the pope argues, is another abuse of human freedom: "By intervening directly and depriving society of its responsibility, the Social Assistance State leads to a loss of human energies and an inordinate increase of public agencies, which are dominated more by bureaucratic ways of thinking than by concern for serving their clients, and which are accompanied by an enormous increase in spending."

John Paul's preference, which is an expression of the classic Catholic principle of "subsidiarity," is for what, in the American context, would be called "mediating structures": "Needs are best understood and satisfied by people who are closest to [the poor, the weak, the stricken] and who act as neighbors to those in need" (48). Such mediating structures—religious institutions, voluntary organizations, unions, business associations, neighborhood groups, service organizations, and the like—are the backbone of what Václav Havel and others in Central and Eastern Europe have called "civil society." And the reconstruction of civil society is the first order of business in setting the foundations of democracy: a message that ought to be taken to heart by those in the West, too.

In sum, what is needed is a public moral culture that encourages "life-styles in which the quest for truth, beauty, goodness, and communion with others for the sake of common growth are the factors which determine consumer choices, savings, and invest-ments" (36). We do not live in hermetically sealed containers labeled "economic life," "politics," and "lifestyle." John Paul insists that it is all of a piece. There is only one human universe, and it is an inescapably moral universe in which questions of "ought" emerge at every juncture: or as the pope puts it, "Even the decision to invest in one place rather than another, in one productive sector rather than another, is always a moral and cultural choice" (36).

And as with economics, so with politics. I have stressed here the importance of "1989" in the pope's historical vision. But by "1989," the pope means a set of events fraught with meaning for the West as well as for the East. John Paul II has vigorously positioned the Church on the side of the democratic revolution throughout the world, not because he is a geopolitician, but because he is a moral teacher and a pastor. The Church, he insists, "has no models to present." But, as an expression of its fundamental concern for "the truth about man," the Church "values the demo-cratic system inasmuch as it ensures the participation of citizens in making political choices, guarantees to the governed the possibility of both electing and holding accountable those who govern them, and of replacing them through peaceful means when appropriate" (46).

Truth and Democracy

John Paul II is almost Lincolnian in wondering whether nations "so conceived and so dedicated can long endure," particularly given the attitude toward the relationship between rights and obligations, between rights and the truth, that one finds in Western cultural elites. It is not as Cassandra but as a friend of democracy that John Paul II lays down this challenge:

> Nowadays there is a tendency to claim that agnosticism and skeptical relativism are the philosophy and the basic attitude which correspond to democratic forms of political life. Those who are convinced that they know the truth and firmly adhere to it are considered unreliable from a democratic point of view, since they do not accept that truth is determined by the majority, or that it is subject to variation according to different political trends. It must be observed in this regard that if there is no ultimate truth to guide and direct political activity, then ideas and convictions can easily be manipulated for reasons of power. As history demonstrates, a democracy without values easily turns into open or thinly disguised totalitarianism. (46)

Still, the pope continues, "the Church respects the legitimate autonomy of the democratic order," and the Church "is not entitled to express preferences for this or that institutional or constitutional solution." Rather, the Church is the Church, and thus "her contribution to the political order is precisely her vision of the dignity of the person revealed in all its fullness in the mystery of the Incarnate Word" (47).

Centesimus Annus is an extraordinary statement of faith: faith in freedom; faith in man's capacity to order his public life properly; above all, faith in God, who created man with intelligence and free will. It may well be regarded, in time, as the greatest of the social encyclicals, given the breadth of the issues it addresses, the depth at which questions are probed, and the empirical sensitivity John Paul II shows to the "signs of the times" as they illuminate freedom's cause at the end of the twentieth century. With *Centesimus Annus*, the "Pope of Freedom" not only marked the centenary of a great tradition. He brilliantly scouted the terrain for the next hundred years of humanity's struggle to embody in public life the truth that makes us free.

Notes

Chapter 1

WILLIAM MURPHY

1. I am indebted to the French Jesuit Joseph Joblin for his basic work in this area. See, for example, his contribution to the symposium *Rerum Novarum—Laborem Exercens 2000*, published in 1982 by the Pontifical Commission on Justice and Peace.

2. John Tracy Ellis, *The Life of James Cardinal Gibbons*, vol. 1 (Milwaukee: Bruce Publishing Co., 1952), 530.

3. The numbers refer to those inserted in the revised Latin text published in 1931; the official internal numbering by the Holy See did not start until *Pacem in Terris* in 1963, and with earlier documents there can be variations. The translation is that of the Catholic Truth Society, published in 1961.

Chapter 2

THOMAS C. KOHLER

1. For a thoughtful treatment of the development of the social teachings generally, see Richard Camp, *The Papal Ideology of Social Reform: A Study in Historical Development, 1878–1967* (Leiden: E. J. Brill, 1969). Also see the frequently cited work of Jean-Yves Calvez, S.J., and Jacques Perrin, S.J., *The Church and Social Justice: The Social Teachings of the Popes from Leo XIII to Pius XII (1878–1958)*, trans. J. R. Kirwan (Chicago: Henry Regnery Co., 1961).

2. For a firsthand account of his work on the encyclical, see Oswald von Nell-Breuning, S.J., "The Drafting of 'Quadragesimo Anno,'" in *Readings in Moral Theology No. 5: Official Catholic Social Teaching*, ed. Charles Curran and Richard McCormick (New York: Paulist Press, 1986), 60–61 [hereinafter referred to as *Readings*]. Though not authoritative, also of interest is Nell-Breuning, *Reorganization of Social Economy: The Social Encyclical Developed and Explained*, trans. Bernard Dempsey, S.J. (New York: Bruce Publishing Co., 1936).

3. Nell-Breuning, in *Readings*, 62.

4. One commentator remarked that "Nell-Breuning is so often quoted in [SPD] party discussions . . . that he has become something of a focal point in

Party theorizing" (Douglas A. Chalmers, *The Social Democratic Party of Germany: From Working Class Movement to Modern Political Party* [New Haven: Yale University Press, 1964], 218, n. 39).

5. On this point, see Thomas C. Kohler, "Lessons from the Social Charter: State, Corporation and the Meaning of Subsidarity," *University of Toronto Law Journal*, Summer 1993, 43.

6. Nell-Breuning, in *Readings*, 61.

7. On Bishop Ketteler's thought and its context, see John Laux (George Metlake, pseud.), *Christian Social Reform: Program Outlined by Its Pioneer, William Emmanuel Baron von Ketteler, Bishop of Mainz* (Philadelphia: The Dolphin Press, 1912); and William Hogan, *The Development of Bishop William Emmanuel von Ketteler's Interpretation of the Social Problem* (Washington, D.C.: The Catholic University of America Press, 1946).

8. Quoted in Edward Cahill, S.J., "The Catholic Social Movement," in *Readings*, 9. Also see Laux, *Christian Social Reform*, 26.

9. Laux, *Christian Social Reform*, 5.

10. Ibid., 31.

11. This aspect of subsidiarity constitutes the principle of autonomy or the duty of non-interference, and is sometimes referred to as "negative" subsidiarity. It represents a point of similarity between Catholic social thought and classical liberal theory.

12. This affirmative duty of intervention is sometimes called "positive" subsidiarity. It is one feature of the principle that sharply distinguishes subsidiarity from classical liberalism. While larger organizations have the duty to assist, subsidiarity insists that intervention should occur at the lowest competent level possible, reserving state intervention as a last resort. This regulation of competencies is known as the principle of hierarchy.

13. An early formulation of the principle might be found in the aphorism of the Jesuit Luigi Taparelli d'Azeglio (1793–1862): "As much liberty as possible, as much authority as necessary." Taparelli was one of the most influential of nineteenth-century Catholic social theorists. He was, incidentally, named rector of the Roman College upon its restoration in 1824, the year that the 14-year-old Gioacchino Pecci (subsequently, Leo XIII) began his studies there.

14. *Quadragesimo Anno*, as quoted in Joseph Komonchak, "Subsidiarity in the Church: The State of the Question," *The Jurist* 48 (1988): 298–99.

15. John Coleman, S.J., "Development of Church Social Teaching," in *Readings*, 183.

16. Komonchak, "Subsidiarity in the Church," 300.

17. Ibid., 298, n.1.

18. Also see the teachings concerning subsidiarity in the "new" catechism, presently available in French under the title *Catéchisme de L'Église Catholique* (Paris: Mame /Plon, 1992), ¶¶ 1883, 1885, 1894, 2209.

19. Komonchak, "Subsidiarity in the Church," 301–2, and sources cited.

20. Nell-Breuning, in *Readings*, 62.

21. Komonchak, "Subsidiarity in the Church," 300.

22. In fact, paragraph 86 of the encyclical specifically leaves the choice of the form of the order of a state to its citizens, subject only to the requirements of "justice and the common good."

23. Chantal Millon-Delsol, *L'Etat Subsidiare: Ingérence et non-ingérence de*

l'Etat: le principe de subsidiarité aux fondements de l'histoire européenne (Paris: Presses Universitaires de France, 1992), 158–59. Also see the somewhat more sympathetic account in Paul Misner, *Social Catholicism in Europe: From the Onset of Industrialization to the First World War* (New York: Crossroad, 1991),169–81, 202–11; see also the remarkably concise account by Franz H. Mueller (a student of Pesch's and a member of the Königswinter circle), *The Church and the Social Question* (Washington, D.C.: American Enterprise Institute, 1984).

24. Chantal Millon-Delsol, *L'Etat Subsidiare*, 153.

25. Nell-Breuning, in *Readings*, 64–65.

26. Coleman, in *Readings*, 174.

27. Ibid. For Nell-Breuning's comments on the significance of corporatism and its decline as a part of the social teachings, see Nell-Breuning, in *Readings*, 64–67.

28. On this point, see Ernest L. Fortin, A.A., "Sacred and Inviolable: *Rerum Novarum* and Natural Rights," *Theological Studies* 53 (1992): 203–33.

29. James V. Schall, S.J., "From Catholic Social Doctrine to the Kingdom of Christ on Earth," in *Readings*, 322.

30. Aristotle, *Nicomachean Ethics*, trans. Terence Irwin (Indianapolis: Hackett Publishing Co., 1985), 1170b, 10–15.

31. Edmund Burke, *Reflections on the Revolution in France*, ed. Thomas Mahoney (Indianapolis: Bobbs-Merrill, 1955), 53.

32. On these points see Thomas C. Kohler, "Individualism and Communitarianism at Work," *Brigham Young University Law Review*, Summer 1993, and sources cited therein.

33. For a more developed statement by the "father" of the communitarian movement, see Amitai Etzioni, *The Spirit of Community: Rights, Responsibilities and the Communitarian Agenda* (New York: Crown Publishers, 1993).

34. See, for example, "The First Communitarian Teach-In," *The Responsive Community* 2 (Winter 1991–92): 21–26.

35. "The Responsive Communitarian Platform: Rights and Responsibilities," *The Responsive Community* 2 (Winter 1991–92): 4–20.

36. In *Laborem Exercens*, John Paul II characterizes the labor union as "an indispensable element of social life, especially in modern industrialized societies" (*Laborem Exercens*, 20). Reiterating the teaching of *Rerum Novarum* and *Quadragesimo Anno*, *Laborem Exercens* emphasizes the contributions unions can make in fostering authentic human development. In his first encyclical, John Paul II also reasserts the Church's long-held position that the state must protect the freedom of employees to form autonomous unions of their choosing, a position that he strongly restates in *Centesimus Annus* (e.g., 7). The labor union, *Laborem Exercens* declares, "remains a constructive factor of social order and solidarity, and it is impossible to ignore it" (20).

37. Steelworkers *v.* Warrior and Gulf Navigation Co., 363 U.S. 564, 580 (1964).

38. Richard Weaver, "Two Types of American Individualism," in *The Southern Essays of Richard M. Weaver*, ed. George M. Curtis III and James J. Thompson, Jr. (Indianapolis: Liberty Press, 1987), 82.

39. Ibid., 85.

40. On the role and application of the subsidiarity principle in the European Community, see Kohler, "Lessons from the Social Charter."

41. An excellent study of the role of mediating structures in the modern welfare

state that is consistent with the subsidiarity principle can be found in Peter L. Berger and Richard John Neuhaus, *To Empower People: The Role of Mediating Structures in Public Policy* (Washington, D.C.: American Enterprise Instutute, 1977).

Chapter 3

ROBERT A. SIRICO

1. The official date of promulgation was May 15, 1961, although the document was not actually released to the public until the summer of that year.

2. Matthew Habinger, O.S.B., provides a concise picture of the "authorship" of *Mater et Magistra* in his excellent study *Papal Teaching on Private Property: 1891–1981* (Lanham, Md.: University Press of America, 1990), 220.

3. The key exchanges among Catholics over the encyclical may be found in *National Review*, 29 July, 12 August, 26 August, and 4 November 1961; *America*, 19 August, 30 September 1961; *Commonweal*, 28 July 1961; and *The Wanderer*, Summer 1961.

4. Thomas Aquinas, *Summa Theologiae*, 2a2ae. 66.

5. As Jean-Yves Calvez, S.J., has noted: " . . . certain aspects of Mater et Magistra are novel in relation to St. Thomas; and the arguments used by John XXIII in favor of private property call for its distribution to a far greater degree than did other arguments put forth in the past" (*The Social Thought of John XXIII*, trans. George J. M. McKenzier, S.M. [Westport, Conn.: Greenwood Press, 1977], 22).

6. For an insightful discussion of the problems associated with economic calculation and the usefulness of the market as a means for the coordination of data contained in prices, see Ludwig von Mises, *Human Action*, 3d ed. (Chicago: Contemporary Books, 1966), 206–11.

7. Michael Novak, *Freedom with Justice* (San Francisco: Harper and Row, 1984), 117.

8. A fine and justly acclaimed discussion of the common good may be found in Michael Novak, *Free Persons and the Common Good* (New York: Madison Books, 1989).

9. Karl Rahner, *Foundations of Christian Faith* (New York: Seabury Press, 1978).

10. See Aquinas, *Summa Theologiae*, 1a2ae. 94, 5, and 105, 2.

11. The various translations of the phrase in the encyclical tradition that labor be treated with the dignity due human beings and not, for example, as a "mere commodity" (*vilis merx*), "chattel," "slaves," "bondsmen," or "tools," lends weight to the distinction Michael Novak draws (based on Abraham Lincoln) between free labor and slave labor. Chattel is a form of merchandise that can be bought and sold. Labor, Novak observes, is different in a free economy: "Merchandise can be bought; it is not hired. The hired laborer retains an independence and a dignity lacking both to the peasants and serfs of central Europe and to slaves in America" (Novak, *Freedom with Justice*, 152).

12. Jean-Yves Calvez, S.J., and Jacques Perrin, S.J., *The Church and Social Justice:*

The Social Teaching of the Popes from Leo XIII to Pius XII (1878–1958), trans. J. R. Kirwan (Chicago: Henry Regnery Co., 1961), 247.

13. Aquinas, *Summa Theologiae*, 2a2ae. 66, 2.

14. F. A. Hayek, *The Uses of Knowledge in Society* (Menlo Park, Ca.: Institute for Human Studies, 1977), 7.

15. Calvez, *Social Thought of John XXIII*, 49–50.

16. A representative selection of their works follows:

Wilhelm Röpke, *A Humane Economy* (Chicago: Henry Regnery Co., 1960);

Ludwig von Mises, *Liberalism in the Classic Tradition*, 3d ed. (San Francisco: Cobden Press, 1985);

Henry Hazlitt, *The Foundations of Morality* (Lanham, Md.: University Press of America, 1988);

F. A. Hayek, *The Fatal Conceit* (Chicago: University of Chicago Press, 1988);

Israel Kirzner, *Discovery, Capitalism and Distributive Justice* (New York: Basil Blackwell, 1989).

17. See Alejandro Chafuen, *Christians for Freedom* (San Francisco: Ignatius Press, 1987).

18. For an extensive discussion of the Church's role in the downfall of communism, see George Weigel's *The Final Revolution: The Resistance Church and the Collapse of Communism* (New York: Oxford University Press, 1992).

Chapter 4

George Weigel

1. John Cogley, "Peace on Earth," *Commonweal*, 26 April 1963, 158.

2. John Courtney Murray, "Things Old and New in *Pacem in Terris*," *America*, 27 April 1973, 612.

3. Reinhold Niebuhr, "*Pacem in Terris*: Two Views," *Christianity & Crisis*, 13 May 1963, 81, 83.

4. Paul Ramsey, "*Pacem in Terris*," in *The Just War: Force and Political Responsibility* (New York: Charles Scribner's Sons, 1968), 85.

5. Max M. Kampelman, *Three Years at the East-West Divide* (New York: Freedom House, 1983).

6. See my essays "Religious Freedom: The First Human Right," *This World*, Spring 1988, 31–45; and "Catholicism and Democracy: The Other Twentieth Century Revolution," *The Washington Quarterly*, Autumn 1989, 5–25.

7. *Sollicitudo Rei Socialis*, paragraph 44.

8. For a more detailed analysis of the Church's role(s) in the demise of European communism, see my study *The Final Revolution: The Resistance Church and the Collapse of Communism* (New York: Oxford University Press, 1992).

9. Even to the point where, in so mild-mannered a country as Canada, renascent and assertive Quebecois nationalism is threatening to undo the Canadian federation.

10. David Martin, *Tongues of Fire: The Explosion of Protestantism in Latin America* (Oxford: Basil Blackwell, 1990).

11. In both cases, it should be added, these refined sentiments are usually

accompanied by one or another species of what would be called, in the vulgate, wog-bashing.

Chapter 5

MARY EBERSTADT

1. Nathan Glazer, "Interests and Passions," *The Public Interest,* Fall 1985, 17–30.
2. Auberon Waugh, "Now We Must Take Action to Keep the Flood of Unemployables at Bay," *The Spectator,* 13 February 1993, 8.
3. Irving Kristol, "Skepticism, Meliorism, and *The Public Interest,*" *The Public Interest,* Fall 1985, 31–41.

Chapter 6

KENNETH L. GRASSO

1. George Weigel, "Catholicism and Democracy," *The Washington Quarterly,* Autumn 1989, 5.
2. For overviews of the problem of church-state relations that place the nineteenth-century problematic in a broader historical context, see Luigi Sturzo, *Church and State,* trans. Barbara Barclay Carter (New York: Longmans, Green and Co., 1939); and Joseph Lecler, S.J., *The Two Sovereignties* (New York: The Philosophical Library, 1952).
3. For in-depth examinations of what might be called laicist democracy, see John Courtney Murray, "The Church and Totalitarian Democracy," *Theological Studies,* December 1952, 525–63; and "Leo XIII: Separation of Church and State," *Theological Studies,* June 1953, 145–214. Cf. J. L. Talmon, *The Origins of Totalitarian Democracy* (Boston: Beacon Press, 1942).
4. On this tradition, see R. W. Carlyle and A. J. Carlyle, *A History of Medieval Political Theory in the West,* 6 vols. (Edinburgh: William Blackwood and Sons, 1936).
5. Pius XII, "1944 Christmas Message" (Washington, D.C.: National Catholic Welfare Conference, n.d.), 3.
6. Pius XII, radio message, 1 June 1941, in *Acta Apostolicae Sedis* 33 (1941): 200.
7. "1944 Christmas Message," 4.
8. For an overview of the evolution of Murray's thought on religious freedom, see Thomas T. Love, *John Courtney Murray: Contemporary Church-State Theory* (Garden City, N.Y.: Doubleday, 1965). For an extremely thoughtful critical analysis of Murray's work, see Keith Pavlischeck, *John Courtney Murray and the Dilemma of Religious Toleration* (Kirksville, Mo.: Thomas Jefferson University Press, forthcoming). An account of the controversy stirred by Murray's essays and his

role at the council is found in Donald E. Pelotte, S.S., *John Courtney Murray: Theologian in Conflict* (New York: Paulist Press, 1975). Richard Regan's *Conflict and Consensus: Religious Freedom and the Second Vatican Council* (New York: Macmillan, 1967) offers an excellent overview of the drafting of *Dignitatis Humanae*.

9. References to *Dignitatis Humanae* are from the translation in John Courtney Murray, S.J., ed., *Religious Liberty: An End and a Beginning* (New York: Macmillan, 1966), which was reprinted from *The Documents of Vatican II* (New York: Guild Press, America Press, and Association Press, 1966). In the parenthetical citations, the page number in the Murray volume is preceded by the article number in the declaration.

10. This phrase is found in the notes Murray attached to the text of the declaration in *Religious Liberty*, 167, n. 5.

11. Cf. Gerard V. Bradley, "Dogmatomachy—A Privatization Theory of the Religion Clause Cases," *St. Louis Law Journal* 30 (1986): 275–330.

12. Richard John Neuhaus, *The Naked Public Square* (Grand Rapids: William B. Eerdmans, 1984), 89.

13. Francis Canavan, S.J., "The Catholic Concept of Religious Freedom as a Human Right," in *Religious Liberty*, ed. Murray, 77.

14. John Courtney Murray, S.J., "The Issue of Church and State at Vatican Council II," *Theological Studies*, December 1966, 599.

15. For some suggestion as to how the line of argument adumbrated by the declaration might be developed, see Murray, "The Declaration on Religious Freedom: A Moment in Its Legislative History," in *Religious Liberty*, ed. Murray, 38–42.

16. John H. Hallowell, *The Moral Foundations of Democracy* (Chicago: University of Chicago Press, 1954), 65.

17. Jacques Maritain, *The Twilight of Civilization*, trans. Lionel Landry (New York: Sheed & Ward, 1944), 62. For a detailed discussion of this point, see Maritain, *Scholasticism and Politics*, trans. Mortimer J. Adler (New York: Macmillan, 1940), 56–117.

18. Alexander Hamilton, James Madison, and John Jay, *The Federalist Papers* (New York: Bantam Books, 1982), 284. For a discussion of *The Federalist's* analysis of the moral and cultural preconditions of democracy, see Kenneth L. Grasso, "Pluralism, the Public Good and the Problem of Self-Government in *The Federalist*," *Interpretation*, May–June 1987, 324–45.

19. Daniel Bell, *The Cultural Contradictions of Capitalism* (New York: Basic Books, 1978), 245.

20. R. Bruce Douglass, "Liberalism as a Threat to Democracy," in *The Ethical Dimensions of Political Life*, ed. Francis Canavan, S.J. (Durham, N.C.: Duke University Press, 1983), 33–34.

21. Jacques Maritain, *Christianity and Democracy* and *The Rights of Man and Natural Law*, trans. Doris C. Anson (San Francisco: Ignatius Press, 1986), 98.

22. Ibid., 89–90.

23. John Courtney Murray, S.J., "The School and Christian Freedom," *Proceedings of the National Catholic Educational Association* 48 (August 1951): 64.

24. For an overview of today's *Kulturkampf*, see James Davison Hunter, *Culture Wars: The Struggle to Define America* (New York: Basic Books, 1991).

25. Cf. John H. Hallowell, *The Decline of Liberalism as an Ideology* (Berkeley: University of California Press, 1943).

26. Michael Sandel, "Freedom of Conscience or Freedom of Choice," in *Articles of Peace, Articles of Faith: The Religious Liberty Clauses and the American Public Philosophy*, ed. James Davison Hunter and Os Guinness (Washington, D.C.: The Brookings Institution, 1990), 75–76.

27. Stanley C. Brubaker, "Tribe and the Transformation of American Constitutional Law," *Benchmark*, Spring 1990, 122.

28. Francis Canavan, S.J., "The Pluralist Game," *Law and Contemporary Problems* 44 (Spring 1981): 23.

29. On the topic of anomic democracy, see Michael J. Crozier, Samuel P. Huntington, and Joji Watanuki, *The Crisis of Democracy* (New York: New York University Press, 1975).

30. For solid analyses of today's rights revolution, see William Donahue, *The New Freedom* (New Brunswick, N.J.: Transaction, 1990); and Mary Ann Glendon, *Rights Talk* (New York: Free Press, 1991).

31. Cf. William Ernest Hocking, *The Coming World Civilization* (New York: Harper & Brothers, 1956).

32. See Allan Bloom, *The Closing of the American Mind* (New York: Simon & Schuster, 1984). "Nihilism, American Style" is the title of Part Two of this work.

33. Will Herberg, "What Is the Moral Crisis of Our Time?" *Intercollegiate Review*, Fall 1986, 9. This essay was reprinted from the January–February 1968 issue of this journal.

34. George F. Will, *Statecraft as Soulcraft* (New York: Simon & Schuster, 1983), 22.

35. Cf. Arthur M. Schlesinger, Jr. "The Opening of the American Mind," *New York Times Book Review*, 23 July 1989. Richard Rorty is, perhaps, the preeminent example of a liberal theorist who recognizes the inability of liberal philosophy to provide a metaphysical foundation for the rights liberalism champions in the political arena. Cf. Richard Rorty, "The Priority of Democracy to Philosophy," in *The Virginia Statute for Religious Freedom*, ed. Merrill D. Peterson and Robert C. Vaughan (Cambridge: Cambridge University Press, 1988), 257–82, and Richard Rorty, *Contingency, Irony and Solidarity* (Cambridge: Cambridge University Press, 1989). Ronald Dworkin would also seem to recognize this fact. See his *Taking Rights Seriously* (Cambridge, Mass.: Harvard University Press, 1978), 81.

36. Thomas A. Spragens, Jr., *The Irony of Liberal Reason* (Chicago: University of Chicago Press, 1981), and Alisdair MacIntyre, *After Virtue*, 2d ed. (University of Notre Dame Press, 1984).

37. Irving Kristol, *On the Democratic Idea in America* (New York: Harper & Row, 1972), 20.

38. Canavan, "The Catholic Concept of Religious Freedom as a Human Right," 71.

39. Jacques Maritain, "The Conquest of Freedom," in *Freedom: Its Meaning*, ed. Ruth Nanda Anshen (New York: Harcourt, Brace and Co., 1940), 636.

40. John XXIII, *Pacem in Terris* in *The Encyclicals and Other Messages of John XXIII* (Washington, D.C.: TPS Press, 1964), 335.

41. Edmund Burke, *The Works of Edmund Burke*, vol. 4 (Waltham, Mass.: Little, Brown and Co., 1866), 51–52.

42. Mary Ann Glendon, *Rights Talk*, 143.

43. "What's Your Best Hope for the 1990s?" *Wall Street Journal*, 27 December 1989, A6.

Chapter 7

ROBERT ROYAL

1. All citations from *Populorum Progressio* in this essay are drawn from the translation published by the U. S. Catholic Conference entitled "On the Development of Peoples" (Washington, D.C., 1967).

2. No one who examines the evidence fairly could believe that the Vatican supported, or was even willing to tolerate, Hitler before and during World War II. Pius XII was much honored and thanked by the Jewish community for his rescue services. But the fair-minded observer Albert Camus has remarked that "during those frightful years I waited for a great voice to speak up in Rome." Camus never heard such a voice:

> It has been explained to me since that the condemnation was indeed voiced. But that it was in the style of the encyclicals, which is not at all clear. The condemnation was voiced and it was not understood! Who could fail to see where the true condemnation lies in this case. . . .What the world expects of Christians is that Christians should speak out, loud and clear, and that they should voice their condemnation in such a way that never a doubt, never the slightest doubt, could rise in the heart of the simplest man. That they should get away from abstraction and confront the blood-stained face history has taken on today. The grouping we need is a grouping of men resolved to speak out clearly and pay up personally. (From Camus's 1948 address to the Dominican monks of Latour Maubourg. He was invited to speak about "What Unbelievers Expect from Christians." The essay was collected in Albert Camus, *Resistance, Rebellion, and Death*, trans. Justin O'Brien [New York: Modern Library, 1960], 53.)

Many have defended the Vatican's approach in this instance as a prudential judgment about the ill effects speaking out would have had on various people, as occurred in Holland after that country's hierarchy publicly condemned the Nazis. That may be so, and the Vatican may have judged the situation correctly. Yet even these explanations suggest that there is something amiss in the issuing of equivocal public pronouncements by an institution essentially wedded to the promulgation of truth.

3. Nearly twenty-five years after the appearance of *Populorum Progressio*, the *spirit* reflected in its style is perhaps more worrisome than any of its practical failings. The great modern poet W. B. Yeats, no mean judge of stylistic overtones, once observed:

> We proclaim that we can forgive the sinner, but abhor the atheist, and that we count among atheists bad writers and Bishops of all denominations. "The Holy Spirit is an intellectual fountain," and did the Bishops believe that Holy Spirit would show itself in decoration and architecture, in daily manners and written style? What devout man can read the Pastorals of our Hierarchy without horror at a style rancid, coarse and vague, like that of the daily papers?

Yeats may be a bit too hard on the bishops of his day and ecclesial solidarity prevents our applying his criticism too rigorously to popes and bishops of our own time. But his exaggeration underscores a kernel of truth: defects of style can also indicate moral, perhaps even spiritual, failings.

Yeats's spiritual-aesthetic complaints and Camus's moral objections to the style of the Church's public pronouncements, however, return us to a classical insight. Spirituality, morality, and aesthetics are related to one another, as the classical world knew in its positing of the True, the Good, and the Beautiful among the transcendental properties of existence. The pope and bishops generally take fair aim at the good. They less frequently achieve beauty of thought and expression. And partly as a result of this failure, when it comes to truth, they are long on moral verities and short on empirical verification.

4. The trendy aid policies of the encyclical were so blinding, however, that its Catholic underpinnings were lost on various commentators. The libertarian Catholic economist P. T. Bauer, writing in irritation almost twenty years later, could still maintain, despite passages like those cited above:

Even the eternal verities are overlooked. The responsibility of a person for the consequences of his actions and the fundamental distinction between mankind and the rest of creation are basic Christian tenets. They are pertinent to the issues raised by the pope; but they are ignored throughout these documents." (P. T. Bauer, *Reality and Rhetoric* [Cambridge, Mass.: Harvard University Press, 1986], 88)

5. See *Quadragesimo Anno*, paragraphs 78 and 79.

6. See *Sollicitudo Rei Socialis*, paragraph 44.

7. Cited in J. O. de Meira Penna, *O Evangelho segundo Marx* (São Paulo: Editora Comvívio, 1982), 45 (translated by Robert Royal).

8. A good survey of the recent literature on this point is Lawrence E. Harrison, *Who Prospers: How Cultural Values Shape Economic and Political Success* (New York: Basic Books, 1992).

9. See John Locke, "Second Treatise," in *Two Treatises of Government*, ed. Thomas I. Cook (New York: Hafner Publishing Co., 1947), sec. 37, 139; and John Stuart Mill, *Principles of Political Economy*, ed. Sir William Ashley (New York: Augustus M. Kelley, 1969), 235. Michael Novak's commentary on these principles in *The Catholic Ethic and the Spirit of Capitalism* (New York: Free Press, 1993), 147–168, is worth consulting.

10. See Paul Craig Roberts, "Up From Mercantilism," *The National Interest*, Summer 1990, 64.

11. See Nicholas Eberstadt, "Foreign Aid's Industrialized Poverty," *Wall Street Journal*, 8 November 1989.

12. See Alan Woods, *Development and the National Interest: U. S. Economic Assistance into the 21st Century* (Washington, D.C.: U.S. Agency for International Development, 1989), particularly Chapter 4, "Nonprofit Assistance to Development."

13. Amy Sherman's *Preferential Option: A Christian and Neoliberal Strategy for Latin America's Poor* (Grand Rapids: Eerdmans, 1992) provides some useful guidelines for judging which governmental programs and which private activities may be of most use in promoting development.

14. Quoted in *The Economist*, 15 September 1990, 93.

15. Hernando de Soto, *El Otro Sendero* (Lima: Editorial El Barranco, 1986).

Chapter 8

JAMES FINN

1. The impact of these travels is suggested by the reaction to one of Pope Paul's early trips, which was followed by a number of reporters of the *New York Times*. Homer Bigart wrote:

Pope Paul VI journeyed to the United Nations on October 4, 1965, to appeal to the leaders of the world for peace. It was a historic mission that transfixed a great city, seized the attention of millions of Americans throughout the country, of people around the globe. . . .

His mission of diplomacy marked the first visit of a reigning pontiff to the New World. It was an occasion that suspended the normal life of the city and affected the emotions of millions of persons of all faiths. . . .

This was the first time that a pontiff had appeared before the United Nations, and the challenge of Pope Paul VI, spiritual leader of half a billion Roman Catholics, to the chief secular organization of mankind, was watched with rapt attention by world diplomats and guests within the high-ceilinged assembly chamber and by a television audience numbering hundreds of millions. ("An Historic Mission," *The Pope's Visit to the United States* [New York: Bantam Books, 1965], 1)

2. Quentin Quade, "America and the World, II," *Freedom Review*, May–June 1993, 45–47. He goes on to say:

Democracy's central justification is that, compared to other political forms, it can perform the essential state tasks and magnify respect for the person at the same time. And in that personalist justification one finds no boundary lines: personhood stops at our border is an absurdity. Civility may stop here, order may stop here, power may stop here, but once we have recognized our own value and said it deserves democratic protections, truthfulness and logic will compel us to say that, abstractly, all deserve it as much as we.

I am indebted to Quentin Quade for some of the remarks about the state that precede the quotation from the article.

3. Samuel P. Huntington, "Democracy's Third Wave," *Journal of Democracy*, Spring 1991, 13.

4. "Few relationships between social, economic, and political phenomena are stronger than that between the level of economic development and the existence of democratic politics. Most wealthy countries are democratic and most democratic countries—India is the most dramatic exception—are wealthy" (Ibid., 30).

Freedom House makes an annual survey of every country in the world, ranking each on the degree of political rights and civil liberties it observes. It also provides a survey of social and economic indicators. The correlation of democracies with capitalist economic systems is very high. See *Freedom in the World: Political Rights and Civil Liberties, 1991–1992* (New York: Freedom House, 1993).

5. *New York Times*, 23 March 1993.

6. Douglas W. Payne writes:

Political cultures do evolve, if slowly. . . . In Latin America today, ordinary people are further along than their leaders in embracing democratic values. They are organizing peasant federations, worker movements, neighborhood associations, and small business, professional legal services, and rights groups. Even those in the burgeoning informal economies, the poorest of the poor, are demonstrating an ability to form social and economic units more democratic and efficient than the central governments that shun them. ("Latin America: Democracy and the Politics of Corruption," *Freedom Review*, January–February 1993, 30)

7. William J. Bennett, secretary of education from 1985 to 1988 and co-director of Empower America, has compiled a list of eight such cultural indicators.

They support his observation that "what is shocking is just how precipitously American life has declined in the past 30 years, despite the enormous governmental effort to improve it" ("Quantifying America's Decline," *Wall Street Journal*, 15 March 1993).

8. Zbigniew Brzezinski, national security adviser to President Carter and professor of American foreign policy at Johns Hopkins University, has commented astringently on aspects of Western cultural life today and what they might portend in our relations with other countries. The failure of what he termed "utopias of total control" has, in the West, given way "to the current antithesis, which is essentially that of minimal control over personal and collective desires, sexual appetites, and social conduct. But inherent in the almost total rejection of any control is the notion that all values are subjective and relative." He adds that "the West's contempt for religion is part and parcel of this mindset. The prevailing orthodoxy among intellectuals in the West is that religion is a waning, irrational, and dysfunctional aberration. Yet religion not only persists but in some parts of the developing world is staging a comeback" ("Power and Morality," *World Monitor*, March 1993, 22–28).

Chapter 9

Robert A. Destro

1. "Man's life is built up every day from work, from work it derives its specific dignity" (*Laborem Exercens*, paragraph 3).

2. "It is only after my stay in the hospital that I have been able to revise it definitively" (*Laborem Exercens*, paragraph 113).

3. "The Marxist solution has failed, but the realities of marginalization and exploitation remain in the world, especially in the Third World, as does the reality of human alienation, especially in the more advanced countries" (*Centesimus Annus*, paragraph 42). The irony in this statement is underscored by the continued suspicion that the assassination attempt was itself a "Marxist solution" that went awry, thus leaving Pope John Paul himself in the ironic position of ministering to the spiritual needs of other survivors. See generally David Wise, "Unraveling the KGB's Secrets," *San Francisco Chronicle*, 27 December 1992, This World section, 8/Z1.

4. Brenda C. Destro, "An Exploratory Study of Twenty Employee Assistance Programs in the Milwaukee (Wisconsin) Area," a thesis submitted for the degree of Master of Social Work, University of Wisconsin-Milwaukee, 1981.

5. David Meakin, *Man and Work: Literature and Culture in Industrial Society* (London: Meuthen & Co., 1976), 1, quoted in ibid., n. 7. Albert Camus made essentially the same point: "Without work, all life goes rotten. But when work is soulless, life stifles and dies."

6. *Centesimus Annus*, 42.

7. *Black's Law Dictionary*.

8. Cf. Bill Jamieson, "The Fatal Bear-Hug: Global Economic Prospects Have Seldom Been Bleaker," *Sunday Telegraph*, 13 March 1993, stating that a Russian political and economic collapse threatens to take the rest of the world down with it.

9. See *Mater et Magistra, Gaudium et Spes,* and *Populorum Progressio.*

10. See Christa Klein, "The Lay Vocation: At the Altar in the World," in *Being Christian Today: An American Conversation,* ed. Richard John Neuhaus and George Weigel (Washington, D.C.: Ethics and Public Policy Center, 1992), chapter 7, including responses by Alberto R. Coll and Robert A. Destro.

11. Gregory Baum, "John Paul II's Encyclical on Labor," *The Ecumenist* 20 (November–December, 1981): 3.

12. Bureau of National Affairs, "Unions Must Change Course, GWU Professor Says In New Book," *Daily Labor Report,* no. 63, 5 April 1993, Current Developments section, A3 (an interview with Professor Charles B. Craver of George Washington University relating the thesis of his newly published book *Can Unions Survive?* [New York: New York University Press, 1993]).

13. See ibid.

14. See, for example, Keller v. State Bar of California, 496 U.S. 1 (1990); Communications Workers of America v. Beck, 487 U.S. 735 (1988). See also Nat Hentoff, "The Pro-Life Professor v. the Pro-Choice Union," *Washington Post* (final ed.), 25 August 1990, A21.

15. See John Holusha, "Unions Are Expanding Their Role to Survive in the 90's," *New York Times,* 19 August 1990, F12.

16. Professor Craver believes the key to organized labor's survival lies in the use of more sophisticated organizing techniques that emphasize "empowerment, worker dignity, participation in the decision-making process," rather than economic issues. See Bureau of National Affairs, op. cit., n. 26.

17. Adam Smith, *Wealth of Nations* (London: Oxford University Press, 1904), 417.

18. The Americans With Disabilities Act (A.D.A.), 42 U.S.C. § 12101, *et seq.,* defines the term "employer" in the same manner as Title VII of the Civil Rights Act of 1964, 42 U.S.C. §2000e, *et seq.* Section §12111(7) of the A.D.A. adopts the definition contained in Section 2000(e)(b) of Title VII: "The term 'employer' means a person engaged in an industry affecting commerce who has fifteen or more employees for each working day in each of twenty or more calendar weeks in the current or preceding calendar year, and any agent of such a person." The Family and Medical Leave Act of 1993, 29 U.S.C. §2601, *et seq.,* contains an even more expansive "small business" exemption: 29 U.S.C. § 2611(4)(A) exempts employers who employ fewer than "50 . . . employees for each working day during each of 20 or more calendar workweeks in the current or preceding calendar year."

19. See Bureau of National Affairs, *Banking Report,* 15 March 1993, noting that U.S. Trade Representative Mickey Kantor is pessimistic on chances of a quick conclusion to the GATT trade talks.

20. One can only hope, as these words are written, that the "culture of death" (*Centesimus Annus,* 39) so clearly evident in the Dutch parliament's recent decision to legalize euthanasia can be re-oriented through the evangelization and collective action of concerned Christians and others. But the signs are not promising in the United States either; the legalization of assisted suicide and euthanasia are being promoted under the rubric of the same constitutional "right to privacy" that gave us the most liberal abortion law in the world. See Hobbins v. Attorney General of Michigan, Complaint, No. 93–306178CZ, Michigan Circuit Court, Wayne County, Michigan., 29; ACLU of Michigan, Press Release, 1 March 1993, quoting Elizabeth Gleicher, lead counsel in its challenge to the Michigan Assisted Suicide Statute, Mich. Comp. Laws § 752.1027 (1992).

21. See James Davison Hunter, *Culture Wars: The Struggle to Define America* (New York: Basic Books, 1991).

22. Joseph Pichler, "Capitalism and Employment," in *Catholic Social Teaching and the U.S. Economy*, ed. John W. Houck and Oliver F. Williams, C.S.C. (Lanham, Md.: University Press of America, 1984), 65.

23. The point has been raised in recent years by two women closely associated with the political process. Nancy Reagan, the wife of former president Ronald Reagan, and Zoë B. Baird, the woman first nominated by President Bill Clinton to be attorney general of the United States. Mrs. Reagan made the point directly: "If you use drugs, even on a casual basis," she said, "the blood is on your hands." Ms. Baird inadvertently made the same point. Though she was denied the appointment because she had hired undocumented aliens to care for her child, the real burden of her violation of the law fell on the undocumented workers who had the misfortune of being caught in the glare of the political process. They were deported within weeks.

24. Healy v. The Beer Institute, 491 U.S. 324, 337 n. 12 (1989), quoting Baldwin v. G.A.F. Seelig, Inc., 294 U. S. 511, 523 (1935).

25. See, for example, Bureau of National Affairs, "EPI Urges Policy to Stimulate U.S. Exports to Third World by Raising Labor Standards," *Daily Labor Report*, no. 48, 15 March 1993, A17, reporting on an Economic Policy Institute study that suggests that the United States could increase its exports by encouraging Third World countries to improve their labor standards.

26. See, for example, "The Pope's Third Way," *The Tablet*, 3 October 1981, 955–56.

27. Marjorie Heyer, "Most React Favorably to Encyclical: Scholars from a Wide Spectrum of Thought Voice Their Approval," *Washington Post*, 18 September 1981, B18, quoting Msgr. George Higgins.

28. J. Bryan Hehir, "A New Era of Social Teaching," *Commonweal*, 23 October 1981, 585.

29. National Conference of Catholic Bishops, Washington, D.C., 1986.

30. Quentin de la Bedoyere, "Man and His Work," *The Tablet*, 5 December 1981, 1192.

31. Douglas M. McGregor, *Human Side of Enterprise: Twenty-Fifth Anniversary Printing* (New York: McGraw-Hill, 1985).

Chapter 10

WILLIAM MCGURN

1. Robert Suro, "The Writing of 'Sollicitudo Rei Socialis,'" *Crisis*, May 1988, 14.

2. Alan Woods, *Development and the National Interest* (Washington, D.C.: U.S. Agency for International Development, 1989).

3. Jan Morris, *Hong Kong* (New York: Viking Press, 1990), 197.

4. Walter Wriston, *The Twilight of Sovereignty* (New York: Charles Scribner's Sons, 1992) 101.

5. Joel Kotkin, *Tribes* (New York: Random House, 1992), 9.

Index of Names